D0764318

LIVING FOR DESIGN: THE YVES SAINT LAURENT STORY

By

AXEL MADSEN

NONFICTION

Billy Wilder
William Wyler: The Authorized Biography
The New Hollywood
Malraux: A Biography
Hearts and Minds: The Common Journey of
    Simone de Beauvoir and Jean-Paul Sartre
John Huston: A Biography

FICTION

Borderlines

LIVING FOR DESIGN: THE YVES SAINT LAURENT STORY

AXEL MADSEN

DELACORTE PRESS / NEW YORK

Published by
Delacorte Press
1 Dag Hammarskjold Plaza
New York, N.Y. 10017

Manufactured in the United States of America
First printing

Designed by Oksana Kushnir

LIBRARY OF CONGRESS CATALOGING IN PUBLICATION DATA
Madsen, Axel.
  Living for design.

  Bibliography: p. 237
  Includes index.
  1. Saint Laurent, Yves. 2. Costume designers—France
—Biography. I. Title.
TT505.S24M32   746.9′2′0924 [B]   79-13818
ISBN 0-440-05358-7

Darling, what is that?
Are you sure it is a hat?
—OGDEN NASH

CONTENTS

1
PARIS RAGTIME

*L*ights, camera, ostentation!

The floating multinationality of press and buyers, Beautiful People and fashion groupies, jet-laggers and photographers festooned with gear, cram into the ballroom for another sensory charge. Fashion Week in Paris is the foremost form of modern live entertainment, ten days of madness, sweep and din and of dead-serious competition among the big names, each wanting to stop the parade. The fashion greats must carry an aura that can be attached to more than mere dress design. Attracting 130,000 visitors, including several thousand buyers whose responsibility is both to enhance the fashion reputation of their stores and to make a profit, Fashion Week is a cash bash that packs every hotel. Fashion Week means nearly a hundred officially scheduled showings and a handful of top shows to which two thousand are invited and another two thousand try to gate-crash. Fashion Week is the City of

Lights becoming Hollywood-sur-Seine, an extravaganza, "for the trade only," of lights and color, hysteria and tension, special effects and overstimulation that each year is *le most*.

The crowd spilling over the gilt chairs on both sides of the raised runway that stretches the length of the ballroom is a celebrity-studded melee of people who have the looks, the self-confidence and the glamour that come with being at the epicenter of social tremors. Here are the attendant groupies—the fashion writers and the women who make a career of chic. Here are the flamboyant fashion women, sometimes taking notes—the idle noodlings of the very hip—and the perspiring retailers more in search of ideas than merchandise. The fashion writers are women mostly, with hard eyes and hard lines around the mouth, who regularly have nervous breakdowns trying to find a new word for *new*.

Everybody seems to know everybody else, and the patter floats in and out of several languages and accents. A theatrical decor intriguingly hides the backstage area at the beginning of the runway. The opposite end is dominated by the television and video crews' own exclusive platform. Celebrities are seated in the first row along the runway, glaring patiently across at each other while they wait for the always late-starting show to begin. Celebrity-spotters jot down the names—Sophia Loren, Princess Maria Gabrielle di Svoia, Ghislaine de Polignac, Barbara Walters, Jacqueline de Ribes, Helene de Rothschild, Ellin Saltzman, Hiroko Berghausen—and play the same name game on the buyers' side. Who gets the front-center seats among the stars from the stores—presidents, vice-presidents, merchandise managers, fashion directors? Behind them are people who know they belong here—a dignified woman who might have been a model for Gabrielle Chanel or Elsa Schiaparelli, a Japanese youth in Tokyo school uniform complete with studded wristbands as if he came directly from the Narita airport riots. Latecomers are rushed to their seats. Here is a photographer who, besides his Nikons and flashguns, carries a neat little stepladder. There is a portly Byron who speaks a lisping Spanish, and next to him, a woman who proves to be murderously fast with felt tip and sketch pad. The hard core whose applause has the precise modulation of bullfight aficionados is the seven hundred writers and two hundred top buyers who come to Paris four times a year—in January and July for the haute couture, or made-to-measure, collections; in April and October for the ready-to-wear shows. With a word—or a word withheld—they can bestow glory and inflict pain on any of the high-fashion houses.

A Karl Lagerfeld show comes with sample perfumes on numbered seats, a Kenzo Takada show is a free-for-all. At a Christian Dior *défilé*, the runway separates media and retailers like the Red Sea; at Ted Lapidus, the hierarchy of who-gets-in-and-who-does-not pretends to be more intricate than in a hot disco. Nina Ricci's is the holdout against music, and the hushed presentation is only interrupted by Duchess Sophie de Wurtemberg discreetly announcing the number of the next creation. At André Courrèges, lavish notebooks come with a Xerox-copy synopsis stressing the highlights to come ("the shape is generally structured; the shoulder is important"). Serge Lepage once showed his line for the House of Schiaparelli in a grandiose display: A massive outside staircase was erected to the second-floor windows of the company's place Vendôme town house, and the models made their entrances through the windows. Pierre Cardin has flown journalists to Lyons to show his models in the futuristic setting of the new Lyons-Sartolas airport. Kenzo has had a white horse carry a damsel in white and golden tulle on the runway. Lagerfeld has simulated a lockup, with models standing in striking poses behind bars until supermodel Pat Cleveland unlocked the stage jail. At the end of their shows, Kenzo and Sonia Rykiel scoot down the runway themselves, holding hands with their models.

The designer's imagination is the Big Bang in the beginning of the complicated creation, into which are fused the interests of textile and garment industries, advertising and accessory franchising around the world. Collections are costume parties, show-biz events where the production values are almost as important as the clothes. They are a front, a costly facade that gives a label sheen and glitter. To get a seat at the top shows is to feel the goose pimples of being where the now is being amplified. It is to rub shoulders with inspiration and devastating assertion.

Accreditation and schedules come from the Chambre Syndicale de la Couture Parisienne, the Chambre Syndicale du Prêt à Porter and the Fédération Française du Prêt à Porter Féminin, the powerful trio that are both management organization and union, and count among their members all the big names. To arrange the schedule for the shows may seem easy until you consider the inflamed egos and superstition of couturiers—this one will not show on any day or hour that includes some specific digit, that one will insist on switching to someone else's traditional date. The designers issue invitations that are often useless; at the height of the bedlam, crashers con their way into shows, occupy the wrong seats and add to the general confusion. Legitimate holders of invitations are sometimes challenged by eager doormen and accused of forging names of wives or husbands on the gilt-edged cards. Somehow, there are always more people who get in than are supposed to.

To the twang of Kurt Weill, the first model skips down the runway to still the small talk and focus the attention. From now on, it is nonstop—always two, four, six or eight mannequins in *savant* poses to emphasize a fashion idea, a color scheme; sometimes accompanied by sultry, sunken-cheeked male models. The girls are a glorious charge of insouciance and vitality. They are a chain of hard-boned, earthy and extroverted goddesses who seem to invent themselves as they go along. They have legs that never end and are what the girls next door try to look like—elusive and cared for, sophisticated and adorable. Curves and limbs crawl sinuously out from a blousy profusion of weightless layers, from sacks, smocks, tunics and skirts; and when the models jump up in the air, they seem to stay there. They can't make a wrong move and seem to work on inspiration rather than slick professionalism. Black, Asiatic, English rose and All-American bounce, they are thrillingly unpredictable and totally beguiling.

The show is on. High red and pulsating purple clash with tangerine and sapphire under the floodlights, blend with lime and azure in a confetti-mix of tactile fabrics and put-on accessories. The colors are rich, and a little two-piece black dress worn over a golden-yellow satin blouse with a fuchsia tie receives the first applause. On the principle that it is better to have audiences titillated or indignant than bored to tears, meanings and messages flow and short-circuit each other in a succession of poetic visions, conjured-up climates and confessed obsessions. Smoky mysteries of satin and silk follow the flirtiest of shirt-dresses. Things that are meant to *feel* pretty to wear succeed exhibitions of tacky tiaras and monstrous junk jewelry.

The music segues to hard rock. Maybe the Chambre Syndicale—or ASCAP—should insist on credits for Wagner, Stevie Wonder, Beethoven and Donna Summer. Girls wearing flat-brimmed priest's hats over masses of fake hair pretend to flirt with boys in Genghis Khan jackets made of iridescent brocades. Witty exaggerations compete with inspirations from clerical vestments, royal robes, tin soldiers and the works of a very mad hatter. A plum satin fur-lined coat over the palest copper satin skirt provides both a spirit of adventure and a concept of richness. A petaled ivory top and slim matching skirt, body-wrapped with gold-foil leaves, competes for attention with a bare-shouldered red panné velvet blouse and double-layered skirt. Elusive and playful, a femme fatale parades in a tender wrap skirt and sheer black hose. A *lycée* schoolgirl with golden fairy-tale princess ringlets to her shoulders hopscotches in tartan and knits.

Mid-cut, the music shifts to *Pomp and Circumstance* oom-pah-pah to accompany a jivey presentation of night-shirt smocks and big, off-the-shoulder tops, d'Artagnan blouses and side-hitched ponchos. A shoestring dress and wrap in black receives vigorous approval. One of the sexiest dresses is a warm, sunset-orange, soft cowl-neck halter, gathered at the waist and slit thigh-high. But a minute later a short, shimmery bias-cut lamé dress with a flippy slit comes dancing in on a girl in sky-high shoes and the sunset orange is forgotten. The music shifts to honky-tonk to underscore villainous chic. Boys costumed as eye-patched pirates lust after nearly bare-breasted gazelles in evening gowns.

Many of the clothes seem too outrageous for anyone to wear—and they are. Only a fraction of what is shown on the runways is actually ordered, and retailers tend to be most interested in the conservative elements. The shows are also exploratory forums for portent by way of symbol. You can imagine the designer creating, between readings of Valéry Larbaud and the *Memoirs* of Casanova or *The Book of Marco Polo*, while listening to Birgit Nilsson singing Isolde's death. Veterans of the *défilés* yearn for the Middle Ages before 1970, when models moved in measured strides like flamingos in a rock garden instead of leaping and twirling; when they modeled clothes instead of fractured spontaneity; and when audiences were encouraged to form impressions about garments instead of being overwhelmed by sensory overload. But the new people love it. Collections are stage productions in color, wit and magnetism, a supersensory vapor bath and a vortex of swirling intoxication. Today's throb is numbing, and the models themselves only look happy when the show is grand, the crowd huge and they can feel themselves to be active stars in a fast, flying success.

Ready-to-wear presentations, which make frazzled observers wonder what can possibly be the sequel next spring or fall, are 280 items long: 280 coats, pants, jackets, boleros, obis, skirts, parkas, sweaters, kilts and suits for day, evening, beach and/or ski wear in new trends, silhouettes, lines, looks and directions. They are made in fabrics that flirt, slide, glitter and move in order to highlight, reflect, anchor, subdue or restore as erogenous zones the ankle, shoulder, waist or hip. The accents are on knits, berets, vests, shawls, boots or glittering jewels in shapes that are subtle, sumptuous, sensuous, sleek, practical and for real. The new people love today's fashion because anything goes—they say anything that is fulfilling can be glamorous. They want clothes to show off great shapes and female hubris.

The applause for the two hundred and eightieth novelty—no longer a bridal gown, as tradition once had it—crackles and bursts in precise decibels. Five minutes later, everybody tramples each other in the race outside for available taxis to rush to the next showing. There are days when ten shows are scheduled, and some designers show their collections in far-flung locations—the Palais des Congrès at Porte Maillot, the Pré Catalan in the Bois de Boulogne, the Ambassadeurs on the Champs-Elysées.

In a noble attempt to bring everything under one roof, the designers all showed their 1979–80 ready-to-wear in a tenty city in Les Halles, but the result was more street riot and sports event than an exercise in elegance and subtlety.

At 9:15, Madame Pompidou is among the first arrivals at Guy Laroche; the stars Mireille Darc and Philippe Clay squeeze in just before curtain time. At 11:30, Jeanne Moreau's seat remains empty, but Catherine Deneuve, Helene de Rothschild and Paloma Lopez-Sanchez are at Saint Laurent's to lead the admirers' claque. At 2:02, Kenzo starts his high-energy production, and at 3:45, a calmer, well-behaved crowd comes to order at Givenchy's (and a journalist from *Ebony* talks endlessly into her tape recorder). At 5:00, Paco Rabanne starts one of his ingenious presentations, and an hour and a half later, survival is again the problem as bodies cram together for Claude Montana's rhinestone-cowboy escapism.

The immensely complicated machinery that coordinates the interests of textile and publicity, dress manufacturing and media has resulted in a fashion pace unheard of even a decade ago. The creative thrust of design is now-to-next direction in so many kinds of clothes, and the force, the energy and the appeal are not only change from and change to, but change for its own sake, change that can change fashion. Today's promotion-cum-celebration happenings have overtaken haute couture in both money and meaning and transformed fashion into a spectacularly profitable business.

In 1665, Louis XIV's statesman Jean-Baptiste Colbert said that fashion is to France what Peru's gold mines are to Spain. Three centuries later, French fashion expands at a 15-percent clip a year, and despite the growth of Milan and

New York, Paris remains the true Delphi of the rag trade. It is toward Paris that those whose choices have worldwide influence gravitate—Halston and Calvin Klein have little influence outside the United States, though the Parisian designers are not necessarily French. Yesterday, Cristóbal Balenciaga came from Spain, Mainbocher from the United States and Madame Grès (née Alix Czereskow) from somewhere in Eastern Europe she doesn't want to remember; today, Per Spook is a transplanted Norwegian, Lagerfeld a thoroughly Parisianized German and Issey Miyake a Japanese who cannot make up his mind whether his heart is in Manhattan or on the Right Bank. Modern collection shows are playful distortions, and what they express are moods and ideas that breeze along to delight and to provoke. The evolution from carriage trade to design consciousness is a totally modern phenomenon.

Haute couture is variously described as condemned, dying or dead. The money is now in ready-to-wear and in licensing of logos to manufacturers of sunglasses, bed linens and cigarette lighters. Here, the earnings increase between 15 and 30 percent a year, depending on the house. Saint Laurent calls his made-to-measure dresses gifts to his wealthiest clients, since the half-million dollars it costs to produce and show such a collection cannot possibly be recouped on the sale of the clothes, even if each dress sells for up to ten thousand dollars. Haute couture is an exercise in public relations. Fifty million Frenchmen know that Anne Giscard d'Estaing has her wardrobe made by Jean-Louis Scherrer. Jacqueline Onassis is "surprised by a photographer" in dark glasses and a coat signed by Emmanuel Ungaro. The caption of the photo showing Olimpia Aldobrandini saying yes to David de Rothschild also mentions the bride saying thank you to Saint Laurent for the wedding dress. Reports of Régine's nights in her newest disco come with notes that her muslin and chinchilla gown is a Marc Bohan creation.

More subtly, haute couture has remained a straw in the wind, a tonic for the designers who can afford it and a haven for exceptional craftsmanship and last-of-their-kind artisans. A made-to-measure show is more sedate but no less mobbed than a ready-to-wear collection. The clothes on the models are usually more daring and more reckless, as designers use couture to sum themselves up and to become poets. Shapes are almost unreal; a butterfly print is so light, so beautiful, that it doesn't seem to matter whether it is in the form of a dress or wings. This year Saint Laurent is a man of the theater; for next winter, Ricci's Gérard Pipart promises a natural woman; Laroche believes in tradition for 1980. You may forget you are watching clothes and think instead of dreams—now misty reveries, now dazzling visions adding up to an impact, a mood. At couture unveilings, the ladies of the press are a snobby inch more exclusive than at ready-to-wear affairs, and instead of a dash for the cabs, they are more likely to rush for the caviar and champagne that are likely to follow the event. The clothes buffs in the front rows are the world's big spenders, not very young and not very audacious, and can include in one sitting Madame Claude Pompidou, Brooke Astor, Sao Schlumberger, Ardishir Zahedi and Bergdorf Goodman's Ira Niemark (who may buy ten or twenty ensembles for a couture promotion). At the end, the models march off the runway to the sound of ear-tingling applause and, hopefully, of rustling checkbooks. Tomorrow, the big-time name photographers move in to shoot their layouts.

The most influential designer is Yves Saint Laurent. Others may invent kilts and boleros, Yves Saint Laurent *launches* them. Through inspiration and imitation, he effects the clothes women—and a lot of men—wear on several continents.

Yves Saint Laurent is the one-in-a-generation designer who divines what we want and, four times a year, conceives it in ways we can't yet conceive of wanting it. His gift for catching the mood a little ahead of the rest of us has made us conscious of the changes we are experiencing. For nearly three decades, this immensely private person has given us a healthy interest in the whims of chic and taught us to have a little more imagination ourselves.

2

ALL
ABOUT
YVES

What I hate are the eternal shows; to present fashion four times a year as a sort of spectacle seems ridiculous. The idea of *shows* kills fashion and gives a false impression. There should be a continuous creation of clothes."

Yves Saint Laurent—YSL to half the world—has appeared from behind a mirrored door at his headquarters at avenue Marceau, wearing carefully pressed slacks, an immaculate shirt and a beige cashmere cardigan over his shoulders. He is worn out from work and people; during the presentation, his nerves were drawn tight as an E-string tuned a shade too high, only to relax with the first applause. He is desperate for a vacation, yet ready to lend himself to questions with bemused reserve.

"Fashion shouldn't be something that you show; it should be something alive. Fashion as we still understand it is out of fashion. For me, there is no avant-garde. I don't deliberately set out to make something new. There are years when I think I do something really new and there are years that are very much an evolution of ideas."

The name *Yves Saint Laurent* means inspired assertion and sensuous allure, contemporary moods and glamorous artifice. He heads an enterprise that both carries and devours him. He is distant and self-avowedly neurotic, but in possession of an extraordinarily fertile and precise imagination. He is more complex than his most elaborate renditions, yet believes in simplicity and classicism. He likes to oppose fabrics and ideas, surface and volume. He knows he has molded an era, but says that style, not fashion, is of the essence. And style, he adds, consists of very little.

In his early forties, Saint Laurent is slight and taut, fair and pale, with myopic blue eyes behind the wide-lensed glasses that have become his trademark. He is six feet two inches tall and, despite his delicate, asthenic physique, he has none of the effete mannerisms so often displayed by designers. His nose is prominent, almost patrician; his mouth is wide, full-lipped and sensual. His chin is firm and, when he smiles, furrowed. Like many artists, he is not a verbal person. It is with his hands that he expresses himself—strong, manicured worker's hands that can draw and drape and are devoted to the exaltation of the female body. With pencil or fabric, he becomes the artist turning delicate social tremors into seduction. To see him cut, with scissors appearing out of nowhere, in satins, taffetas and muslins and, in a fire of inspiration, to drape, pin and drape again a model like Mounia Orhozemane, is to understand the mysterious mix of the ephemeral and the basic, the beautiful and the useful.

His own most outstanding traits, he says, are nostalgia and a need for luxury. "I need opulence as others need oceans and mountains, but I know, of course, that this is a guilty, forbidden passion." His smile is crooked, as if to intimate that you shouldn't take everything he says too seriously, or perhaps to show that he is not sure he can totally trust you.

Since he was twenty, he has been on top. Where he leads, others follow—some protesting, others insisting they are actually going in the opposite direction. Saint Laurent has consistently created decisive changes in the way women dress. He is the initiator of pants for elegant evenings, and he launched the chemise, Cossack romanticism and the skirt below the calf. He introduced fishermen's shirts, turtlenecks and pea jackets to couture and started the nude look with see-through blouses. He made pop-art prints and bathrobe coats into universal fashions, invented peasant opulence and endorsed nailhead studs, vinyl raincoats and visor caps. He popularized the safari suit, the long scarf and hip boots, and likes to say that his only regret is that he didn't invent blue jeans. He was the first of the Parisians to sense that youth had replaced money as a psychological and social touchstone—that the lady wants to look like her daughter, not the daughter like a junior version of her mother. He was the first to shift his loyalty to the popular front of ready-to-wear and to sense that feminine liberation shortened the distance between being and appearance, and that it meant mix-'n'-wear fashion that would make the wearer more important than what she wore. The next revolution is obvious. Since men will have to learn to please, the next frontier will involve the masculine half of humanity.

Yves Saint Laurent believes that life has to be *made* interesting. His secret—if a secret is possible in a profession full of built-in glare—is to question himself, to use the world's art, history and folklore as the fountainhead of his inspiration and to listen to the very young. He is not always sure he understands the very young. In the mid-1960s, he saw his generation shake off old taboos in clothes, in outlook, in behavior—and wasn't sure he was part of it. His regret is that success swallowed him up when he was twenty and that he never had a chance to be rebellious. "Sometimes, I feel trapped, a prisoner of success, I suppose. I've never had the time to be young and carefree."

Fashion is a business in which you can never allow yourself to be wrong, he says. "You can't even allow yourself to be three or four years ahead of the times, to be right in three or four years. Designers are asked to feel what is happening, what *will* happen, and to translate that."

His use of the plural is rare. The Parisians don't exactly

consider themselves a brotherhood of couturiers. Instead, each thinks of himself as a unique artisan-artist and of his creations as the result of personal expressions of modern sensibilities. "Yves understands that a kind of craziness possessed him and now he even knows how to use it," says Loulou de la Falaise Klossowski, the woman who perhaps knows him best. "But he's a person who can't live in today's world because it is too flat, too commonplace."

Yves himself says that he adores woman and that his career, which isn't exactly improvised, is dedicated to her enchantment. "If a woman isn't fragile, she's not a woman," he says, adding that it is no contradiction to say that the strength of a woman is timeless, different and—self-evident. His eyes never stop, he says, and he refuses to limit his emotions. "I'm a collector, but not of one period. With me, it's a question of reaction. I react to things that are too 'in.' I break away, even from things of my own making."

When he is asked about influences, he crosses to a Second Empire desk strewn with his drawings. "I've always had a lot of imagination," he begins, picking up one of his sketches. "I think about Ingres, Delacroix when I accessorize. I've imagined the dress that Vermeer's *Young Lady Adorning Herself with a Pearl Necklace* was wearing. It's not copying; it's transposing, picking and choosing."

He is both at the peak of his profession and in the grip of depressions and self-doubts that have had him in and out of hospitals. He is a creator pared down to pure function and can design a collection in three weeks so perfectly that not a bead has to be changed. Yet his subtle, sumptuous and jubilantly feminine *paisana* look of 1976 was partially designed in a psychiatric clinic.

When you wonder if artists don't always grow through the conflict with their predecessors' achievements and the struggle with their former selves, you are met with a stare that may mean you are crossing forbidden boundaries. But he smiles and says there is reason in all his designs. "They evolve, they don't leap wildly out of nowhere. My choice of fabrics and colors doesn't rest on any scientific theory; it's based on observation, on felt experiences. I used to be entangled in tradition. We're all changing. I think it's important that I use simple fabrics for showy clothes. That's what it means to be modern, to adapt. Take cotton; it's my newest theme—shiny cotton that you can set off with a shantung scarf, a T-shirt for dinner wear that you can set off with a classical jacket, gilt sandals or a harem turban. I like clothes to be sober and accessories to be wild. I add and subtract and embroider on my themes. To advance is to impose new forms but there is also a destructive, almost demoniacal side to art."

He smiles and hastily adds that his art is a minor one—an applied art which is meant to enhance and to reflect attitudes. He doesn't think of himself as a designer, really, and likes to simply say, "I work with clothes." While he talks, he picks up a stiletto-sharp pencil and doodles on one of the seemingly finished sketches, drawing flowers in the hair of a floating silhouette. As an afterthought, he adds cross-over laces to the ankles; two quick strokes.

His sketches are crayon renditions of long-necked, long-legged women. The faces are quick allusions, the traits somehow masculine except for exaggerated big lips. The drawings make you think of Matisse and Cocteau pen-and-ink compositions of their happier periods.

He talks about himself and his work with difficulty, he says. "Fashion is very bizarre today. Fashion should be following society's moral evolution, but it doesn't."

He doesn't like to talk about the future and claims he only lives in the present. "I hate to have plans, to anticipate," he says, but with a bit of urging he *will* project a little. These are perplexing times, he feels, unoriginal times, without character. People are close to reality, especially to the reality of their bodies. The body used to be hidden by all sorts of conventions in clothes, and you can no longer shock people with anything in fashion. Modern, keyed-up people want to look rich—but very casually so. They want to be different things by day and by night, since it is now smart to be self-disciplined and hard-driving during the day and to get wrecked in a throbbing disco at night.

He wishes women would be more confident about clothes and that elegance would be better understood. "Those who buy my things must have imagination, too. Elegance is in the mind." When asked what his woman of 1980 will look like, he says she will be ambivalent. He has a feeling that feminism is entering a bourgeois cycle, that to be too serious is a bit old-fashioned, that women are becoming confident and self-assured enough to wear provocative styles. "The woman of 1980 wears sensible, businesslike classics for daytime, and by night she becomes mysterious. She wears black, things that are transparent. At night, she starts to fascinate me. Her heels are very, very high. She is very feminine but with the spirit of a man. She is not at all punk, but . . ." He interrupts his train of thoughts to say that there is such a thing as nightmare fashion, but that is not what he means. To look sexy doesn't mean dim-witted. If anything is modern, it is brainy sexiness, and a sex object must be a person who can choose as well as be chosen. "Real fashion doesn't change, it anticipates. Fashion is beauty, people's manners and attitudes. To function in our fractured society, we both need to find ourselves and to be stimulated."

Wit is part of Yves's psychic makeup, and in many of his designs, there are dashes of humor, details or touches that try to say these are clothes that shouldn't be taken too seriously. His true groupies instantly recognize the gags, such as the Carmen Miranda look, the hooker look and the golden-falsies look, which featured a model appearing in a skirt and a couple of molded metal breasts. It was rumored that the famous Verushka had posed for the breastplates, but Yves gallantly refused to confirm that.

His life with Pierre Bergé, his business partner and intimate for fifteen years, is as harmonious as most marriages. Since fashion is also a business, Bergé is the man in charge of the money tree. He is a stocky, cocky and cultured entrepreneur who is four years older than YSL and looks it. Where Yves is introspective and given to walking into crowded rooms sideways, Pierre is incisive and thrusting. Yves has been both projected and protected by his associate, whose circle of friends comes from the arts—writers, painters and people from the theater and the movies. When they met, Yves found this milieu more congenial than the *tout Paris* limelight. Of late, Pierre has bought a theater and learned to fly a helicopter, while Yves increasingly spends his carefully measured time writing a book.

Increasingly, too, he spends his off-hours with his two muses—Loulou and Betty Catroux. Betty, who first inspired him to do men's clothes with femininity for women, is a former Chanel model and the tall, lithe wife of an interior designer. Betty traveled with Yves to New York in 1968, when he inaugurated his first American beachhead at 855 Madison Avenue, and she says the nicest things about him: "I love Yves. He's one of the kindest, most decent people in the world. He's shy with people with whom he has no empathy. He detests all the phony small talk and he's not at ease talking to chichi types or pompous businessmen or women who gush over him." Betty is part Irish-American and was born in Brazil, where her Italian father was a diplomat. She and Yves met in 1966 at Régine's, where he used to go dancing all night.

Loulou, he says, is his little miracle. "It's important to have Loulou beside me when I'm working on a collection. I can't explain her job . . . it has to do with her manner, her straightforwardness." When they met in 1972, she was "one of those rich hippies from London," a gilded night bird with sure taste and a surer sense of humor. When she married writer Thadée Klossowski, the son of the artist Balthus, Yves gave them a wedding party in the Bois de Boulogne where two thousand guests were boated across a lake to a lavishly decorated isle. "My working methods are lighter and less anxious now that Loulou is here," says YSL.

He and Bergé are quick to defend each other's contributions to success. Says Yves: "Pierre acts as my ramparts, fending off bad elements and seeing things through."

Bergé knows all too well that the easiest explanation is that *he* made YSL, that the success is essentially an exercise in hype and public relations. "The contrary is the case," says the unsmiling Bergé. "Yves had the essential—talent. He would have expressed it without me."

The truth is more complicated. Bergé is an extraordinary character with a supreme skill for keeping Saint Laurent famous although always behind a muslin veil, for maintaining Yves's mystique without ever giving it away.

Fashion designers, of whom society demands more sheer output than of authors, painters, movie directors or other artists, are endowed with vigorous narcissism. Each is naturally persuaded that he is the only important one and is usually quick to let the world know. Yves, too, needs to project a brilliant and flattering image of himself. He is easily called temperamental, if not tyrannical. Inevitably. The fame given to his name the world over, the way he is received when he travels and the way his approval is fiercely sought, the adulation of society leaders, the celebrity hunt— but also the faith he must have in himself—have created a *monstre sacré.* He takes criticism with difficulty, and has declared himself the last of the great couturiers.

Like royalty, Yves carries no money. From their shared Left Bank duplex apartment, Pierre has himself driven to avenue Marceau in a Rolls. Yves used to drive himself to work in a Volkswagen. Reaction, again. But of late, he has taken to having himself chauffeured across the Seine, sitting up front next to the driver. To sit in the back like a high-power executive would be a little too gross. These ten-minute rides between the opulent rue Babylone garden apartment and the avenue Marceau town house are his only contact with workaday Paris.

His collaborators worship him, his two sisters vaunt his sense of family, his nephews and nieces his generosity. He lights his memories as if they were candles and is surrounded by beauty of his own choosing. He has all the enthusiasm of someone who claims he stayed an adolescent until forty. He loves dance, theater, breakfast in bed, unusual people and objects and dark colors because they have depth. He has a fascination for the mad King Ludwig II of Bavaria, and his solitary pleasures include listening to Wagner and reading Marcel Proust.

"I always have paper and pencil on me, but I don't necessarily begin by making sketches of dresses. I drape them. I can't work without the movement of the body. A dress reflects our time and it can't be static; it must have rhythm."

He pushes some of the sketches back and sits on the edge of the desk. "I need insecurity; that's how I work. Anguish is my best friend; it stimulates me . . ." He doesn't always finish his sentences. His French is contemporary Parisian, without elaborate convolutions, and he speaks like someone who knows he is successful and right on. "My work is my passion," he says gravely. "I have never loved anyone in the way I love what I do."

Crossing his legs, he says that this is the age of the working woman. This is the age of making order out of chaos, of back to nature, of appearance over substance and of a more pulled together, more grown-up society. He lights a mentholated cigarette—mentholated to nurse a kind of perpetual cold—and says he discovered that what is modern is not so much drastic changes each season as simply good clothes—the best cashmere sweater over a classic crepe de chine shirt, a pair of well-cut jeans, a muslin T-shirt with a little gold glitter under a beaded jacket—which doesn't mean that fashion shouldn't provoke and titillate common sense.

"I know I'm too expensive, but it's because of the fabrics and the labor, which is marvelous. I do my ready-to-wear as I do my haute couture, with the same will to perfection. In couture, I have my own factory where I personally formed people over a period of fifteen years. What goes on there doesn't change. Certainly, there are things you can't do in ready-to-wear, but I give myself entirely to my ready-to-wear collection as much as to the couture collection. I have tried to give women a chance to make a universal wardrobe, to make so-called investment fashion. When I dressed women as men in vests and blazers and pants, it was practical and sensible. Then I suddenly needed fantasy. I was tired of the humdrum that was so serious I felt paralyzed. I knew women wanted to dress up, to be sensuous, free-flowing, which doesn't mean I'm against what is classic.

"I'm very instinctive. I never let my ideas get ahead of the women in front of me, ahead of the body I'm supposed to dress, because I think the body is more important than the clothes you hang on it. It's out of the body's movement that the dress is born, not the other way around."

His tastes are those of today, he says. He thinks that the truly modern woman, who is self-possessed and may sometimes appear arrogant and aloof, creates beautiful drama and tension. Political theories don't interest him, but he is preoccupied with the consequences of political action. If that sounds contradictory, he says he hates politics because politics separates people and destroys human relationships by destroying our capacity for feeling for others. There are really no beautiful and ugly people, intelligent and stupid people—only people. He sees a lot of movies and listens to all kinds of music while working and on jukeboxes in cafés, but admits to reading little besides Proust, whodunits and the occasional bestseller. When asked why, he says it is because fashion designing is, on his level, a hellish occupation.

"There's an extraordinary drain of your thinking faculties. It's depressing. There are so many things which escape you that you'd like to do but never get around to. I, for example, often feel incapable of communicating with people, even those I love and admire, because I don't have the time and because I can't escape the lockstep of the business, the meshing cogs which cut short many relationships I could have with friends, family . . . lots of things. There are moments when I tell myself I'm not putting enough distance between myself and 'fashion.' There are moments I wish this business would change even more radically than any of the young designers hope for, that this whole circus of collection shows and verdicts by a few hundred specialists will disappear. Why can't we blow our stereotypes sky high like they do in other fields?"

What should be the easiest in designing is often the most *casse-gueule,* the likeliest place for a designer to break his neck. Very few—YSL and Hanae Mori, say veteran observers—can make a dress that looks like anything, yet a good-looking dress should be any designer's biggest success, because all a woman has to do is pull it over her head and she's dressed. He considers this for a moment, while blowing blue smoke toward the ceiling. "The more ideas you have, the worse it is," he smiles. "I imagine what it must be like for a writer trying to write a novel or a director making a film. I wish I could present my work in Volume One and Volume Two. For me, the big thing is simply to pull it all together."

Discreetly, he fails to mention that in addition to pulling

everything together in presentable form four times a year, he is under the very special pressure of being the trend setter. Store owners, buyers and journalists create it for him: at the beginning of each season, everybody lies in wait for him because he sets the tone. He's copied so much it is embarrassing.

To be the trend setter in an industry that revolves around making women feel good—which they rarely can unless they think they look good—is to understand the subliminal instincts that shape their thinking. Fashion is a business that revolves directly around the female mind and body, subjects of endless diversity and fascination, and Yves's feat is to possess a talent powerful enough to hold together what is at best a series of disconnected bright ideas that must always win immediate consent from the buying public, even though they appeal to emotions that are only partly conscious.

His humor is his self-defense. Sometimes his gags are misunderstood, however. In 1971, when fashion anarchy was at its highest, when middies coexisted with hot pants, hair was fuchsia pink or lime green and everything was for decoration, the media declared his 1940s revival a total fiasco; worse, an offensive miscarriage of fashion. Seven years later, his forties style was back and hailed as Exaggerated Chic or Noel Coward glamour.

YSL reacts against personal neglect both by men and women, and thinks a woman should spend a lot of money on herself—a lot of money, that is, in relation to what she has to spend in general. "Making up is a rite. I love rites. I love theater masks. Makeup is a mask. It takes time and shows personality. I like to think about the woman under the mask and what makes her paint her face in a certain personal way. I find a girl of twenty boring with her unmarked, unmadeup face. How much more interesting a woman of thirty with her artifice. Women become beautiful when artifice begins."

When he is asked if there was a time when he didn't understand femininity, he looks at you as if to let you know you may again be trespassing on some invisible threshold of his mind. Like the ideal self, the ideal woman is something that cannot be, he begins. It is a concept that has no place in a global culture like ours. You may have an ideal concept of clothes, of luxury, of quality in human relations, but women are too diverse for one visionary heroine. "The greatest change for me came when I discovered my own style without being influenced by others, and that came with the dinner suit and the transparent blouse. Ten years ago. That is when I began a dialogue with women and began to understand better what a modern woman is."

Gabrielle Chanel proclaimed him her successor around that time. She believed that, like herself, he has a way of thinking of women that is different—which didn't prevent her from trying to steal away Bergé to manage her perfume division for her.

He anticipates the next question by asking, "What do I look for in a feminine silhouette?" His answer is light and smiling. "Straight shoulders like those of Egyptian goddesses, long, very long necks and legs. The way a woman walks, too, the stride. I'm obsessed with black stockings."

When asked if inspiration is reciprocal, if the women he designs for influence his creation, he gets up. It is difficult to pinpoint inspiration, he says, putting out his cigarette. "My creations are more a feast that I offer myself. Egotistically, I express my dreams, my paintings, opera, ballet. It's almost psychotherapy. It's an escape."

He stops. "With people of talent, those with whom I surround myself, talk is rarely essential. There is a complicity of intent, an understanding. I'm ill at ease with people who talk and explain themselves too much."

3

THE
EMPEROR'S
NEW
CLOTHES

*I*f Yves Saint Laurent can guess what we will want, it is
because he knows that the first law in fashion dynamics
is both to contradict and to mirror unexpressed urges
for display and ecstasy. If it is hard for him to accept criticism, it is because what he creates seems to him to be logical, inevitable and a matter of course. As Paul Poiret said,
"You make a designer suffer if you point out to him the
inanity of his daring."*

Poiret was a couturier and eccentric who made—and
lost—a fortune creating one of the richest periods of fashion.
He had a marvelous way of describing the wonder of fashion: "When a woman chooses a dress," he wrote in *En habillant l'époque*, "she believes her choice is free and personal,
which of course it isn't. It's the mood of fashion that inspires and guides her impulses. Of course she would react

---

*Paul Poiret, *En habillant l'époque* (Paris: Grasset, 1930).

to such a putdown by saying, 'Women aren't total fashion ninnies. Proof? We don't follow a fashion we don't like.' And there's the miracle! Fashion is always captivating, always sweet tyranny. We always agree with it, thereby forcing it to change—all the time."

It is in the nature of authority to be unjustified and of the fashion of the day always to be the most bewitching and, if not the most reasonable, the most definitive. It is useless to ask ourselves where the line is to be drawn between what is natural and what is artificial, because no such line exists. Fashion is an unacknowledged world power, guiding us with a soft yet insistent voice from an outworn past, developing new tendencies, subversive and centrifugal movements, giving us new expectations and introducing new ideas of beauty, which provide us with a welcome freedom from compulsion and necessity. A man of genius, said Bernard Shaw in another context, is not a man who can do more things, or who knows more things, than ordinary men; "he simply is a man who sees the importance of things." The unjustifiable, all-justifying authority of the designer rests on seeing the importance of things. His gift is a kind of social radar.

Saint Laurent's sense of the times has been unerring. Since he chose a Second Empire decor for his avenue Marceau apartment in 1972, he has led us up to, in 1980, a celebration of ornament, a celebration that connotes a deep need in all of us for embellishment, for glitter and playful ways. The less-is-more of the last half-century in the arts is yielding to a more-is-more that intrigues. Instead of being sugary excess, ornamentation is becoming Exaggerated Chic. In Yves's perspective, we become accustomed to visions that are otherwise barely perceptible, to shifts and to shapes that are not yet totally here.

We may disagree with a designer's particular line, we may totally reject its forms and palette, but if it has the mark of the true creator, we cannot *not* recognize a feel for an overall unity, its author's *griffe*—that powerful French word that means "claw" and, by extension, "indelible mark," like an eagle's haughty scratch, but that in English becomes the tamer "label" and, by extension, "logo." Although we do it all the time, it is difficult to judge clothes on their beauty. The function of fashion is to create new scales of values. The danger of judging a collection on esthetic grounds is that we apply yesterday's yardstick. A truer test, as veteran fashion observer Bruno du Roselle has said, is whether a collection makes us take sides, whether it shakes us out of our indifference.

Fashion allows us to be different, to express new facets of ourselves, to project an idealized image of ourselves. Today we dress first and add jewelry later, but, historically speaking, accessories came first. Body decoration came before the loincloth. Clothes originated not so much in the need for warmth or protection, say anthropologists, as in the magical powers ascribed to artificially altered appearances. In the broadest sense, fashion is our oldest art. To be able to change our identity as well as our appearance is a basic human wish. To have style is to have ascendancy, personality and a feel for the pleasures of society.

The business of fashion is sociable, outgoing and a response to ever-changing interactions of people, events, creative minds, prevailing attitudes and the ways in which all this rebounds. Fashion is a worldwide business in which the final word is spoken by someone saying, "This is what I want." Design may be personal, but it can never be private. It is not a lonely art; it is a creative business.

The designer emerged in 1860, when English-born Charles Frederick Worth became the couturier of France's last crowned head, Empress Eugénie. Before him, couturiers had been tradesmen producing clothes the rich and the powerful told them to execute. With Worth, whose house on rue de la Paix lasted a hundred years, couturiers began telling the rich and the powerful how to dress. But the majority of women—and men, in response to female attire and, increasingly, their own—reject fashions that talk down to them. We tend to make a distinction between the voluntary "This is what I want" and submitting to dictates, but the difference is more subjective than real, since we eventually follow novelty anyway. Today, no woman would be caught in a miniskirt and no man in knee breeches.

After World War I, the aging department store tycoon

John Wanamaker brought Poiret to Philadelphia and had "La Marseillaise" played everywhere the Frenchman went. After Poiret had been fleeced out of his couture house, he was back in America, on the lecture circuit, and in Chickasha, Oklahoma, advised a gathering of young women not to look in fashion magazines to find out how to be beautiful, but to look in their mirrors. "Observe the colors that highlight the luster of your skin and those that make it dull. Adopt the colors that favor you and if you look good in blue, don't feel obliged to wear green because green is the rage right now." After spending an hour on this theme, he asked if there were any questions—and was asked what next winter's fashionable color would be.

Most women make a distinction between "fashion" and "what suits me." A recent French poll showed that 3 percent of women automatically follow fashion, 63 percent follow fashion "when it suits me" and 34 percent follow it not at all. Teen-agers and young women made up most of the 3 percent; women over sixty totally rejected fashion, while the when-it-suits-me attitude was common to most adult women between the ages of thirty and sixty, regardless of income group.

For Saint Laurent, fashion seems to work in mysterious ways. His big chemise of 1974 was the hit of the year when blue denim was in for jeans, jackets, bags and shoes and even skirts. His 1965 Mondrian look, inspired by the painter who saw everything in squares of color, in turn "inspired" a million copies of checkerboard dresses. If Yves creates by reacting, fashion itself is full of contradiction. It is constantly illogical, and its charm is in the way it provokes common sense—sometimes to the despair of its creators. Courrèges's crisp, geometric miniskirts and flat white boots of the mid-1960s were so mercilessly plagiarized that he shut down his salon in anger, reopening a year and a half later with his own ready-to-wear line.

But there are no guarantees that any of the novelties in a collection will ever transcend the runway. Of the two hundred and eighty fresh ideas in a collection, newspapers and newsweeklies will reproduce one or two, fashion magazines maybe six or eight. To be a fashion designer is to square the circle of the too-far-out and the too-simply-suggested. Powerful forces work for conformity. Making a lot of one thing and selling it widely make the assembly line as tempting for the garment industry as planned obsolescence. Get there first, get there fast. Rake it in, then go on to something else again. The market out there is at once fickle and easily bored. We all want to be entertained. Poiret's sweet tyranny.

For the industry, the freedom of the designer is a necessary evil. He shouldn't exist at all, yet designing sense is being expressed more and more forcefully every year, and not only by the "name" hotshots, but by mass-production designers who increasingly manage to get label credit.

At the top of the rag trade, the bets are not only larger but more daring than in any of the other consumer arts. The leading designers cannot get away with the movie- or TV-industry formula, which proclaims that the larger the investment, the less you want to offend anyone in the audience. There is no safety in numbers in fashion, since clothes are supposed to express each consumer's individuality, to be a backdrop against which each will fill in the fine lines of taste. Two people are not offended because they discover they are reading the same book, but if they wear identical dresses, they make mental abstractions of each other's accessories, eye color, makeup, height or size of pocketbook. We are never *ever* supposed to look alike.

At the top, the magic of authority doesn't come from hedging bets; nor does it come from covering them all. America's great leap forward has been to make clothes *available,* says New York's fashion doyenne Diana Vreeland, but besides blue jeans, nothing has really been created in the United States. In France and Italy, where most fashion is created, she says, there are revolutionary tendencies that influence fashion because upheavals are, by definition, upsetting and provocative. "I think you can feel revolution in the clothes before you can see the revolution in the street," she says.

But authority isn't sociology. Nor is it shrewdness. If there were a formula, if success could be programmed, the eighth and sixteenth arrondissements of Paris and Manhattan's Seventh Avenue would be paved with gold (and Hollywood peopled with millionaires). Ritualistic, high-power media packages bomb as cheerfully as PTA amateur nights, because our responses are not totally Pavlovian. In fashion, everything is excess and convention.

How is it that YSL nearly always comes up with exactly what we want at exactly the right time? When he dropped skirts to the knee in January 1969 and showed coats that fell to the ankle, he was clearly excessively out of line. The hemline controversy was unresolved, with younger women reluctant to abandon the miniskirt, but he persisted and six months later went all-out for the midcalf skirt and the Maxi coat. By the fall, the mini had, in fact, begun to lose some of its appeal, and fashion experts agreed that Yves was right. The mini was dead.

In 1976, anyone could foresee the day women would be tired of dressing like men, perpetually in pants. Industry leaders could even pinpoint the approximate season—Saint Laurent himself has a theory that real change comes in seven-to-ten-year cycles—and logically deduct that a latent urge for something "feminine" and "romantic" must be out there. But what new femininity, what new romanticism? Direct recycling is impossible. Clothes of 1970 today look odd in our eyes because we have come to appreciate a new set of colors and contours. The garments of 1960 look "funny" in a nostalgic way, while those of 1950 have reached the age where those who originally wore them consider them hideous. If their daughters are ready to adopt them, it will be as a reinterpretation according to contemporary, not historical, tastes. Yves's inspired solution in 1976 was the Fantasy Look, imbued not so much by the past as by the exotic—a lush, extravagant and theatrical Orient.

Fashion is arbitrary, not reasonable, and it isn't made by J. C. Penney store managers, Bloomingdale's cost accountants or Madison Avenue copywriters. They, like the rest of the industry, are downstream from the wellhead, where the initial spark originates. So are the collection shows. What the buyers, journalists and fashion groupies see on the runways has originated in somebody's mind.

The big buyers think Yves's influence today is both mainstream and totally worldwide. Koko Hashim, vice-president and fashion merchandise director of Dallas-based Neiman-Marcus, thinks YSL is the most international designer. "He picks up inspiration from different attitudes and styles of dressing," she says. "I don't think of him as typical of Paris. He works from a total world point of view." Kal Ruttenstein, Bloomingdale's vice-president and fashion director (and the only male in the front ranks of American buyers), agrees that Yves's influence is the main worldwide influence, while Bergdorf Goodman's Dawn Mello thinks of him as a designer not only of apparel but of new ideas, new concepts. What they and their colleagues, who must create and sustain a store's fashion image, expect from YSL is not merely direction, but, beyond specifics, a spirit of design. They expect the unexpected: the trendier clothes, a firm lead in color combinations and collections that are truly collections—that is, shows that anticipate, say what is new and interpret such novelties well and with good quality.

What goes unsaid is that they also expect him to say when a trend is over. Poiret thought very few people could recognize the end of a fashion, although it was quite simple: all excess in a fashion means it is over. "If I one day announced that henceforth hats would be plain, it's because I had realized they were full of leaves, flowers, feathers and ribbons," he said. "Nevertheless a delegation of industrialists, manufacturers of artificial flowers, leaves, fruits and ribbons came to see me and stood, like the burghers of Calais, supplicating me to go back to trimmings. But what can anyone do against a woman's wish, a woman's yearning?"

Fashion is the emperor's new clothes, appearance and sleight of hand that we applaud even when we can't see how it is done. It is extremes that are necessary to move things along—items that may not necessarily even be purchased. It is an expression of a personal statement, and it is what we don't expect.

Saint Laurent is not afraid of calling himself a classicist. To him, the term implies sacrifice, introspection and a belief that art is perhaps the only reason to think we can transcend ourselves. Classicism implies a certain stubbornness, a need to return to the same problem, the same situation, the same work, a will to try for perfection. As a designer, he is not afraid of limiting himself to one well-defined area of creation and to apply intelligence rather than inspiration. Design is symbolic and has always been a subtle conflict between appearance and reality, between inspiration and its power to impose. A compulsory, lifelong reader of *Remembrance of Things Past*, he believes, like Marcel Proust, that creation is more "real" than life.

Many of Saint Laurent's traits are Proustian. If he isn't as frail as Proust or riddled with suffocating allergies and isn't keeping himself alive with drugs and willpower, he does share something of the novelist's little-boy-lost febrility and desire to speak and create candidly while being aware of a need for concealment that makes many daily adjustments hazardous. Like Proust, he has an uncanny power of accumulating ideas that reaches back beyond his own birth— his focus of inspiration is the mid-1920s, which he claims continue to vibrate in all the arts. If he doesn't share Proust's nostalgia for childhood, he feels deeply that we are living the end of an era, the transformation of an older order, and that he has a sense of what our time is about.

Of late, Saint Laurent has come to identify haute couture with a splendid Proustian sunset of things past, with a disappearance of luxury and elegance that he has a hard time accepting. The Chambre Syndicale puts the number of women in the world who buy their wardrobes in haute couture at five thousand, a figure everybody else thinks too high. Sonia Rykiel, the leading theoretician of the Parisians, thinks there are only a thousand women still dressing in haute couture, and Ungaro thinks there are no more than a hundred. Significantly, Ungaro and Saint Laurent are, with Hubert de Givenchy, the only ones to claim they aren't losing money on their made-to-order salons.

Couture is totally unsuited for the instant obsolescence of throwaway fashion and the new tastes and attitudes of fashion consciousness. With Courrèges, Saint Laurent was the first to sense the growing anachronism of haute couture, predicting in 1966 the demise of the fashion edict. "Now that women have liberated themselves from our dictatorship and the corset of other people's ideas," YSL said in 1971, "they themselves become more important than the clothes they wear."

For a year after that, he experimented with doing away with haute couture altogether, only to reinstate it in 1972. Since then, he has settled on reversing the creative importance so that his haute couture dresses, selling at ten times the off-the-peg versions, are actually high-priced "knockoffs" of his own ready-to-wear originals. More subtly, he has started trends in rtw—as *Women's Wear Daily* trendily abbreviates ready-to-wear—that he then "finishes" in couture. There are years when the two are totally separate, when he says he has "to clear my mind" of one before beginning work on the other; and there are years when rtw has, in effect, become daytime clothes and couture evening clothes.

The shift to rtw has not been easy. He has had to learn his trade over again and almost do violence to the very gifts that brought him success in the first place. Haute couture is essentially a carriage trade. For a couturier, ready-to-wear is a quantum jump into the totally modern concept of design as intended for mass production. Indeed, on the lower rungs of the process, the accuracy of design can multiply annual sales by a factor of ten. Karl Lagerfeld, who was just one year behind YSL at the Chambre Syndicale trade school, took twenty years to make his breakthrough in rtw, but he never had to readapt.

To those aspiring unfortunates who spend uncounted hours knocking on doors, Yves's path to glory was enviably short, and his story can be told as a fairy tale. At ten, this supergifted child, born in sunny North Africa, put on a miniature *Carmen*, making the sets and costumes for his puppet theater himself. At fourteen, he was fascinated by the theater, cut up one of his mother's dresses to make clothes for his younger sisters' dolls. At sixteen, he told himself that within a year, he would have his name emblazoned in neon on the Champs-Elysées. He almost made it. Four years later, the shy, bespectacled youth was acclaimed and adulated and, on a balcony a couple of blocks from the

Champs-Elysées, made an appearance to wave to the cheering crowd.

So much for the fairy tale. The real story is more complicated and much more interesting.

4

THE
BEGINNING

Yves Henri Mathieu Saint Laurent was born on a summer morning in a beautiful big house on the North African shore of the Mediterranean. The date was August 1, 1936. The place was Oran, the second largest city in Algeria.

The French had been in Algeria for a hundred years and the Saint Laurents for a half-century. Yves's father was a shipping agent in the busy port city, the fifth and youngest child of Marie-Jules Mathieu Saint Laurent, who had settled in the land of hard sun and inky shadow in 1883.

The Saint Laurents were an old family of the law from Alsace. Their lineage dates back to the quarter-century after the Thirty Years War, which, in 1648, had made the rich German-speaking province on the western bank of the Rhine part of Louis XIV's domain. Alexandre André Mathieu was born in 1672 in Andolsheim, near Colmar, and was the father of a lawyer. His grandson was a judge and the first to add "Saint Laurent" to the family name. The judge presided over the nuptial rites of Napoleon Bonaparte and Joséphine in 1796. The judge's son and grandson were lawyers in Colmar, where Yves's grandfather was born.

When Marie-Jules was nine, Alsace ceased to be French. The Franco-Prussian War of 1870–71 proved disastrous for France, achieved unification for Germany and lit the long fuse that exploded in World War I. German public opinion and Kaiser Wilhelm's military command wanted to crown the victory with tangible gains, and when a humiliated France sued for peace (and dethroned Napoleon III and his fashion-conscious Eugénie), Alsace and Lorraine became part of the Reich.

Like so many young French-Alsatians, Marie-Jules couldn't wait to leave, and when he was eighteen, he emigrated—not to France but to the nearest of its overseas territories. The mood of Victorian France was optimistic and expansive, and although colonialism never excited the minds of the French as it did the British, most of North and Central Africa was becoming French, as was Indochina and a smattering of Pacific islands. The British wanted territory; the French wanted more people and set out to make the indigenous populations into so many black and yellow Frenchmen.

In Algeria, land could be had for pennies, Arab labor was cheap, and those who knew how to work hard were already pushing back the arid rim of the Sahara and planting vineyards, orchards and barley and wheat fields. The key word from the policymakers in Paris was *assimilation*. Algerians and Tunisians and, later, Moroccans would become swarthy, Moslem Frenchmen. Marie-Jules knew nothing about agriculture, so he settled in Oran, 150 miles west of Algiers, near the Moroccan border. Famous for its beautiful natural harbor—and eventually for being the place where Albert Camus set *The Plague*—Oran was a bustling center of commerce. Marie-Jules went into business. It was only eighteen years later that he found time to marry. His wife was Joséphine, née Charrin. When Charles was born, four months before the outbreak of World War I, Marie-Jules was fifty-two and a wealthy man.

Charles Mathieu Saint Laurent was, even in his youth, a somewhat distant businessman whose only regret was that he was not a lawyer. His presence in the big seaside villa and in the life of his young son was benevolent and distracted. Charles's world was in town, and he and his pretty wife were an intensely social couple. "My father was very fairminded," Yves would recall in adult life. "He let me do what I wanted," meaning that Charles didn't insist when his son announced he wouldn't study for the bar.

Although nothing on the paternal side predisposed Yves toward a career in fashion, on his mother's side, it was another story. Yves's young mother (née Wilbaux) was elegant, impulsive and in love with clothes and parties. When Yves was six, a baby sister, Michèle, was born, and three years later, Brigitte came along. The precocious, honey-haired boy grew up in an atmosphere of cuddled femininity, of motherly example and abetment and of sisterly acquiescence. Yves adored his pretty mother, was extremely timid with strangers and came to see the world not so much with the eye of the innocent as with the goblin eye of someone developing in playful and protected isolation. His universe was not the alleys of the casbah, the bustle of the harbor or the boulevards of the European quarters; it was the big house by the sea and his own room.

"Now it can be told: Yves Saint Laurent was a sissy when he was a kid," *People* magazine would write in 1974 when he was rich and famous. More subtly, Anthony Burgess, who profiled YSL for *The New York Times* Sunday magazine, would sum up the early years as an inward escape from sunbaked harshness to "the softer lights of the theater, Maeterlinckian shadows, the fantasy of decor and costume." Yves adored solitary games, to play in his room with scissors and crayons, but his childhood was no lengthy excursion into fey, ascetic preciosity.

As Jean Cocteau wrote in a preface to *Le Bal du Comte d'Orgel*, "What family doesn't have its child prodigy! The word was invented by families." When three-year-old Yves decided a Punch and Judy show was his favorite toy, his parents smiled encouragingly. When he was seven and built a puppet theater, they applauded. But he was never allowed to become a child monster. The house rang with laughter, and he was not an only child.

The Saint Laurents moved in the best of Oran's colonial circles, and when Maman dressed for an evening out, Yves and Michèle stood in the hallway in rapt attention. Lucienne was to swear that her son was only four when, on one such occasion, he made an aunt change clothes and accessories before she was allowed to go out with his parents. Once the adults were off, however, a native nurse put the pint-sized Beau Brummel to bed, because the next morning it was off to school like every other kid.

His interest in the theater never waned. After the Punch and Judy show and the puppet theater came a time when he struggled with costumes for marionettes. World War II passed over his head. He was three when it started and six when American, British and Free French troops landed in Oran in the Allied push east toward Tunis and the invasion of Italy. Three years later, Yves began to paint. One of his first efforts was a scene of a village fair, a watercolor that thirty-five years later was to decorate a wall in his mother's Paris apartment. Later, he imitated living expressionists and executed a portrait of his sister Brigitte, "in the manner of Foujita," and landscapes in the style of Utrillo. Sketching and theatrical arts came together in fashion, and Yves began to draw dresses for Maman and Michèle.

He was thirteen when his parents took him to see Molière's *School for Wives*. The year was 1947, and the play was a road-company production of Louis Jouvet's perennial Athénée Théâtre classical hit. The magnificent Jouvet, whose melted caramel voice and illuminating interpretations on stage and screen had charmed French-speaking audiences for decades, was himself playing Arnolphe, who wants to marry his student Agnès and therefore brings her up in total ignorance (which doesn't prevent her from preferring young Horace in the end). *L'Ecole des femmes* enchanted everybody at the Oran Municipal Theater that night, but what left Yves speechless was Christian Bérard's sets and costumes. When he got home, he had to try himself. "I was impassioned by the elegance and simplicity of the sets and the same with the costumes," he was to remember. "Back home, I invented the costumes over again, taking little pieces of paper and scraps of fabric. I didn't know how to sew, so I cut them out with scissors and pasted them together. Let's not say they were dolls. They were personalities made of cardboard which I sketched and dressed and which I alone saw."

Indeed, Lucienne was to recall that no grown-up was ever allowed to see any of Yves's productions. "We let him turn an empty room into a theater," she was to remember. "He wrote and directed plays, designed and made all the sets and costumes with his sisters and cousins as actors, but he never let his father or me see any of his productions."

School was not a happy time for this limpet adolescent, who was an easy target of other boys' taunts and sarcasms. Intellectually and emotionally well-developed, he was shy and introverted, with occasional outbursts of nasty temper and skulking pride. Later in life, he would call his years as a schoolboy "tragic" and date his ambition to reach the top to a need to get back at his tormentors. "I suffered so much in school because of my colleagues, and when I was despondent I would tell myself, one day I'll be stronger than you. You'll be nothing. You'll be down there and I'll be up here. I think that's what gave me strength."

Adolescence enlarged the horizons and made him realize that he was a provincial—worse, that he was a colonial. "I felt especially strong about all this since we were living in Algeria," he would say. "When you're from the provinces, you develop an acute sense of what you're missing. And of what you're not." He was not a Parisian, and he smarted under the derisive *pied noir* (literally, "black foot") that Frenchmen from France called French settlers in North Africa. He realized he had an accent and that, in pure *pied noir* fashion, he added *"n'est-ce pas?"* (isn't that so?) to every other sentence.

Algeria was not the *"patrie intérieure"* it was for his most famous compatriot, Camus, whose renown was reaching its zenith as Yves entered the Oran *lycée*, and who hated Paris, suffered recurring attacks of tuberculosis and made an inhospitable, dirty Paris, a rainy Amsterdam and a sinister

Czech village images of prison and exile where pale hard bodies longed in vain for light. Yves would always be drawn to the sun-baked lands, and in his maturity would choose North African models for their warm, more-than-Mediterranean sensuousness, but his attachment would not be to his fellow *colons,* and he would never share Camus's sense of tragedy during the long Algerian war of the 1950s and 1960s, which would see the *pieds noirs* come down on the wrong side of history, the last French colonialists, in the end loathed by the majority of Frenchmen.

Entering the *lycée,* Yves decided to major in modern languages. Paris beckoned, but before his mother took him there as a treat for passing his philosophy exams, he read about it. From his sixteenth birthday on, this skinny college student in search of heroes bought and devoured newspapers and magazines from the capital. French *Vogue* was his favorite. The big monthly wasn't just devoted to fashion, although he copied hundreds of its sketches; it covered theater, ballet and, to a certain extent, whatever concerned the decorative arts. The first gods of this adolescent mythomaniac came largely from these pages. Chanel and Victor Hugo, a couple of well-dressed society ladies, one or two models, Christian Dior and Schiaparelli were, after Bérard and Jouvet, the people he admired.

Not that Yves neglected school. While achieving better than passing grades, he took to spending his free time locked in his room, copying and tracing drawings, inventing and sketching, and realizing that to approach his deities, he would have to know how to cut fabric, how to hold a brush, how to light a stage.

He was properly impressed with Paris and became speechless when Maman managed to have the two of them invited to a fashionable cocktail party on avenue Montaigne, a few doors from the salon of Christian Dior, whose newest look was the princess line. Together, mother and son "did" the Faubourg Saint-Honoré and the place Vendôme, looking at dresses at Lanvin and Schiaparelli, and visiting the brand-new boutique twenty-four-year-old Hubert de Givenchy had opened in rue Saint-Florentin after four years of designing for Elsa Schiaparelli. Next door, Maman ordered a sea green organza gown from Jean Patou and, with Yves, tiptoed through the avenue George V salon of the haughtiest of them all—Cristóbal de Balenciaga.

All too soon it was back to Oran. Yves's imagination was brimming with impressions and with ideas of exaggerated, geometric shapes, boldly asymmetric and stylized dresses and sculptured formal designs.

He kept sketching and preparing for his baccalaureate. With his mother's encouragement, he sent one of his sketches to Paris—not to any of the couture houses but to the International Wool Secretariat, which annually organized a design contest open to everybody regardless of age or nationality. The number of contestants each year was around six thousand. The winner didn't get any money but saw his or her design executed by one of the leading houses. When the 1953 winners were announced, Yves was in third place. The next year, he won first prize with a black, asymmetrically cut cocktail dress. The runner-up, winning with a coat design, was a sixteen-year-old boy from Hamburg named Karl Lagerfeld.

Yves's cocktail dress was made by Givenchy in a fine wool crepe and, with Maman, Yves traveled to Paris to accept his winner's certificate and to be photographed with a mannequin modeling the dress. One of the judges, Thelma Sweetingburgh, was to remember him as "an ugly, ungainly, overgrown boy with thick glasses, and so horribly shy he couldn't take his eye off the floor." Augustin Dabadie, *Le Figaro*'s fashion editor, was to be a little more polite: "He never opened his mouth. He was the true *'enfant prodige,'* intense, restless and, like a young fawn, easily frightened."

The next step was to try and meet Michel de Brunhoff, the director of French *Vogue*. Brunhoff was a great snob who dressed impeccably and was nicknamed Phineas Fogg because of his enormous snow-white sideburns. He was of an Alsatian family long associated with publishing, and his sister had married Lucien Vogler, the founder of the *Gazette du Bon Ton*, possibly the best fashion periodical ever produced, which, until its demise in 1925, had given a free hand to such artists as Raoul Dufy, George Lepage and Edouard

Benito, allowing them to interpret the latest fashions in original drawings. More important for Yves, Brunhoff was famous for having helped young persons getting started in the business.

Edmonde Charles-Roux, the future author and biographer of Chanel, was cutting her journalistic teeth at *Vogue* that year, and she was to remember being given a letter from Oran, accompanied by a letter of introduction from a North African department store owner, specifying that a seventeen-year-old local youth and his mother would be seeking an appointment with Monsieur Brunhoff. Charles-Roux was also to remember the arrival on the appointed day. "He was an adolescent cut like a giraffe and constantly struggling with huge glasses that kept sliding down his nose. He had a false air of idleness about him. In fact, he was more reserved than timid."

The interview with Brunhoff was brief and to the point. Yves never opened his mouth and it was his mother who showed the portfolio of sketches. Brunhoff declared himself impressed but wondered aloud if it wasn't best for the silent young man to graduate first.

Yves returned to the *lycée* in Oran. Sketching was exciting, but fashion was not his dream. The theater was. When he wasn't cramming for exams, he locked himself in his room and sketched endlessly, and when he wasn't studying or sketching, he tried to turn his visual ideas into dresses and had Michèle and little Brigitte model his efforts. Working in fabrics, however, was something else. But, he told himself, his goal wasn't to become a couturier—which didn't mean that the shortest way to stage design couldn't pass through fashion illustrating; Brunhoff had been encouraging, and hadn't Bérard himself done fashion illustrations? Theater and fashion did overlap. Paul Poiret had let himself be inspired by Léon Bakst's fabulous sets and costumes and had clothed Isadora Duncan, Eleanora Duse and Sarah Bernhardt for the stage; Lucien Lelong had designed Marlene Dietrich's wardrobe, Jeanne Lanvin had devised theatrical costumes for Arletty, Schiaparelli for Greta Garbo and Mademoiselle Chanel (as everybody respectfully called the now-retired designer) had invented costumes in Hollywood while her poet friend Jean Cocteau had sketched his own costumes for his movie *Orphée*.

Four months after the meeting with Brunhoff, Yves graduated, with a major in modern languages. In June 1954, he went to Paris—alone—to see the *Vogue* director. This time Brunhoff thought the young *pied noir* should stay, and a few days after his eighteenth birthday, Yves had his first job. Since he had a knack for drawing pretty heads and pretty coiffures, *Vogue* made him its illustrator specializing in hairdos.

Charles-Roux was to remember that Yves had grown even taller in the intervening months—"one meter eighty-four of slinky precocity, total muteness, sixty-five kilos of juvenile impatience." Brunhoff took an interest in the young illustrator who signed his sketches Yves Mathieu Saint Laurent, specifying that he didn't like to see the *Saint* abbreviated to *St* and that there should be no dash between *Saint* and *Laurent*. The boy blushed at anything, but he obviously had talent. Patiently, Brunhoff explained that the difference between *illustrator* and *modelist*—as a designer working for a name couturier was called—was technique. *Technique* meant a solid knowledge not only of cutting, sewing and draping but an understanding of surface and volume. It meant knowing how to design for men, women and children, how to design accessories and furs, how to drape on a dummy and how to cut on the table. In short, it meant going to trade school.

In the fall of 1954, Yves enrolled at the school run by the Chambre Syndicale. The private school occupied three dingy floors in a commercial building in the rue St. Roch off avenue de l'Opéra, and Yves hated every minute of it. But he was in Paris and the school was only blocks from the rue Cambon, where the most exciting event of 1954 took place— Chanel's reopening after a sixteen-year hiatus. Mademoiselle, who didn't admit to being seventy-one, had closed her house in a huff in 1939, when her workers had threatened a strike. Her attempted comeback came seven years after Dior's New Look, which in one stroke had outdated everything, and her casual chic was far removed from Dior's lady-like elegance. Chanel hated Dior and said so. To mark her second coming, she gave him and other couturiers a caustic going-over in a series of snappy interviews.

For Yves, however, 1954 was anything but exciting. When school was over, he wouldn't tell Brunhoff he had learned anything. All he would say was that it had been the most difficult and boring year of his life. The school administration would remember him as its most talented and glamorous student—together with Lagerfeld, who entered the year Yves left.

Luckily, there were the vacations. Yves spent the summer of 1955 in Oran and began to dress his sisters again, this time with better results. When he was by himself, he sketched a whole collection—evening gowns and daytime dresses, beachwear and accessories. One idea he was particularly fond of was a slim tunic with a long jacket reaching to the knees over an even slimmer skirt.

The summer was glorious, but the mood of Algeria's French was somber. The Algerian War, which had started in 1954, showed no signs of abating as terror, mutilations, counter-terror and torture took place on both sides with increased savagery. There was no middle. You were either *pied noir* and sworn to keep Algeria—and everything you had—French, or you were Arab and equally committed to a cruel struggle for independence. "It's better to suffer certain injustices than to commit them," Camus said, but as a *pied noir*, he, too, hesitated to come out on the Arabs' side as Jean-Paul Sartre and almost all of France's intellectuals increasingly did.

Politics didn't interest Saint Laurent, although he did his best to understand. His parents felt little guilt for being in Algeria and thought they could decently stay. Yves was irresistibly drawn toward Paris and, at the end of the summer, left with fifty sketches. The first day back at *Vogue*, he showed them to the boss.

Brunhoff was stunned. Without contact with Paris, Yves had come up with the H line that Dior had just invented. Only two days earlier, Dior himself had shown Brunhoff his personal drawings for his winter collection, which included a knee-length jacket over the narrowest of skirts. What happened during the next hours was to be written in 1961, complete with dialogue, by Agence Dalmas journalist Michel Borry:

"Have you seen anybody besides me?" Brunhoff asked incredulously.

"No, Monsieur," Yves answered.

Brunhoff got Dior on the phone. "So far I've never asked you anything," Brunhoff told the couturier at the other end of the line. "But now I want you to meet—and I mean right away—a young man who is in my office here!"

Dior answered that even if the young man was a genius, he, Dior, couldn't see him. "I'm sorry but I'm exhausted and I'm leaving tomorrow."

Brunhoff insisted. "I don't care. You must see his work. I'll bring him over right away!"

Before Dior could answer, Brunhoff hung up, grabbed the sketches and pushed the nonplussed Saint Laurent ahead of him down the stairs and into a cab.

Dior was equally stunned. From the sketches that Brunhoff put in front of him, his own new line stared him in the face. But this young man who practically hid behind Brunhoff knew nothing of what Dior himself had just invented and apparently hadn't even sketched his collection ideas in Paris. Within twenty-four hours, Yves was hired as a modelist on a three-month trial basis at 60,000 francs, or $120, a month. After the probation period was up, he was put under contract and told his duties also included sketching the House of Dior Christmas cards.

If Yves was a cherubic nineteen-year-old who looked like a romantic seminarian, Dior was, at fifty, an overworked and overweight pink little bachelor who had the world in his hand. Women obeyed Paris because of him, because no one could forget that his New Look had turned the page on the war and its drab aftermath in 1947 and in one swish of newly discovered stiffened nylon swept away thirteen uninterrupted years of the square-shouldered, military, Schiaparelli-inspired look. "We are saved," wrote Susan Mary Alsop in *To Marietta from Paris*, after attending the memorable February 12 show where models with yards of fabric in their skirts spun up the aisle to the sound of rustling petticoats and the crashing of ashtray stands. "Gone the stern padded shoulders, *in* are soft rounded shoulders without padding, nipped-in waists, wide, wide skirts about four inches below the knee. And such well-made armor inside the dress that one doesn't need underclothes."

One hundred percent financed by textile tycoon Marcel Boussac, Dior, the one-time art dealer and former Lelong modelist, had opened his salon in pristine premises at 30 avenue Montaigne and in one afternoon restored world confidence in Paris as fashion leader. He and his staff had worked eighteen-hour days to accommodate I. Magnin, Bergdorf Goodman, Bendel and the first famous customers, the Duchess of Windsor and Eva Perón. In quick succession, lines had followed lines—the envol line, the princess line, the tulip line and now the H or I line, all adding up to a stylized fashion with grand geometric and exaggerated shapes and great if contrived glamour. Behind the success, fundamental changes revolutionized the House of Dior and, by repercussion, Paris haute couture. With trepidation, Dior put his name on nylon stockings and on men's neckties, opened a shoe department and put his imprint on scarves, gloves and custom jewelry. Following Chanel's lead, he launched his own perfume. Together with Givenchy and Pierre Balmain—another Lelong graduate who had opened his own salon—Dior created clothes that had body and shape of their own and were popular with retailers for their "hanger appeal." Chanel was the focal point of the opposite camp, of clothes that had no existence apart from the women wearing them. Mademoiselle's conviction was that clothes should be easy to wear and, together with Patou, the House of Lanvin and sometimes Balenciaga, she emphasized clothes made in soft jersey and silky tweeds.

Dior realized that his young modelist was hypersensitive and blushingly shy, but also that there was nothing evasive about him when he discussed what interested him. Others were less charitable. The art critic Pierre Schneider was to remember Yves as a "well-behaved, tremendously overgrown schoolboy sleepwalking his way through a world of grown-ups." Yves himself would remember his first year with Dior for its fascination. "I had just left my province behind me and I was literally captivated. I was very timid and I didn't open my mouth. No one can any longer imagine what couture was in those days—the dash, glitter and glamour of the House of Dior!"

He soon learned who was who among the fifteen hundred employes. As *directeur-général*, Jacques Rouet was the architect of the expanding concept of fashion and, as general manager, Henri Fayot was the purse strings and *éminence grise* of the aging but enthusiastic Boussac, whose millions were coming tumbling back to him and whose textile mills were working overtime. Dior's trio of intimate collaborators were Raymonde Zehnacker, who represented order; Marguerite Carre, who supplied technique; and Huberte Bricard, who produced the flights of fantasy.

Yves was given a corner in the back office but was soon moved "upstairs" and told to work at a small desk in Dior's own workroom. His output was enormous. For the 1956 summer collection, he submitted nearly four hundred sketches. Dior himself did many more, and the result was a combination of ideas. Acknowledgment came in the form of a long-term contract and the title of artistic director. Yves even got his own assistant to concentrate solely on the ready-to-wear for London and New York—Marc Bohan. Eleven years older than YSL, Bohan had worked for Patou, designed for Swiss ready-to-wear makers and tried—and failed, because of insufficient capital—to establish his own house. "It marked me," Bohan would say later. "It was an enormous disappointment."

Most couturiers are superstitious, and Dior was almost as bad as Charles Worth, who feared March 10 for some reason and died on that day in 1895, and Chanel, who attached the greatest importance to the date of her birth—August 5— showed her summer clothes on February 5, her winter collections on her birthday and called her perfume No. 5. Dior had to touch wood before and during the elaboration of any new line and, with a somewhat morbid sense of premonition, told Lucienne Saint Laurent that her son would replace him.

The pace was grueling. The buildup of public expectation exerted tremendous pressure, and Dior, who already had two heart attacks behind him, kept gaining weight and some days looked more like a seventy-year-old than a man in his early fifties. He had no financial or domestic worries, but he had to "deliver." Behind the facade of luxury, 30 avenue Montaigne was a business organization where records were kept with the efficiency that only a self-made millionaire like Boussac could impose on such a *fantaisiste* trade as high fashion. The House of Dior was incorporated in five countries, farmed out franchises in five others, and Dior himself was sent on endless overseas publicity tours. Each Paris collection included 250 creations, broken down into 60 for the salon, 110 for the Fifth Avenue boutique and 80 for the West End outlet.

Master and pupil had a strangely silent relationship. Each morning, Saint Laurent went to Dior's spacious office, sat down and silently watched the sketches being created. The two men almost never spoke.

"I learned more than I can ever say," Yves would remember, "simply by observing. He seemed to have a lot of confidence in me and I had some ideas that followed along with his. We worked without even discussing or talking. If I had an idea, I would design it, and show it to him—and he would nod, or shake his head, or sometimes point to details with a pencil, or perhaps redraw it on a fresh sheet of paper. Between us was a silent power."

Saint Laurent adopted—for good—Dior's ecclesiastic manners. Unlike most designers, who leap about, scream, beat seamstresses over the head with yardsticks and throw tantrums, Dior was gentle, reserved and retiring. Already less than outgoing and never given to raising his voice, Yves had little difficulty assuming the former art dealer's gestures.

After showing a collection, Dior invariably left Paris, and not even Boussac would know where to get hold of him. He was somewhere between Biarritz and Cannes; and if he phoned Yves or anyone else on the staff to find out how things were and was asked where he was, he would laughingly reply, "At Albi. I've been to the museum to see the Toulouse-Lautrecs, but I'm leaving in an hour. I'll call you again."

Before World War II, Dior had had a brief career as an art dealer in the Faubourg Saint-Honoré. There he had shown the work of painters like Leoni and Eugene Berman, Salvador Dali and Montmartre's poet-painter Max Jacob. In 1934, Dior fell ill. He was obliged to give up his little gallery and to spend a year convalescing. The sale of a large painting by Raoul Dufy, *Le Plan de Paris,* which he had bought from Paul Poiret, tided him over, but the question of earning a living had to be faced. Encouraged by a friend, he made his first sketches and sold hat designs to Agnès, a famous milliner on place Vendôme. From his first job as a stylist for Robert Piguet, he entered the House of Lelong.

Yves liked to hear about the gallery days and about Dior's friends. Christian Bérard had been a friend. Yes, Bérard had been a gross, nonchalant and much-loved figure, a diabetic and an opium addict. Chanel had called him Bébé Bérard because he had become an addict in the company of the black American boxing champion Panama Al Brown. Colette had called him the guy who, without ulterior motives, guided Paris's infatuation with such good fortune that everybody loved him. After the war, Dior, Bérard, Cocteau and theater decorator André Dignimont had worked together to launch Paris as a fashion capital again. To show that despite the ordeal of the Occupation, Paris had remained the center of couture, they had put together a Theater of Fashion. The first performances had been in 1945 in the Musée des Arts Décoratifs, and people had come from everywhere and made the show a success. A year later, Boussac had offered to finance Dior, and the rest was history. Dior still had Bérard's drawings of the New Look.

The atmosphere was casual at avenue Montaigne, despite Dior's reserved manner. Most members of the inner circle used the familiar *tu* instead of *vous* in addressing each other. Madame Raymonde and Madame Marguerite had come with Dior from Lelong, and with them, he made a selection from the hundreds of sketches he and Yves produced. Dior came to work at nine thirty every morning, and after going through the mail and donning a doctor's white smock, he settled down in his studio. He stayed at his desk all day, usually even eating lunch there and, in the afternoon, overseeing the nonstop parade of models and fitters from the various workrooms. Using a teacher's pointer that he always carried, he indicated where the dresses in progress were wrong, and as the day went on, there were more and more alterations to be made. This must be recut, that gotten rid of completely, he would say.

"Nothing escaped his eagle eye," Yves would remember. "And although people began to groan, often surprised by his dissatisfaction, his obstinacy was justified. In the end, they found a way of correcting what by now was obvious to them, too."

Dior was a hard taskmaster for his modelist, too. When Yves showed his first sketches, the great couturier threw a hundred of them on the floor, saying they were "too exaggerated." "One must not push things too far," was one of Dior's admonitions Yves would remember, "because one of the first secrets of elegance is genuine simplicity."

The 1956–57 winter collection was politely received. The featured waistless chemise dress that narrowed toward the hem was called a refinement of Givenchy's "sack," but the breakthrough of the season was that of Pierre Cardin, who had set himself up in business in 1949 and whose first client had been none other than Christian Dior. Moved to tears, Dior ordered a lion's costume for what turned out to be the last costume ball of the patron saint of the surrealists, Count Etienne de Beaumont.

Yves lived in a single room in a large apartment owned by an old woman on avenue Pierre 1er de Serbie, a leisurely ten-minute stroll from avenue Montaigne. The days, and sometimes evenings, were exhausting, and he often fell into bed to sleep around the clock. But he also went to the opening of most new plays, to the ballet and the opera. More often than not, he was in the company of Suzanne Luling, a sales director at Dior, who was even taller than he.

Suzanne, a big, awkward-looking girl with a full-throated laugh and an appetite for life that made it impossible for her to go to bed before dawn, was known by everybody in the business. She had a sense of the picturesque, and the stories she told were always about people, never about places or things. For Yves, she became the initiator into the rites of the fashion business, where everybody was on terms of the greatest intimacy, called each other by first name, kept nothing to themselves and where, as in the theater, difficulties were quickly overcome. Everyone got angry without quite knowing why and, a few minutes later, called each other my angel and my darling.

Yves was also seen with Phillippine de Rothschild, the daughter of the baron and baroness. There were rumors that he was thinking of marrying Phillippine, but he squelched those by saying, "I don't think I could make a good marriage because I am so shut up within myself."

Brunhoff had introduced him to Jean Cocteau, the homosexual poet, novelist, illustrator, filmmaker, drug addict and socialite who was a friend of everyone who mattered. Now Yves discovered the plays of Cocteau and Giraudoux, the acting of Jean-Louis Barrault, and began going to the theater every night. The stage was becoming an obsession again as he soaked up colors, impressions, surprises. As Charles-Roux would write in a *Figaro Littéraire* piece on Yves fifteen years later, "Let us pay homage to the boss who could admit and understand this divided interest. God knows it is not a common trait. Dior did better than that, he encouraged his assistant's passion for the theater while at the same time using more and more of his sketches." Of Dior's 1956 winter collection, 50 of the 180 finished creations were pure Saint Laurent.

One evening, when he and Dior were working late, the boss sighed and said he would like to retire to his newly built but rarely visited Colle Noire villa in the hills above Cannes. Another time, Dior asked, "What are you waiting for to send me off to pasture?"

Politely, Yves answered that he was there to learn and simply considered himself very lucky.

"Either you're a true creator or you're indeed an idiot who's been lucky," Dior said. "In any case, I need proof before I retire. You'll design the entire spring collection!"

Dior never got his proof. In October 1957, while visiting

the Montecatini spa in Italy for his obesity, he died of a heart attack.

The news caused consternation at avenue Montaigne and a tremor at the Paris stock exchange. Yves went into seclusion. When friends tried to call, he refused to answer the telephone.

Even before the near-national funeral from the St. Honoré d'Eylau church where Yves flanked Boussac and the rest of the braïn trust, a stockholders' meeting took place. The consensus was to call in an experienced couturier; but, someone pointed out, any such outsider would have to learn Dior's technique, and there wasn't much time. The spring collection was scheduled to be unveiled January 30. Boussac suggested they go with the young artistic director who knew the house and the Dior technique. When someone objected that "the boy is too young," Boussac grunted that he, too, had started at a tender age and, one might say, hadn't done too badly.

Yves still dreamed of a career in stage designing, and when the offer came, he hesitated. Everybody told him he would never be forgiven if he turned down the offer, that even to hesitate was a crazy self-indulgence. Not to talk about the money—630,000 francs, or 15,000 1957 dollars, a year. And it was understood that if he was successful, he would be elected a director of the company within a year or two. The pressure was tremendous and his nerves were shot. When he said yes, he managed to extort the permission to go to Oran for a quiet week.

He was back before Christmas with a new line. The backbone of the collection was a simple black silk-and-wool dress with a bow marking a high waist and with the hem raised to just above the knees. The gently flaring design was judged not too different from Dior's A-line but just different enough, and put into rushed production.

"Yves knows exactly what he wants, and gets it," said Jean-Claude Donati, an executive at the house. When a made-up dress was first brought to him, Yves imitated his late master's bearing and stood back, arms folded, and scrutinized the garment. If it didn't please him, he had it destroyed, regardless of cost. Said Donati, "I've seen him tear up patterns that other top designers would have given a year's salary to have produced." But Yves wanted perfection, and was quoted as saying that he tried to look at everything as if Dior were still looking over his shoulder.

He made few changes in the work routine. The shyness was still there, and when he didn't want to commit himself on something, he politely said, "I've never asked myself that question." But he couldn't be pushed around. When a woman in charge of accessories kept trying to convince him to use a certain alligator bag to go with the dress he was inspecting, his answer was mild but definitive. "We will not use the bag, Madame."

The expectations and the media curiosity were tremendous. Yves Mathieu Saint Laurent, who just weeks earlier had been an unknown, was suddenly a starlet compared with Brigitte Bardot, Françoise Sagan and the wunderkind poet Minou Drouet. He was variously called Christian II, young Mozart and, less indulgently, the New Sad Child. Madame Raymonde and the other chiefs of the twenty-eight workrooms were billed as "the stepmothers." Gossip columnists said he was getting fan mail, including poems from rhapsodic ladies and, after it was reported that he had a cold in wintry Paris, homemade cough drops from less ethereal admirers. He was reported being recognized standing in line at a Champs-Elysées cinema.

The big day would be January 30, 1958, and Yves told his mother that although Michèle and Brigitte begged to come to Paris for the occasion, it would be too much for him to have his sisters in the audience.

Christine Tidmarsh, an English girl who was later to become a designer in Milan, was one of the models working for Yves on the collection. "He was wonderful to work for," she was to remember. "He knew exactly what he wanted, but he'd always ask what *you* felt about a particular dress or color. And he'd listen. Very rare. He was fun, too. He knew everyone by name and the atmosphere was marvelous."

On January 30, 1958, an impressive and skeptical crowd filled the cream-and-ivory-colored salon on avenue Montaigne. Svetlana, Victoire, Christine and seventeen other models made a succession of fresh clothes spin and flutter.

People cried, laughed, clapped and shook hands. When it was all over, no one wanted to leave, and for nearly an hour, it was what the headlines of a conservative London newspaper called "an amazing scene." Saint Laurent was forcibly hauled out of his hiding place behind heavy drapes and up onto the runway, where stage star Madeleine Renaud kissed him. In the rush forward to embrace and congratulate him, Pamela Churchill was trampled and Madame Arturo Lopez fell off one of the chairs she and others had climbed up on. Finally, Yves was forced to appear on the balcony waving to the crowd outside, a gesture even Dior himself had never received. When he retreated into the building, the cheers became more insistent. "Go out again," a friend urged. Yves shook his head. "No," he said, "that wouldn't be right. It's not me they are hailing—but the memory of Dior."

For the first time in three months, Boussac and the brain trust breathed and said, "But of course. . . ." By midnight, the $180,000 that the trapeze line had cost was recovered via unending telephone orders, and by dawn, Paris newspapers cried that the great Dior tradition would continue, that Saint Laurent had saved France.

At twenty-one Yves found himself perched on the million-dollar edifice of the most influential fashion house in the world. With his first collection, he had kept his balance.

_____ *5*

MONEY,
MONEY,
MONEY

The empire Yves Saint Laurent controls today is as different in substance and structure as the late 1950s fashions are from the styles at the dawn of the 1980s. Despite its artistic director's enormous success the first time out, the House of Dior was rudderless in 1958 and faced an uncertain future. Its founder was dead and it was totally beholden to the powerful Boussac textile interests. Today, the YSL touch commands such respect—and such prices—that the House of Saint Laurent is the only major house in the world entirely owned by its two founding partners.

The headquarters and nerve center is the three-story avenue Marceau town house a few hundred meters up from the Seine and the place de l'Alma. Here, Yves hunkers over a small, folding worktable. At his left is a stack of white sketching cards; on the floor sits Hazel, his beige Chihuahua. Puffing on a Kool, he plucks a dagger-sharp 2-B pencil from a pot to his right and swiftly, unerringly sketches another grand tomorrow, one year stopping the parade with high-camp fashions that are impractical, fantastical and egotistical and the next leaving others to undo themselves in the flamboyance he has abandoned for an inspired return to basics.

From the glass-door entrance, the visitor is greeted by an opulent 1860s decor. The walls are in scarlet moiré, the floors covered with sea green carpets and the furnishings are spare settees, a Louis XV desk and the traditional gilt chairs. The lighting is modern track, bounced off marbleized walls and fringed white draperies. An imposing staircase leads to the more private second floor, where Bergé's vast office dominates the landing. Bergé's executive desk is directly under a bigger-than-life portrait by Andy Warhol of Yves without glasses. YSL's own worktable is behind mirrored doors, in a cubicle overlooking the garage courtyard. Ostentation is not a necessity when he works. He can curl up almost anywhere to sketch, and calls the town house a folly.

"The most ruinous of empty gestures," he said in 1974 when he and Pierre bought the building and spent $400,000 redecorating it. "But since haute couture is condemned, let it die in style at least." When asked if haute couture couldn't survive as a craft if it abandoned all this pomp, he said no. "Haute couture can't be modernized. It is a fiesta; it needs pomp and display, rites, the full orchestra, the fireworks."

Saint Laurent spends his working day out of public view, with his intimate crew and his models. Anne-Marie Muñoz is the "guardian of the temple," as he says, and Ida Fayoll is the chief of the workrooms. Both have been with him since the House of Dior days, as has Gabrielle Busschaert, who heads the YSL public relations. Jean-Louis Derbord is the youngest member of the crew, a thirty-year-old wizard of a tailor who is responsible for the thousand-and-one rolls of silk and satin with which entire rooms are laden. Madame Felisa, who worked next to Balenciaga from the time she was thirteen until his retirement in 1968, is the newest member.

"It is through Madame Felisa that I discovered *flou*—the soft, floating technique of making dresses—as it relates to the hips and shoulders," says Yves, who is called Monsieur Saint Laurent by everybody here.

A quartet of models are under year-long contracts, because Yves never works on dummies or forms. "To work on a woman's body is the only way to develop *flou*, movement, imagination in clothes. A good model can save you ten years of work. I need a woman to try my things on. I work it out with her, I don't 'create.'"

He considers himself lucky to have the collaborators he has—Loulou de la Falaise, Muñoz, Fayoll, Felisa, Derbord and the models. "Together we make a stewing pot. Things bubble and brew. There's a lot of ESP and trust in the stew—among us, we get the collection done. It took me a long time to realize this is the only way to work. Collaboration is everything; a team of people who respect each other and are good at what they do, each pulling for the team with confidence in themselves and in each other. No jealousy, no competitiveness. I'm lucky, but I'm severe with myself as well. I'm incredibly lucid about what I do. I constantly eliminate."

The corporate Yves Saint Laurent, S.A., has 230 employes, but only 5 collaborators, and the mannequins are part of Yves's own team. The rest are under chief of personnel Maurice Pittet, who is under administrative director Christian Rivero, who answers to Bergé's second-in-command, Jean-Sébastien Szwarc, a vivacious technocrat, who is flanked by Marc Vincent and Yves Faro.

Yves Saint Laurent, S.A., gives employment to ten thousand men and women worldwide. Eighty percent of the ready-to-wear sold under the Saint Laurent Rive Gauche label is made by C. Mendes, S.A., an old-time manufacturer with head offices in rue d'Aboukir in Paris's old garment district, and factories in and around Angers. The production is quality-controlled from 5 avenue Marceau, and is priced in the lower end of the couture-labeled ready-to-wear—in France, somewhere between Daniel Hechter and Christian Aujard. The price range is deliberate. "A label can no longer sell anything and everything," says Bergé.

Although YSL is rather removed from the business end, the cost of ready-to-wear has been a concern of his for years.

"How to get the Rive Gauche coat that costs nine hundred francs down to four hundred?" is one of his existentialist questions. When a reporter asked him, in 1973, what the difference was between a made-to-order coat selling for four thousand francs and a Rive Gauche coat selling for one tenth that amount, he disarmingly said, "With the exception of the fabric, none at all."

"When you can get such similar-looking fabrics," he added, pointing to a picture of himself between two dresses that were identical except in price, "no one wants the expensive one." This is one reason he has lost interest in haute couture and, in 1971, nearly closed the salon altogether.

From the moment he became independent, Saint Laurent began to turn away from the idea that Paris must remain a mecca for those who can pay as much for a dress as most will pay for a car. Since the mid-1960s, he has said that he would like to turn his back on the very rich; that if he keeps his private clients, it is to keep his seamstresses employed, not to satisfy wealthy egos—and other statements guaranteed to offend the traditional, albeit shrinking, clientele. As the House of Saint Laurent grew in strength and reputation, his philosophy became more and more affected by the aspiring young rather than the privileged few. Yet his feelings toward haute couture remain ambivalent. He listens—and occasionally nods—to the opposing views, to those who say that haute couture is the last refuge of craftsmanship and that with its death, something very precious will disappear —and to those who say that with its arrogant clients and exploited work force, it is the last bastion of ugly capitalism. To those who speak with melancholy about a dying craft, he retorts that with machine stitching, haute couture is no longer very haute. To those who want to let the outmoded old lady die because exciting things are happening in textiles, he says he never tires of watching creative hands.

If he wants to come down in the middle, he says the meaning of luxury itself is changing. "To mean what it means, luxury must be in short supply. Time and peace are luxury items today, not hand-stitched hems." He acknowledges that the agony is also industrial. The specialized couture work force has shrunk from ten thousand to three thousand in ten years, due to retirement, attrition and less than brilliant wages. Few young people feel any calling. It is already hard to find pleatmakers, embroiderers or specialists in ornamentation and trimming, he admits.

But haute couture represents less than 5 percent of the turnover of any of the Paris houses. By clever scheduling of deliveries, Bergé has nevertheless managed to turn the biannual January and July haute couture presentations, which cost a half-million dollars to stage, into something like subliminal publicity reminders. The same week fashion writers are talking about the glories of YSL's haute couture, the ready-to-wear line, trade-shown three months earlier in October or April, is hitting the YSL boutiques and department stores from Kuwait to Rio de Janeiro. This reversal of the traditional sequence of high fashion followed by the mass-manufactured ready-to-wear version is the true revolution of the House of Saint Laurent.

The menswear division is by far the most profitable. Saint Laurent's men's clothes are made and marketed by Bidermann–Prouvost Crepy. Maurice Bidermann is number one in men's clothing in France and the most admired, criticized and envied person in the young ready-to-wear trade. It was Bidermann who, after two years in the United States, came knocking on Bergé's door in 1975, saying he would guarantee five thousand American outlets in ten years for YSL-labeled menswear. The brother of disco queen Régine, Bidermann says his ambition is to be able to sell YSL suits for men for under two hundred dollars and go aggressively into women's rtw, which, he thinks, hasn't really been industrialized yet.

Maurice Cau manages the YSL Rive Gauche chain, which has nearly a hundred outlets worldwide, including a dozen boutiques in the United States. The Rive Gauche stores exist independently of the franchised boutiques in department stores (which, in the United States, run the gamut from Bergdorf Goodman in New York to Younker-Kilpatrick's in Omaha). The Rive Gauche shops sell bags, belts, scarves, jewelry, shoes and linen, and, frequently, menswear. Yves is almost jealous of the accessory designers, saying that they have more creative freedom than designers of clothes because the choice of materials in handbags and jewelry is as wide as anyone can wish for. Bed linen is "edited," as he likes to say, by Zucchi in Italy, and the newest product—wallpaper—is also farmed out.

Juliette Maubras had been with Saint Laurent Perfumes for more than ten years when, in 1978, she oversaw the plunge into makeup. For the lipstick, nail polish, eyeshadow and foundation bases, Yves supervised every detail and spent hours working on the shape of the display box and discussing the publicity blurb (translated from the French: "Yves Saint Laurent is a symbol, a name, a renown . . . a certain complicity with women the world over"). The cosmetics' packing—gold, red and black and very similar to the packaging of his Opium perfume—was inspired by the evening bags of the 1930s. To do his publicity pictures, he chose Heidi Morawitz, a young Austrian who had worked at French *Vogue.*

Bergé believes passionately in the talent he is selling and is cautious when it comes to new products and new boutiques. He regards the YSL *griffe* as a precious badge not to be distributed like a decal. The name is attached to glasses, stockings, umbrellas and costume jewels—fifty-eight products in all.

"A name is like a cigarette; the more you puff on it, the less you've got left," Pierre likes to say when the question of franchising and merchandising comes up. "You've got to know how to say no. There will be no YSL automobile tires, although we've had a request from America. In couture, we're first. In ready-to-wear, we're first, and in franchising, we're in the lead, with Dior and Cardin."

It all adds up. Since 1977, earnings have increased yearly at a rate of 30 percent. Worldwide sales are approaching a half-billion dollars.

Yet there are moments when Yves would like to walk away from it all. "It has happened," he says, and smiles. "But couture is a mistress I can't live without. Also, I feel responsible to the people who have helped make my success and the house."

The collaborators are more important to him than the

structure and hierarchy of the organization. Besides Loulou, Muñoz, Fayoll, Felisa and the models, the *premières* or heads of workrooms, the fitters and Derbord are his most important staff. With the exception of Derbord—Jean-Louis to everybody—they are all women.

Under the overall direction of Muñoz, the *premières* execute his concepts and must know how to assimilate his intentions and translate them into fabrics. He pays Muñoz $70,000 a year because he feels she must be able to afford a life-style that reflects the elegance and mood he tries to give his clothes. "A good première must have a sense of the *meaning* of a detail," he says. "She must know sewing, of course, but also have an instinct for composition, line and volume."

The *vendeuses*—all older and reassuring as hospital nurses—are the made-to-measure sales personnel. They must have sufficient ascendancy over very demanding clients and inspire immediate and lasting confidence. "They must have the patience of angels and know how to channel a client's taste," says Yves of this endangered species of couture personnel. "They deal with women who have a highly developed sense of their own attractiveness and of what enhances their appearance. In general, women possess the instinct—original but perfectible—for deciding whether a detail is right, whether it is important and in the right color. If a fitter doesn't have this gift, she is worthless," says YSL.

Sales to professional buyers are no less complicated. Yves shows a 280-piece collection, but in the showroom, there may be over 2,500 possibilities, because of different colors and styles. Sonja Caproni, fashion director of the San Francisco–based I. Magnin, says it takes her about three days to buy a YSL collection.

The least known, but to Yves third most important, collaborator is Derbord, who buys and receives all fabrics, materials and accessories and orders everything for the six studios, as the creative workrooms are called. There are studios for soft dressmaking—one for grand *flou*, one for tailored *flou*—studios for Rive Gauche prototypes and a studio for all-out tailoring where Georges Tyvaert is the "grand premier" (and where all those 1978 "Broadway" spencer suits were made).

For a number of years, Yves has been determined that a woman should appear feminine even in a tuxedo, and the tailored, or structured, *flou* has been his most recent challenge. When designers say a garment is structured, they mean it is adjusted to the body or that there is a fitted form built into the dress. Saint Laurent was trained in the school of Dior, a school of tailoring where the body is not emphasized, and, as he said in 1978, he had a hard time learning to make clothes that move, that is, clothes that combine both structure and loose-fitting, free-flowing elements. "Fluid clothes are feminine because they are sensual," he says. "Highly structured designs are very rigid. I wanted to synthesize certain elements from those two opposing traditions." Together with Courrèges, he is considered not only a superb craftsman on paper but a top sewing expert who knows exactly how to structure clothes, in contrast to younger designers who have grown up in rtw and whose effect of free, loose clothes is sometimes considered disarmingly easy.

"With Yves," says Muñoz, "the fabric helps in finding the right expression."

The most important nonresident collaborator, Gustav Zumsteg, lives in Zurich. The head of Abraham Fabrics, he creates all those extraordinary fabrics that Saint Laurent—and other couturiers—use. "Yves is my joy," says Zumsteg, "because he gives life to my fabrics."

Yves is more lyrical. "Gustav is my good fortune. For the last collection, I designed everything with care, including the accessories; then I went to Zurich and, in his plant, we dyed everything. I said I wanted a kind of steamy orientalism, all in red—rose red. Then we walked back there in his factory behind the office and there are the fabrics. Beaming with pride, he lets me touch.

"For me, fabrics are never in or out of fashion, but you must know how to choose the right materials for ready-to-wear, you must be sure of the result when you use the same fabrics repeatedly. I'm tired of muslin; it's soft, difficult to work with and has no weight. Gustav and I feel the same currents and trends at the same time—he in Zurich, I here in Paris. Geography has nothing to do with talent. Once, when we met after several months to discuss ideas, I talked about a fabric I saw in my mind—an idea for a dress—and he pulled that fabric right out of his pocket!"

Saint Laurent is neither the first nor the only of the Parisians to have discovered Zumsteg; Abraham materials were the highlight of Ungaro's 1967–68 collections. The newest "in" designer of fabrics is Gimmo Etro, who commutes between his native Milan and London.

Although most seamstresses and tailors are completely loyal to their houses and take immense pride in feeling that they contribute to a successful line, everybody working on a collection is sworn to secrecy. Piracy, the flattering ransom of success, has been a problem as far back as the eighteenth century, when Versailles courtesans tried to bribe Rose Bertin, Marie Antoinette's dressmaker, to reveal details of the queen's latest gown before she wore it for the first time. The first law specifically protecting fashion creation was passed in 1920, and couture designs registered with the Chambre Syndicale are accorded almost the same protection as literature, films and patented inventions. But that's only in France. Elsewhere, fashion designs cannot be patented or copyrighted.

Despite the careful screening of buyers, press and private clients who attend the shows, stealing designs has been a fine art since the 1930s. When cameras are banned from shows, teams of two or three legitimately accredited sketch artists work separately on specific portions of a silhouette—one concentrating on sleeves, the other on necklines, the third on the skirt treatment. Then, right after the show, they assemble the total look. And small knockoff houses work extremely fast. The sketches are handed to pattern makers who, in no time, can tool up and produce hot items weeks before larger manufacturers have had a chance to gear over their means of production, months before the designers have had a chance to sell a collection.

Counterfeiting is a global business, concentrated, according to the Union des Fabricants, in Italy, South Korea and

Taiwan. There are fake Chanel, Givenchy, Lanvin and Nina Ricci "boutiques" in Seoul, and Taipei is the center for export to Latin America of inferior imitations of French labels. In 1969, the House of Saint Laurent took legal action against a rtw firm in Bologna for putting the famous YSL logo on ripoffs, and recently, Givenchy received a parcel with six of his own patterns, reexpedited by the Italian post office, which couldn't decipher the addressee. The parcel led to the discovery of an Italian copy service of purloined haute couture patterns. In Florence, Aldo Gucci has successfully hauled fourteen Italian manufacturers to court for making Gucci knockoffs.

To get more protection for the industry, the Chambre Syndicale has assisted in the formation of a Groupement de Mode. Bergé is the president, and the members are Dior, Kenzo, Emmanuelle Khanh, Ungaro, Jacqueline Jacobson of Dorothée Bis, Sonia Rykiel, Lagerfeld and Saint Laurent.

YSL is the most influential designer today, and whenever he presents a collection, his ideas, through inspiration or imitation, affect clothes everywhere. In 1976, he designed his opulent fantasy look, partially in reaction to the constant ripping off. "I was fed up with opening magazines and seeing clothes I thought were mine but had in fact been done by somebody else," he told *Time* magazine that year. "I made a decision to make a dramatic departure."

It takes the House of Saint Laurent six weeks to make a collection. First, YSL designs the new line in some six hundred sketches. This solitary task is often done far from avenue Marceau. Sometimes he sketches the collection in his new and very secret condominium apartment in avenue de Breteuil, behind L'Hôtel des Invalides, but more often, he retires to Morocco to do it. He still feels drawn to the silky, sun-baked lands of his childhood—no longer Algeria, now an austere socialist state, but to laissez-faire Morocco next door. Near Marrakesh, Yves and Pierre own an elegant five-bedroom house. It was in Marrakesh that Yves really discovered color.

The collective work begins when Yves returns and pins his six hundred sketches on the walls of his workroom. He is the first one to say that the sketches are not all that important, that it is the three-dimensional effect, the cut, that counts; that a good design can make a bad dress, and vice versa. A lot of thinking goes into the choice of fabrics, and there are years when Yves personally sees twenty thousand samples. He chooses embroidery and evening accessories with Muñoz and Loulou, "the accomplices who understand me, stimulate and help me." A little later, he designs collection jewelry that is farmed out to Scemana and consults about shoes, all the while continuing to modify sketches, sometimes at home, sometimes at avenue Marceau.

Two weeks later, the first fifteen sketches have been made up in muslin *toiles,* and the long and laborious fittings begin. As the designs take form, changes are inevitable, and it is not unlikely that the collection be revamped ten days before the deadline. The first fitting is crucial. Here, Yves and Muñoz see how the fabric moves on the body. "With Yves, the fabric helps find the right expression," says Muñoz. "And, of course, we always look for the right proportions on the body. When you cut a tweed, it's not the same as a muslin or a velvet."

La pose—the interminable standing that the model must do while effects are viewed and alterations suggested— generally begins in December for January couture collections and in June for July showings, meaning that haute couture models spend six or seven hours of the coldest January days in the flimsiest organzas and the hottest July weeks in woolens and occasional furs. As the pace intensifies, mannequins are on call constantly, catnap whenever and wherever they can. Loulou, Muñoz, Fayoll and Derbord are with Yves in this stage. Everyone talks in near-whispers, no phones ring, no one enters or leaves without a good excuse.

Saint Laurent and Muñoz understand each other almost without words. They have been together so long that she understands his style perfectly; she knows what he is aiming at and what themes he is working on. When a dress doesn't have the effect he has anticipated when it is modeled by one of the girls, they modify it together, making the skirt narrower, shortening it by changing a panel. They may decide to change the bodice. But if they do, then what is the point of the dress in the total scheme of the collection? Muñoz may defend the dress, knowing that lots of creations are discarded at this stage.

"The back's very pretty," she murmurs.

The model bends and looks over her shoulder to see herself in the mirror. She agrees. It is pretty and there is something elegant about the top. Suppose the back were opened up a little, Yves says. The center seam is ripped open and slopes off in a huge V. Without Muñoz, W has intimated, the studios of YSL might crumble. She is the first person with whom Yves checks every morning before the working day begins.

They may admire one another, but the creation is a give and take. If everything stayed within the limits of decorum and good taste, if Muñoz and the workroom crews acted with the same common sense as the customers' husbands, if YSL invariably behaved with the studied elegance he affects in the company of clients and journalists, Muñoz, Fayoll, Madame Felisa and Derbord might long ago have guessed that his talent was used up. Says Loulou, "This is the period when Yves is afraid—afraid of not having time enough to express all his ideas." Says he, "I know I'm dragging my feet here, but I want too many things."

Buttons, flowers and feathers are selected and embroideries chosen. As the days tick away, the pressure builds. Lunch is grabbed in the studio, and the work hours stretch to eight or ten in the evening. For the 1978–79 winter couture collection, Yves didn't have a free morning for four weeks; ten days before collection showtime, the entire house reported to work on Saturdays. "I usually end up every evening at around seven thirty," he says of the last days of the countdown. "I come home, have dinner alone and try to relax for an hour. And every night I go back to the studio and work alone, most of the time until after two A.M."

The models' "cabin" is staffed by five full-time mannequins, currently one blond and four Mediterranean beauties. A great model, Yves feels, must not only have a pretty profile, beautiful movements and charisma; she must understand the clothes she is wearing. She must captivate on the runway, but also, she must know how to work with him during *la pose,* when the individual dresses are being created and recreated, sometimes for an hour at a time. Certain girls give the impression of understanding the esthetic value and the social functions of a beautiful gown; others are only themselves. He remembers one tall, rather ungainly model who achieved an astonishing plasticity.

Yves calls his models *jeunes filles* and treats them with respect. His current passion and muse of his 1978 Broadway Suit collection is Mounia Orhozemane, a pale black North African. His latest star mannequin is the younger Kirat, a haughtily strong-featured brunette with a penetratingly calm gaze and long, long, skinny legs.

Saint Laurent's preference for Mediterranean, African and Brazilian models is an almost unconscious homage to his childhood, but also reflects a wide-awake awareness of the growing internationalization of fashion. Nationality means less and less. There is no such thing as a separate fashion for the Japanese woman, the European or the American woman, he says, and if black models, with their broad shoulders, long legs and extremely fluid and sensuous movements, are giving fashion a new élan, it is also because they incarnate the provocativeness rather than the aggressiveness that very modern women want. "I take for granted that a woman is completely free," he says. "Systematically, I look for girls who look right for the moment, girls or women who are practically glued to their time. Some years ago, I had Danielle, a girl from Lyons, who had done very little modeling. I realized her body, her gestures were typically those of today's woman. It was all there. I had nothing to teach her; on the contrary, it was she who inspired me to get rid of all sorts of obsolete references. An exchange happened between us. Maybe I transformed her, but her attitude, her behavior never changed. Everything I did on her that didn't work, I realized I had to get rid of once and for all. She made me progress."

Each house mannequin gets to model the dozen dresses made on her, while the star of the cabin gets to present as many as thirty creations. The clothes easily become "my bolero" and "my silk flounced tunic," says Liane Viguié, who worked for Bohan, Chanel, Balmain, Lanvin, Givenchy and, briefly, for Saint Laurent. "Nothing belongs to you; everything is on loan, but you flesh it out and, for the duration of the collection, you monopolize it, often with ferocious jealousy. A house model has lived with a dress from the first fitting of the *toile*. When we put it on, our bodies react to it. We can feel where the changes will be made, because you get into the mind of the person you work with." It has happened that on the eve of the show, one of the dozen dresses created on one girl is taken away from her and given to another, not because the second girl is prettier but because she knows how to be more eye-catching.

Runway models for ready-to-wear are hired hands, appearing in a two o'clock Jean-Charles de Castelbajac showing and in Lagerfeld's lineup at six. They, like house models doing couture shows, must know how to change extremely fast. They have calculated that "from pantyhose to pantyhose"—that is, from the moment a girl, wearing only her pantyhose, is ready to put on a dress, to the time when she has shown it on the runway and is ready to slip into the next dress—no more than three minutes have elapsed.

Some of them are more in demand with photographers than others. Sometimes a very good house or runway model is less photogenic than photo models or cover girls, who sometimes are incapable of showing off a dress in a salon. YSL prefers house models because the clothes seem to matter to them. Cover girls, he has noticed, don't really care about the dresses they model, only their own looks, their next job, their careers. Press-agency photographers use house models because the house supplies the girls without charge, although it does pay its employes extra for this chore. Name photographers borrow dresses from the collection and photograph them on their own models and charge everything to the magazines they sell their layouts to (Richard Avedon shot the winter 1978–79 YSL couture line on Janice Dickinson for *Vogue*).

Ready-to-wear models are sometimes "cast," like TV-commercial actresses, not to look too overwhelming. Paris-Planning, Elite, Models International and Cosa Nostra (sic) are the leading Paris agencies, although the field is increasingly dominated by the big New York agencies—Eileen Ford, Wilhelmina and fast-rising John Casablancas. The current "in" appeal is vitality and narcissism; strong, wonderful bodies; thick, shining hair; and a sense of well-being. With the exception of blacks, American girls don't go with the exotic aura Parisian couturiers are currently trying to express. In the 1950s, it was Suzy Parker, in the sixties the London peaches-and-cream look. Now, say the top agencies, it's North African, Brazilian and some Oriental models that everybody is looking for. The "new woman" that sells is taking the world for all she can get, and the new models look very tall and assertive, striding along with angry glances and free movements to project a near-androgynous sexiness. For male models—for years, Yves has used a black South African with closed-cropped hair—the look that sells is the surly scowl.

The fitting in the workrooms is finished when the *premières*—Madame Felisa in the *flou* studio, Monsieur Georges in the tailored studios and Madame Catherine and Madame Ida—feel a dress is ready to be sewn together. Sometimes models wearing a dress slip into oversized white dust covers when they walk through the sales floor and the public hallways for fear that a spy—a "friend of the house," a passing journalist—might get more than a glimpse of next season's new colors, fabrics and style. Chanel claimed on television that she had surprised people going through her trash cans on the eve of collections looking for swatches that would tell them what fabrics she was using.

During the week before Collection Day, the models shuffle between Yves's studio and the workrooms for constant corrections, without ever sitting down for fear of wrinkling the creations. A kind of collective psychosis permeates the house. Nothing seems to be ready; tempers flare. All private life ceases to exist and everybody is at the total, round-the-clock disposal of Yves. "We breathe with him," says Loulou. "If he's happy, we're happy; if he scowls, no one budges. We're a team, living and breathing in unison."

After the dress rehearsal, three days before the show, lights burn until dawn, and Yves admits it is just as well that a collection deadline is set. Otherwise, he would never stop revising and getting new ideas.

On D-Day, says Viguié, all designers go crazy. "Some of them want to be left alone, some want to be surrounded, some even have to be supported—literally—and, once the show is over, be carried toward the crowd to receive the congratulations of rapturous friends. The state of jangled nerves and madness, however, reaches its paroxysm during the last two hours before curtain time."

Bergé gets involved backstage during the countdown. While Yves becomes a mad genius of an accessory worker who, with a tug of a scarf, a flip of a collar, a snip of a ribbon turns the girls into goddesses, Pierre acts as the stage director. "Now you, now you and you!" Yves is extenuated, drenched in sweat. Pierre seems furious. Together they watch the show on a closed-circuit television monitor, Pierre holding his long cue sheet. What they really watch for is the crowd's reaction. Behind them, the *habilleuses*, or dressers, help returning models out of and into new creations with lightning speed. Girls strip to pantyhose and are dressed again. One *habilleuse* per model, each knowing the sequence on Pierre's master cue sheet and which accessory goes with which number. The dressers are like the girls' best friend and mother, and before anyone else, they seem to be able to read the returning models' faces and tell whether "the juices are passing," whether the audience out there is being electrified.

During the show, Yves has been known to hide behind plants, curtains and loudspeakers, in balconies and basements, but somehow always within earshot of the audience. Visibly, the tension drains from his face at the first burst of applause.

6

ALL
THOSE
YVESDROPPERS

S aint Laurent got his feathers ruffled in New York recently when he was made to wait at the high-security entrance to Steve Rubell's disco, Studio 54. Rubell and his doormen failed to recognize the tall, bespectacled Parisian as one of the high-tone trendies when his limousine-load of special guests arrived. Someone eventually realized who Yves was, and he and his entourage were whisked in to join an invitation-only party.

Or so said the gossip columnists, including the Los Angeles *Times*'s Manhattan celebrity spotter, who swore she saw Rubell apologize to a "peeved" Saint Laurent and escort him personally "to the private basement office where only Liza Minnelli, Andy Warhol, Bianca Jagger, Halston and other Rubell-approved swells are allowed."

Saint Laurent's relationship with the media is a rollercoaster love affair full of gooey gushings, back-handed wrist slappings, occasional tiffs and one or two blowups. Couturiers need the attention—and not only during the quarterly collection shows—and the media need fashion stars to fill the fashion pages, talk shows and celebrity columns. The closer the symbiosis, the more incestuous the relationship, until, in French *Vogue* or *W*, editorial attention seems in direct column-inch proportion to paid-for advertising. One double-page ad for Saint Laurent's Rive Gauche boutiques in *W* is matched with photos of Yves, Pierre, Loulou and Anne-Marie Muñoz attending Paloma Picasso's wedding to Rafael Lopez-Sanchez, with the text quoting Yves's raves over Lagerfeld's red bridal gown. The gossip column accompanying the photo spread also mentioned that Yves and Karl danced together.

From the beginning, Saint Laurent was the darling of the press. At the height of the hysteria that followed Dior's death, journalists and photographers besieged avenue Montaigne so forcefully that the Dior brain trust had to smuggle the twenty-one-year-old successor in and out under a canvas in the back of a truck. *Vogue* has called him the genius who knows how to achieve perfect balance between change and continuity, and both *Time* and *The New York Times* have called him the world's most influential designer. *Women's Wear Daily*—*WWD* as it is chummily called—has been good to him. This monopolistic trade paper, with the edge on the fashion news and therefore the most influence, has called him the man of provocative chic while bitchily inquiring into the "subcultural influence" around him (it has called Loulou de la Falaise Klossowski's image "a marked-down version of Marisa Berenson").

Saint Laurent has had to learn to live with criticism. Reviewing clothes in anything but the most euphoric terms is something new and American that the Parisians were not used to when Eugenia Sheppard began covering shows for the New York *Herald Tribune* in the late 1940s. "Maybe designers are more spoiled than other artists who are reviewed and criticized," Sheppard told *W* at a New York party in 1978. "It has not been a tradition to be severe about Paris. When I first criticized Paris designers they were terribly upset. They just weren't used to taking the criticism."

Although surrounded with the power elite of the fashion

world, Sheppard managed to get herself banned from the House of Saint Laurent several times for panning collections. "He's so silly to be mad at me because he's the idea man of fashion right now and I've recognized that," she said two years later.

Once Saint Laurent and Bergé tried to separate buyers from fashion writers so the latter couldn't influence the former. To discourage buyers or spies from copying designs without buying the originals, store buyers and manufacturers pay $1,500 for the first two persons from the same organization (and $750 for each additional staffer) to even *see* a show. When a buyer purchases originals from the collection, however, the fee—called a caution—is deducted from his bill. In 1965, after reviews of the previous summer's collection were less than flattering and the bad press cost them $100,000 in canceled orders, Yves and Pierre got the idea of banning the media until the buyers' orders were in. The press was invited weeks after the buyers' show, but the idea backfired when so few journalists bothered to show up, and quietly, Saint Laurent and Bergé abandoned it.

Yves still feels that there is a love-hate relationship between himself and his critics, but he *is* learning. "I'm less sensitive to criticism than I used to be, but I'm not indifferent to it. Sometimes they've been unjust, like in 1971, when my fashion was inspired by the 1940s and *Time* called it my ugliest ever. That was very hard; it took me a while to forget."

The most disdainful reporting is often done by those who don't cover the shows. The New York *Village Voice*'s Blair Sabol thought Yves's Oriental fantasy look of 1977 might have earned him "a degree in art history—or a curatorship at some museum—so we can get onward and upward out of this loop of costumery"; she thought the most newsworthy report out of Paris was that Yves's maid had found him passed out one preshow morning.

He is often misquoted, possibly because he doesn't like interviews, and journalists find it easier to make up their own quotes. When Helen Lawrenson saw him for an *Esquire* piece in 1970, she was able to have him deny such howlers as the printed quote that he had designed his 1968 collection "in mourning for Vietnam." The injurious "People who ride the métro and work in offices—my collection is not for them" keeps cropping up in various rewrites, most recently in *Time:* "My clothes are addressed to women who can afford to travel with forty suitcases."

Fashion writers try to become celebrities in their own right, and, with fellow designer Sonia Rykiel, Yves wonders how many of them are qualified to judge fashion. What he deplores is the general lack of information in the fashion magazines. He believes there is a curious time lag between the magazines' craving for novelty and their readers' capacity for absorbing it. The flip side of novelty is its erosion, and the speed with which fashion is downgraded and dismissed can be frightening. There is neither anger nor resentment in his voice, only a hint of regret as he discusses this.

The year *Time* called his collection the ugliest ever was a year of confusion and contradictions. In 1971, Zandra Rhodes presented fantastic follies, Lagerfeld showed tap dancers in silk gym suits, Mary Quant had wrestlers' jackets and Kenzo Takada began to make his influence felt with tucked and quilted white cottons. YSL revived the 1940s, with tweed suits and padded shoulders, and was savaged. In her report for the *New York Post* and twenty-four other American newspapers, Eugenia Sheppard wrote: "What a relief to write at last that a fashion collection is frankly, definitely and completely hideous." *The Guardian*'s Alison Adburgham chimed in, calling the collection "a tour de force of bad taste . . . nothing could exceed the horror of this exercise in kitsch," and even *Women's Wear Daily* called his work "poor" and urged him to "shake off the weirdo and kooky influences." When *WWD*'s Paris correspondent sought to interview the victim, he was turned away by press secretary Gabrielle Busschaert, who said, "You're trying to destroy Saint Laurent . . . you've broken windows." In self-defense, Yves said that his fashion corresponded to the brutal and vulgar mood of 1971. As usual, he was prescient. Shorn of some of his excesses, the tailored look was indeed back the following year.

The 1971 pans, which *Time* headlined YVES ST. DEBACLE, made him announce that his August haute couture collection would be his last. Henceforth, he said, he would devote himself exclusively to ready-to-wear. The decision seemed to make sense, given the loss-leader status of made-to-measure, but by year's end he was backtracking, and a couture show was announced for January 1972—with new ground rules for admission: only buyers would be admitted, plus representatives from one magazine, *Paris-Match*.

So no press and no ballyhoo attended the hushed presentation of his 1972 summer couture collection, which, he insisted, was only for the eyes of a few choice clients anyway. The glossy magazines could take photographs of the beautiful things he would continue to make for a handful of people, but only if they reproduced the photos without criticism and without comment. While *Paris-Match* took advantage of the offer and took pictures of Marisa Berenson modeling the new YSL line, the women of the international press threatened to picket his premises. *Le Monde,* whose fashion editor had been banned along with Sheppard and the fashion reporters from *Combat* and radio station *Europe 1,* reacted with a short but biting editorial taking to task those couturiers "who love to adorn themselves with the attributes of the artist, overzealously seek publicity and have no greater desire than to see themselves honored with the accolades and applause that their genius deserves, nevertheless cannot accept the least criticism."

But Saint Laurent and Bergé remained unperturbed. The YSL summer look was a combination of white gabardine pants with cutaway red-and-navy vests worn with big straw hats and bright espadrilles. "All nice girls love a sailor suit," cooed British *Vogue. WWD* called the new line "a certain triumph."

Saint Laurent's fine-honed contempt for the working press is as acute as ever, and he tries more and more to escape the worst of their prying impertinence. Not that he is always successful. *Facade,* a new Parisian punk magazine, has closed in on the Beautiful People's gamier nightlife and reports in paparazzi pictures and risqué one-liners on Kenzo in drag, disco queen Grace Jones's crotch, Yves and Karl embracing, Paloma and Loulou dancing. In self-defense, corporate YSL buys full-page ads in *Facade* and in

W, whose chic black correspondent in Paris, André Leon Talley, can report that Yves was *not* seen crawling on all fours at the Palace disco in rue du Faubourg Montmartre but went backstage, tore off Grace Jones's ill-fitting body stocking and plastic moon clothes and, with a cashmere evening scarf and some of Loulou's jewels, created a *flou* costume that made Jones look more dramatic than ever.

The price for American financial backing—first, private capital; later, investment by Lanvin–Charles of the Ritz—has been business trips to the United States to meet manufacturers, store owners and the press and submitting to cocktail parties in Atlanta, Dallas, Los Angeles, San Francisco (which he likes), Kansas City, Chicago and Washington. When Helen Lawrenson asked him how he could stand it, he said it was horrible, that he didn't say much, just smiled a lot. Lanvin–Charles of the Ritz has not been totally happy with his attitude toward public relations, and its former president, Richard Salomon, has called him the worst traveler in the world.

Though it hasn't come to blows for Yves himself, Pierre has scuffled with members of the press. During the presentation of the 1978–79 winter ready-to-wear, Bergé staged an unprogrammed curtain raiser when he had kneeling photographers move back from the runway so first-row VIPs could see. All packed their gear and faded into the crowd except Remy Labbé de la Mauvière. Bergé picked up the Associated Press photographer by the collar and tried to throw him back bodily, but the crowd sided with Mauvière and Pierre retreated. By the time the show began, the other photographers were back at ringside.

Saint Laurent is the despair of scandal sheets. His friends have never felt the urge to tell raunchy stories—if there are any to tell—nor have present or former employees detailed incidents of tyrannical behavior or monstrous tantrums. As the proverb says, no one is a prophet in his own backyard, and Yves's fame is greater abroad than in France. To the French in general, he is a very successful couturier to whom no particular whiff of scandal, or even notoriety, is attached. Typically, when *Le Point* and *Saga* do cover stories on him, they introduce him to their readers by quoting *WWD*'s John

Fairchild's assessment that YSL is at the height of his influence, and by having correspondents in Munich, Rio and Tokyo feed back professional and popular opinions on him (Director Sally Marx of the Rive Gauche boutique in Washington's Watergate complex: "Clients mispronounce his name, but they know his work and his reputation").

Yves's tortured psyche, his depressions and moments of moody discouragement, have caused concern, and his nervous breakdown and hospitalization during the year of the exuberant fantasy look made Bergé and Busschaert tighten the already-formidable antimedia barrier.

The circumstances *were* morbid. It began with the October 1975 ready-to-wear show. Reporters were less interested in Yves's short smocks than in sizing him up when he took a bow at the end. He looked ghastly, they decided, as he stood at the runway curtain with his hair disheveled and with glazed eyes. A few months later, he added to the unwholesome curiosity himself by confiding to *Le Point*'s motherly Barbara Schwamm, "I'm very, very sick," and admitting that he had designed part of the 1976 couture collection in a psychiatric clinic. "It's only during the last days that they've allowed me to leave the clinic and to work in the atelier." At the January 1977 haute show, he still looked weak, although not so wasted. At one point, Bergé told him to sit down. *France Soir* attributed Yves's apparent vertigo and inability to stand up to a toothache.

Then, he was rumored to be dead. Nobody knew how it started, but there it was. Yves had committed suicide, or he had been stabbed to death in Marrakesh. Reporters assailed avenue Marceau, and Busschaert repeated, endlessly, "Monsieur Saint Laurent is alive and well and working on his new collection." The rumors kept flying. Bergé was livid. *Le Figaro*'s Hélène de Turckheim and *Stern*'s Barbara Larcher made him hit the ceiling when they trooped to avenue Marceau and demanded to *see* Saint Laurent. Bergé made the two fashion editors follow him inside, opened a door to a room where Saint Laurent was draping a cossack dress on a model, and shouted, "Yves, move your arm so they can see you're not dead!" De Turckheim got to embrace Saint Laurent and, with a profusion of apologies, she and

Larcher tiptoed out. Turckheim told her readers that YSL had "red cheeks and there is no death stare" in his eyes. Larcher called it "my most beautiful morning." Still the rumors wouldn't go away. It was specified that he had died suddenly either Wednesday, March 23, or two days later, in the afternoon.

Bergé was forced to issue a statement: "It is true that for two years Saint Laurent has been suffering a nervous depression and that he still needs another year's care to be completely out of it. But I assert, on my honor, that he has neither cancer, nor is suffering any other serious illness nor anything else that needs to be concealed. In any case, the brief hospitalization at the American Hospital for in-patient treatment hasn't prevented him from creating more and more brilliant collections that a lot of healthy individuals envy him." To help squash the rumors, Yves escorted Helene de Rothschild to the reopening of the Normandie-Lido nightclub.

Intrigue or collective psychosis? No one would ever know. Three months later, when *Le Point* did a cover story on him, Yves could laugh with a sour edge in his voice. "My death finally left me indifferent," he told the news weekly. "What's annoying is all these people—even friends—who opened the door to *see* if I was alive."

The depression and the stay at the American Hospital in suburban Neuilly made Saint Laurent take up writing. The book was started partly as therapy, partly to explore and extend his artistic grasp. It is about himself, he says, but it is not an autobiography. He is shy about showing the manuscript, but *Le Point* was allowed to print an excerpt in its cover story, a lyrical description of an operatic Mongolia swathed in satin and silk, tasseled and tufted, brocaded and beaded, that inspired his romantic look of 1977:

> Fabulous boyards, grandiose samurais, wild Mongols, a whole epic poem of golden brocades, coarse-grained silks and grosgrains that are sharp-edged as scimitars, choking Barbarian furs. . . . The shadow of the Great Wall against which I shatter myself is more terrible than Genghis Khan's bronze shield. The vapors

from my slashed mind makes all the dynasties come alive with their furor, their arrogance, their nobility, their grandeur. I finally manage to pierce the secret of the Imperial City and to liberate my esthetic ghosts, my queens, my divas, my whirlwinds of fiestas, my nights as black as ink and crepe, my lacquerware from the Coromandel Coast, my artificial lakes, my hanging gardens.

From the gates of Heavenly Peace flow wild silks which irrigate the temples and the tea houses with their voluptuous fluidity. From the terraces and from the pagodas of the Red Pavilion I can see my dreams dance on the silvery waters of the River of Love.

When Maria Callas died in 1977, *Le Monde* got to publish another excerpt, showing that besides introspection, the book would also be part observation of his famous friends. The piece was both homage to the diva and her voice— "burning, solemn and high-pitched, strident, supernatural, baroque, miraculous," and to opera, "struggling to rediscover its ostentation, its prestige and splendor." He called Callas the "diva among divas, empress, queen, goddess, witch, working magician and above all, divine . . . Queen of Sheba who visits us, empress of China and all the Russias, queen of Spain . . . Cleopatra, Aïda."

To be published by Grasset, the book was, for a while, an all-consuming effort, making Saint Laurent spurn friends and such daily pleasures as reading newspapers and watching television.

"It's a book on me, on my profound aspirations. Words exert a true fascination on me. I study them, look things up. I always wanted to write but the click never happened. I also have two plays in my head, but time is short. I have to navigate on an ocean of illusions."

He cannot give in wholeheartedly to the temptations and, with disillusion in his voice, he says he has a feeling the book will never be finished. "Actually, to finish it I'll have to fall sick, like Proust."

7

FRIENDS
AND
GROUPIES

When Loulou de la Falaise Klossowski throws one of her famous parties, Saint Laurent shows up late, at one A.M. All the "chums" are there much earlier—Pierre, "queen bee" Helene de Rothschild, Paloma Picasso and her Argentine playwright-husband Rafael Lopez-Sanchez, Betty and François Catroux, Lucienne, supermodel Pat Cleveland, movie critic Jacques Chazot and Rudolf Nureyev. Loulou, who is making herself into a legend like Nancy Cunard, Daisy Fellowes and Bianca Jagger, likes to give costume balls that end with an eight A.M. breakfast.

At the end of Fashion Week for winter 1978–79 collections, she threw one such party at the Palace disco on boulevard Montmartre. Kenzo showed up as a bird of paradise, his business manager Gilles Raysse as the devil. Helene de Rothschild was a fairy queen, Régine came as Carmen Miranda, David Sulzberger as a *Star Wars* character, Marina Schiano as Bloomsbury groupie (and one-time mistress of

Bertrand Russell) Lady Ottoline Morrell, while Anna Piaggi of Italian *Vogue* came as the wife of Emperor Bokassa I of the Central African Empire. Loulou herself was a fallen angel, her husband an angelic angel with white wings, and Javier Arroyuelo, a playwright and fellow-Argentinian exile, a flamenco lesbian. Lagerfeld found an authentic Josephine Baker sequined costume and pinned it over his street clothes. Disco owner Jacques de Boascher came as Icarus and actor Jean Lafont as a Magritte brick wall. YSL came as himself.

Nothing is more dangerous than success, and Yves is a radiant and vulnerable cult object. In its cover story on him, *Le Point* quoted one of his intimates as saying that his entourage resembled a Byzantine court with everybody vying for the prince's attention. In reality, he likes to live slightly offstage from the glare of the capriciously taxing *beau monde*. Invitations never stop, and hostesses always try to pull off the considerable coup of having him and Bergé at intimate dinners. "Darling, did you say Pierre and Yves will be there?" The suspense can last for days.

He prefers people who have personality to society hostesses, *mignons* and hangers-on. "I am interested in people who live their lives their own way, without restrictions, who have an art of life. I don't like people who are playing with their lives." Among his friends he counts filmmaker Alain Resnais and his wife Florence Malraux, Andy Warhol, the theater couple Madeleine Renaud and Jean-Louis Barrault, perfume heiress Helen Rochas, sculptor François Xavier Lalanne, *France Soir* movie critic Jacques Chazot and Jean-Claude Binoche, an opinionated auctioneer who scouts antique sales for him. Others are Jacqueline de Ribes, the wife of one of France's richest bankers, Elie and Helene de Rothschild, Emile and Charlotte Aillaud, Helmut Newton and Helmut Berger, Paloma and Rafael Lopez-Sanchez. Yves sometimes says that Paloma, the daughter of Pablo Picasso and Françoise Gilot, is the only woman who knows how to be rich in an original way, and he is happy she finally got her $24-million inheritance from her father's embattled estate and that she and Rafael are going to use part of the money to produce films (and the plays Rafael and Arroyuelo write together). Yves has known Paloma since the time she was poor, twenty-one and her father's name was not very relevant in her life. She was beginning to design jewelry—shooting stars and other pop shapes—and he bought some of her eccentric accessories for his 1971 collection. He was the first invited to the premiere performance of *Succès*, the Sanchez-Arroyuelo satire of glamour and fame, for which Paloma contributed outrageous costumes, sets and makeup. The play was a short-lived hit in 1978. Paloma is the link between Yves and Lagerfeld. For her wedding ceremony, she was dressed by Yves, and for the wedding dinner, by Karl. Her own style is quirky and flamboyant, and although she can now afford it, she never shops in haute couture, not even YSL's.

The intimate circle is anonymous, a Proustian coterie of elegant and bright young men and women in whose midst Yves doesn't have to make an effort. Paris is a city where it is chic to think, and the YSL entourage is passably highbrow. Conversations are subtle, the jokes are sly and the allusions pointed. The dramatic pressures are urbane and build up under the surface of intimate party chat. There is a disdain for celebrity, and tricks to unmask and deflate are relished. The charm that is appreciated is the kind of elegant despair that is combined with attractive self-mockery. Perhaps because fashion is also sets of circumstances and influences, Yves is good at creating contexts, not in a self-conscious search for life-style but as a feel for the right mood matching the right group of people at the right time of day.

Evenings may end at Yves's in rue de Babylone, in the Oriental room which is a shell of smoked mirrors jammed with lamé pillows and presided over by a sixteenth-century Ming bronze Buddha. The room, says Yves, is "the late, late night spot for candlelight and intimacy."

Loulou has been the antidote these last years to a certain preciosity, radical anxiety, exoticism and visions of moral erosion. Eleven years younger than Yves, the London-born social queen is a vivacious and stimulating woman of unerring taste. Together with Paloma, she is a tonic example of the new womanhood, and Paris's high society seeks her company for her confidence, charm and wit.

"Things have been wonderful since Loulou came," Yves admits happily. "I trust her reactions. Sometimes they are violent but always positive. And there is a lot of humor. We laugh a lot, especially when the going gets rough and we are tired. She's the sounding board. I bounce ideas off her and they come back clearer and things begin to happen." He admits he consults with her on virtually all his designs and spends the last sleepless twenty-four hours before a show with her at his side. "She's never wrong. She has a sense of fashion—like her mother and her grandmother."

Grandmother was the stylish Lady Rhoda, née Rhoda Mary Pike in County Carlow, Ireland, the wife of New Zealand-born Buckingham Palace court painter Sir Oswald Birley. Her mother is Maxime de la Falaise, award-winning British designer and social catalyst. Her father is the Marquis de la Falaise, whose brother successively married a pair of 1930s Hollywood stars, Gloria Swanson and Constance Bennett. Loulou's parents split up when she was three, and for the next twelve years, she was shunted from London to Paris to New York to finishing school in Gstaad. At fifteen, she was kicked out of school, allegedly because her St. Bernard ate a visiting woman's poodle. To get over the trauma, she spent time in therapy with a New York psychiatrist, and soon became the driven darling of a group of artists that included Marcel Duchamp and Saul Steinberg. "They loved young girls," she told *People* when the magazine profiled her in 1978 and called her YSL's Gilded Muse. At eighteen, she married an art expert at the Victoria and Albert Museum and, when they divorced, moved to New York to become the roommate of photographer Berry Berenson. She was hanging out with Warhol, Halston and Elsa Peretti when she tried modeling. "I was hopeless," she says. "I had total stagefright. The minute it was time to go on, I had to pee."

She began working for Saint Laurent in 1972—as any Seventh Avenue cynic will say, it can never hurt to have a social type acting as your assistant whatever—and now Loulou divides her time between avenue Marceau and the artist's atelier she and her husband Thadée Klossowski have had renovated on Montparnasse. Klossowski, whose literary endeavors include translations of English astrology texts, is the nephew of Pierre Klossowski, the author of novels and works on the Marquis de Sade. Thadée is as subdued as his wife is the life of any party. At her costume ball at the Palace disco, the gold-tipped wings of his costume were still unruffled the next morning.

Fashionable Paris thinks Loulou is divine. Says Bobby Peligry, the exquisite woman who runs the International Wool Secretariat, "I've seen Loulou carry off a dress with trains of fox plumage. Well, carrying that off is like eating crayfish at a dinner table. Either you can or you can't, and Loulou can." Bitchier tongues have it that in her social climb, Loulou is using Yves more than he is using her.

But all designers, in a sense, have their Loulous. Sharp-eyed collection watchers realize that the explanation for a slightly over-the-hill model in such and such a lineup is simply that she is "a girl who inspires the boss." Of late, Beautiful People have formally joined the image business. Valentino has made Princess Ira von Furstenberg president and director-general of his perfume division, just as Chanel put Catherine Deneuve under contract and Nina Ricci put Andrea de Portago on its publicity payroll. YSL executive vice-president Marina Schiano is in charge of business operations in the United States. The former Milanese model, who started as head of the YSL boutique in Manhattan in 1971, also provides public relations for Yves in New York.

Once or twice a week Yves has lunch or dinner with his mother and once a month sees his father. Since the Saint Laurents lost everything they had in Oran when Algeria achieved independence, Charles has preferred to live in Antibes, the winter resort across the Baie des Anges from Nice while Lucienne lives permanently in a ground-floor apartment in the sixteenth arrondissement. Today a director of La Foncière Civile, a real-estate investment firm, Charles comes to Paris once a month and never misses any of his son's collections, although he always leaves before anyone can recognize him. Lucienne lives totally for her son and now-married daughters. She wears an all-YSL wardrobe, treasures clippings about him and has every letter he ever sent her. "I can't help it, but I'm simply not capable of being critical as far as he is concerned," she says, admitting that she is terribly hurt when he is criticized. She is often at avenue Marceau, knows her son's collaborators intimately and laughingly says she must know about everybody's health, if not amorous affairs. She feels especially attached and almost responsible for the original YSL boutique in rue de Tournon, visits it often and chooses all her clothes there.

Bergé is Yves's oldest friend, the gray-flanneled *éminence grise* of the hierarchy, the necessary foil. Says Yves of him, "Pierre combines some of the characteristics of King Edward VII and Svengali," meaning that he combines long-suffering patience with hypnotic persuasion, a sure grasp of what is happening with an astute and often overpowering personality.

The son of an Internal Revenue inspector, Pierre likes to affect hopeless confusion when it comes to figures, but if anybody is responsible for turning talent into gold, it is this emphatic native of the storm-tossed island of Oléron on the Atlantic coast. When he and Yves met in 1958 at a dinner party given by Marie-Louise Bousquet, the Paris editor of *Harper's Bazaar*, Bergé already had a varied career behind him on the fringes of the artistic and literary world.

As a tax inspector, Bergé senior was assigned to many parts of France, and Pierre's education was somewhat chaotic. He rarely spent more than three semesters in one school, and never went beyond high school. Like Yves, self-awareness came at fourteen, when World War II raged across France. At one school, he became the editor of a short-lived school newspaper that happened to attract the attention of the writer Jean Giono.

Once out of school, Bergé was next associated with Gary Davis, the American ex-bomber pilot who in 1948 renounced his U.S. citizenship on the steps of the Palais de Chaillot, where the newly formed United Nations was in session, and declared himself a citizen of the world.

Davis was a Broadway actor with a promising career when he founded an organization of what he called World Federalists and said he could no longer give his sole loyalty to one nation. "I love the United States and want to see the democratic principles on which it was founded extended to the whole world," he said, announcing that he would go to Germany to seek forgiveness for having been part of the Allied war machine. The French government refused the State Department's huffy request to expel the renegade New Yorker, and Davis's unorthodox bid for peace through world government rallied an imposing list of French writers, including André Gide, Albert Camus, Jean-Paul Sartre and André Breton. Bergé was eighteen, loved things American, and soon became a volunteer editor of the French-language version of Davis's World Federalist newsletter. He even managed to have himself arrested, together with Camus, when the two of them helped Davis pitch a tent on the Palais de Chaillot grounds during a United Nations session.

World citizenship was an idea whose time had not yet come, and after editing *La Patrie mondiale*, Pierre sold rare books while gravitating toward the effervescent postwar scene on Saint Germain-des-Prés. From literature, Pierre drifted toward art and a meeting with a painter his own age whose career he was to influence.

Bernard Buffet had had his first private showing when he was twenty, and immediately hit on a spare, lifeless, rectilinear style that pleased because it was instantly recognizable. He was under contract to the Maurice David gallery to produce a hundred canvases a year. Part of his output was stockpiled each month by David so as to make the demand exceed the available art. Bergé was fascinated by art dealing and soon became Buffet's agent, pressuring the crafty David to increase the painter's percentage.

Buffet's art earned him a studio in the Batignolles section of Paris, a sports car, a manservant and a country estate in southern France. He affected to be solitary, yet had more than one private exhibition a year and, with the promotion of David and Bergé, sold everything he painted. At one point, Pierre himself owned eighty Buffets.

To write the text for a coffee-table book on Buffet's paintings, Pierre went to live with him at the country place near Manosque, in the Durance Valley in the foothills of the Alps, some forty miles northeast of Aix-en-Provence. Pierre was soon introduced to Manosque's native celebrity, Jean Giono. The writer vaguely remembered the school newspaper he had liked during the war and the very young editor with whom he had exchanged a few letters.

Giono had just made his comeback with *Hussard sur le toit*, a latter-day *Barry Lyndon* saga about an eighteen-year-old cavalry officer's adventures in nineteenth-century Italy. Like Louis-Ferdinand Céline, Giono had suffered harrowing experiences at the front during World War I, but instead of Céline's misanthropic invective, his hallmark became a lifelong pacifism. His popular 1930s novels were filled with pacifists, anarchists and an expressed love of age-old peasant culture. His idealization of rural life and nature's secret life forces, and his loathing of the masses and mistrust of ineffectual French parliamentary politics, made him turn toward fascism. At France's defeat in 1940, he gave every appearance of finding the Germans no more repulsive than the French. During the German occupation, he wrote for a collaborationist paper, went briefly to prison at the Liberation and was, when Bergé met him, just re-emerging in the new guise of a bestselling historical novelist.

If Buffet tried to be a hermit, Giono was a total recluse, living with his wife and nineteen-year-old daughter nearby. When he talked about going to town, he meant Manosque, five hundred yards away, which he visited once every two months. Pierre told Giono he wanted to write a book about him, but instead of becoming Giono's biographer, he became his personal secretary, shuffling between Manosque and Paris. The secretaryship was short-lived, but Pierre discovered a talent for representing recluse artists. He was good at explaining others, at "selling" them. "I wanted to be a physician," he once said, "but everything in my life has happened by accident."

Through the 1950s, he dabbled in the arts, buying and selling paintings and original editions, writing essays on Giono, Jean Anouilh and Henry de Montherlant and moving in the circles of those who, like Cocteau, set the artistic tone and knew how to astonish and surprise. He visited Céline in Meudon and was nearly eaten up by Céline's dogs—the author of *Journey to the End of the Night* was afraid of Communists—but was not involved with the posthumous revival of Céline's popularity. (Céline's writing has since come to be regarded as among the most significant in contemporary French literature.) By the time Bergé met Yves—on the rebound from Buffet's sudden marriage—he was ready for what was to become the biggest selling job of an artistic talent. He had a profound understanding of art and of the need to build around an artist, to manage and promote in order to turn a creation, *any* creation, into a commercial success. More profoundly, he understood the artist's guilt when dissipating energies on worldliness, and that the true helping hand a friend and associate can offer is not only the imposition of discipline but the ability to make the artist's talent less accessible and to nourish the mystery surrounding him.

Today, Bergé still promotes. He has never been afraid of spending money to make money and throws fascinating parties to sell the House of Saint Laurent, taking over Maxim's, for example, to launch the Opium perfume line in Paris, or spending a quarter of a million dollars on the New York premiere of the perfume line.

"I never have three-martini lunches and I never send flowers to clients," he says, adding that the key to the success of the House of Saint Laurent is that Yves—and he—control everything. "Everything is controlled by Yves Saint Laurent himself, from the decoration of avenue Marceau to the last item the house produces. There are no modelists; everything must be submitted to him so that there is a unity of tone and style."

When Yves gives parties, the reason usually has nothing to do with the label. A few months before Pierre's bash for Opium, Yves celebrated his own debut as a theatrical designer. The occasion was the revival of Cocteau's *L'Aigle à deux têtes* at Louis Jouvet's old Théâtre de l'Athénée, now owned by Bergé. Yves had designed the costumes for a handful of plays and movies over the years, but until 1977, he had never fulfilled his adolescent wish of doing stage design. For his debut, he chose to accentuate Cocteau's dramatic intensity and troubling doppelgänger effect, with sets all in blue, brown and purple and costumes in white, gold and black. For the premiere of *The Two-Headed Eagle*, he invited everybody for a backstage sit-down supper. The stars were there—Genevieve Page, who plays the queen who is as much a prisoner of her crown as of her past; and Hugues Quester, who is the anarchist who looks exactly like the murdered king and comes to kill the queen, only to fall in love with her. The actors and director Jean Pierre Dusseaux were there, together with Loulou, as were such old friends as Catherine Deneuve (for whom Yves did his first movie costumes, for Luis Buñuel's *Belle de Jour*) and Zizi Jeanmaire's choreographer husband Roland Petit. It was for Zizi that Yves had made his first stage costumes and for Roland that he had made his first television sets and costumes. The year was 1961, and Yves had just gone through the worst period of his life. "We're going to do two ballets for television; do you want to do the sets and costumes for us?" the Petits asked. The offer couldn't have come at a better time, and Yves had tears in his eyes when he accepted.

8

DOWN, DOWN AND UP

*E*ugenia Sheppard had written that the January 30, 1958, show "was the best Dior collection I've ever seen," and the following Sunday, *France Dimanche* had told the world that on the fateful day, a Dior saleswoman had given birth to a 3.2-kilo baby boy and promptly named him Yves. For the twenty-one-year-old crown prince, however, the glory was to be short-lived. In six months, the boy wonder had become the boy monster.

Bernard Buffet had been in on the triumph, turning journalist-illustrator for the weekly *Arts* to report on the trapeze collection, and Pierre had introduced the two to each other. When the painter opened his 1959 one-man show, it was Yves's turn to be quoted ("*C'est magnifique!*"). Yves's triumph led to a publicity-blitz tour to Brussels and his first trip to America, to receive the Neiman-Marcus award (which the French press called the Oscar of couture) in Dallas. In February 1959, he was dispatched to London, where the press nicknamed him The Choirboy, and three months later, he was in Moscow, where Nikita Khrushchev's de-Stalinization was in full bloom and the House of Dior presented an eighty-item collection.

Yves was under pressure to top himself.

Besides the "body lines" in the forms of *envol, I, H, A* and Yves's tulip lines, fashion during the fashion-conscious fifties was a matter of hemlines. No woman could forget that with one collection, Dior had made her entire wardrobe obsolete, and by the late 1950s, women were rather defensive about a too-abrupt hoisting and lowering of hems; so much so that the Paris houses allegedly had a tacit understanding not to change the length of their hems by more than two inches per season. The trapeze line had had a hemline just covering the knee, and by fall, the rest of Paris had adopted Yves's length. In 1958, the House of Dior had sold more than half as much again as all the other Paris houses combined, and Boussac, Jacques Rouet and Henri Fayot wanted an encore.

Wanting to be original and to offer a real alternative to the careful but insignificant modulations of hemline lengths, Yves unveiled a winter 1958–59 collection that dropped the hemline to three inches below the knee. Describing the stony reception that replaced the cheers and kisses of six months earlier, one British fashion editor commented that after looking for half an hour at these new long skirts, the gloomy audience resembled "drug addicts done out of their dope." The confidence invested in Yves was swept away by the outcry of the press. *Vogue* presented his collection in the kindest words: "When a new line is greeted with cries of indignation, it's a healthy sign. . . . It means that the fashion world is alive and kicking."

The psychological winner of the season was the seventy-five-year-old Mademoiselle Chanel, who offered a shrewd alternative to "lines." "In a time of great insecurity," wrote Georgina Howell in *In Vogue,* "she provides a glamorous, easy-to-wear, recognizable head-to-toe look that doesn't date. Her cardigan suits with chain-weighted jacket hems, beautiful linings and real pockets to hold cigarettes and keys leave the wearer free from clothes-worries and give enormous self-confidence."

"The tension on avenue Montaigne was so thick you could cut it with a knife," Saint Laurent was to remember. The Dior executives flew into tempers, while Raymonde Zehnacker sniffed that they had been wrong in handing over the fate of the house to a kid after all. Marc Bohan didn't say anything but began to see his chance. Impassively, Yves worked and worked. At eight P.M., he was still at his tiny desk, his necktie undisturbed, a crayon in one hand, facing the general staff, who were asking for the umpteenth time if he was sure.

The only pleasures were wholly extracurricular—evenings with Pierre and his friends and, with Leonor Fini, working on the sets and wardrobe of *La Parisienne* at the Comédie-Française. Fini was a formidable painter-illustrator-poetess and author whose surreal works were suffused with suffocating seductiveness and morbid eroticism. The Buenos Aires–born Leonor lived at Montparnasse and, together with Yves, managed to give the revival of Henri Becque's 1885 satire on bourgeois adultery a suffocating sumptuosity. She already had several movie costumes and sets behind her, including Renato Castellani's 1953 *Romeo and Juliet,* and told Yves all about it. He would love to try. Wasn't Cardin designing bias-cut, long-jacket suits for Jeanne Moreau in *Jules and Jim* and Givenchy making high-bosomed princess dresses without sleeves and belts for Audrey Hepburn in *Breakfast at Tiffany's?*

Instead of film costumes, he got to make sets and costumes for Roland Petit's *Cyrano de Bergerac,* an assignment that showed he could make brilliant things and that his creativity was becoming authoritative. It almost caused a break with the dancer-choreographer. The story was told with gusto and direct quotes by *La Presse.*

Yves had been in on all the rehearsals and knew each dancer's steps, each note of the music, each choreographic nuance. At the dress rehearsal, everything seemed to work smoothly until the costume designer's voice was heard shouting "Stop!" from a seat in the darkened orchestra. The dancers froze, and Yves walked down to the ramp and, pointing toward a dancer in a cadet officer's uniform, said, "We've got to change this."

"Impossible," objected Petit. "In that case, we'd have to redo the three other cadets' costumes."

Yves's voice was soft but firm: "Even if we have to start all over again, even if we have to cancel the invitations, I wouldn't change my mind. I just realized what it is that doesn't work and I know what to do. If you don't agree with me, I'll withdraw my costumes!"

Petit and company remained stunned. To postpone the preview, cancel more than a thousand invitations to the premiere, pay overtime, revise contracts, take out cancellation ads, would all add to the production deficit. Petit shouted, threatened, begged. The young costume designer remained adamant. The solution was finally to send out squads of taxis to round up enough seamstresses to remake the offending cadets' uniforms. Yves worked through the night with the seamstresses. At dawn, everything was saved but nobody had slept a wink.

At Dior's, the pressure was immense to recoup so as to make the previous season appear to be a one-time fumble, and for the 1958–59 winter collection, Yves did what would normally be a smart move—he reversed himself and came out with a hemline shortened to the knee. Called the puffball skirt, the short dress was gathered over the hips and tightened at the knee. As a publicity stunt, it was great, since the media immediately jumped on the hemline debate and began quizzing women about their reaction to the knees-or-not issue. As a marketable line, it was less than popular. Saint Laurent's next—and last for Dior—was his "beat" or Left Bank collection for 1960, featuring leather suits and coats, knitted caps and high turtleneck collars, all in black, on models with pale, zombielike faces. It was the most unpopular look in Paris (*Women's Wear Daily* described the silhouette as resembling "a toothpaste tube on top of a brioche").

Then, the grim realities of the Algerian War burst in on

him personally. Unlike the faraway Indochina War, which had ended with France's defeat in 1954 and the temporary division of Vietnam into separate states, the Algerian conflict was fought with draftees led by officers determined not to let the humiliations of Vietnam happen again in North Africa. Twice the war was nearly won. In 1957, the feared paratroopers of General Jacques Massu, using torture on a scale that shocked and sickened the home-front French, destroyed the Front de la Libération Nationale (FLN) underground network, and two years later, punishing French raids shattered the morale of starving, undersupplied Muslim units in rural strongholds. Many of the FLN cadres seemed ready to sue for peace, and with some justice, French commanders complained that decisive thrusts were frustrated by the waffling of politicians in Paris. In 1958, the demoralized and near-seditious army, aided and abetted by the million *pied noir* settlers, threatened to let events run away with themselves unless World War II hero Charles de Gaulle was brought into the government. In May, the towering sixty-eight-year-old general became France's new, strong president, and a year later, he tried to bring about peace by offering "self-determination." The FLN's reaction was far from negative, but the *pieds noirs,* who in the end would be forced to choose between "the suitcase and the coffin," answered de Gaulle with barricades in Algiers, a wave of violence in Algeria and metropolitan France and a succession of plots on his life.

Part of de Gaulle's effort to build morale for the badly bruised army was to clean up deferrals of too highly visible young conscripts. In the tradition of Brigitte Bardot's then twenty-year-old pop-singer husband, Jacques Charrier, who had been excused for reasons of nervous tension, the heads of Dior and Boussac had obtained a series of deferments for their most prized employe. Half of the much-needed money that France earned from its fashion industry came from Dior, now the General Motors of Parisian couture, and with two thousand jobs depending on the young designer, the deferments had been routine. With Charrier's much-publicized discharge for nervous tension, however, the media heat became too much for the army, and on September 1, 1959, Yves was sent to boot camp while Bohan took over as the House of Dior artistic director.

It is difficult to imagine a more unlikely recruit than the twenty-four-year-old Saint Laurent, thrown into basic training with a bunch of nineteen-year-olds, but the induction was more for public relations than for the necessity of adding one more man to the fighting force, and the next two months were the most painful in his life. Two weeks after the induction, he had a mental breakdown, and a week later, he was transferred to the Val de Grâce military hospital in Paris. The national sensitivity was as exasperated as Yves's nerves, and the transfer from boot camp to psychiatric ward was greeted with a swirl of scathing press innuendos suggesting that the army was giving its star recruit the kid-glove treatment. Stung by this criticism, the army sent obviously biased psychiatrists to the bedside of the famous recruit. Lucienne made desperate attempts to have her son released, but the army answered her request by transferring Yves to a military hospital in Saint-Mandé, east of Paris, where he was committed to solitary psychiatric confinement. It was only in December that the army gave up and allowed a less than honorable discharge of the now too notorious conscript.

Yves emerged shattered and emaciated from what he would always call his "nightmare," and, at doctors' orders and the army's strong suggestion, disappeared from public view. In January 1961, paparazzi spotted him convalescing on the Spanish Balearic Islands. Then the second shoe fell. The House of Dior told him his services were no longer required. His deputy, Bohan, was doing fine and the house had no intention of giving Yves back his artistic directorship.

Saint Laurent sued for $150,000 and was eventually awarded $40,000. In an about-face from the reportage on his military career, the press developed a new interest in the running drama of the fashion designer, who was now cast as a young rebel taking on the fashion Goliath.

Every young couturier's dream is to have his own house, and with Dior's "abusive breach of contract," as the court eventually ruled, Yves was forced to think of working under his own label. Hubert de Givenchy, the tall, handsome *grand seigneur* who had started in Schiaparelli's boutique, had owned his own house since 1952, Pierre Cardin since 1953, and André Courrèges, who had worked for Balenciaga, was rumored to be about to open his own "design firm." But what about Bohan's early go-it-alone failure, as well as the failures of Max Sarian (who had managed to get Rita Hayworth and Juliette Greco as clients), Alwyn (who had taken over the House of Jacques Fath at Fath's premature death), or one-armed Jean Pomarède, or Frédéric Sennes, Jean Gando or Georges Apothelose. The only recent success story was that of Guy Laroche, maybe because he had dared call a loft a couture house, had rented models by the hour instead of the day—but made a hit with his first collection. Laroche's clients now included Empress Saroya of Iran, Michèle Morgan, Bobo Rockefeller and Lily Pons, and he had just brought out his own perfume.

Yves discussed the pros and cons with Bergé, and the more they talked the more Pierre was convinced that if Yves didn't want to be a twenty-four-year-old has-been, the only solution was a House of Saint Laurent. All it took was money, and talent and luck. Givenchy had started in a salon furnished with two rows of canvas chairs, had not had the money to buy beautiful silks and expensive woolens, but had persuaded Bettina, Fath's top model, to leave Fath. It had been this charming redhead whose entrance had seemed to bring fresh air to the hothouse atmosphere of the salon and had electrified the bored buyers. Cardin had opened his boutique in the Faubourg Saint-Honoré in 1953, but it was only three years later that he had had his first hit. Yves also talked to his mother in Oran via long-distance telephone. She was encouraging, he told *France Soir* in September, when, still alone, he was trying to set up a tiny couture house in a two-room rented apartment in rue de la Boetie. "I'm much more afraid than I was before," he admitted to the newspaper.

Pierre didn't want to be an agent, but an associate, a full partner in the artistic-commercial endeavor. He had no money, and once the lawyers' fees were deducted from

Yves's settlement with Dior, the damages wouldn't go far enough. Pierre began to look for financial backing in Switzerland, on the theory that the further from recent Parisian headlines the money came from, the fewer the questions. In November, he went to Zurich.

"When I think I almost missed the plane," Pierre was to say years later. "There might never have been a House of Saint Laurent!"

He was eloquent, but the gnomes were not persuaded. The creation of a couture house, even with a wunderkind designer as its artistic pillar (and, incidentally, its only asset), was a proposition that was a little too risky for conservative bankers. Before leaving, however, Pierre was put in contact with an American who was in Europe scouting investment possibilities. The man was a thirty-seven-year-old insurance executive from Georgia with a mellow accent and zero knowledge of couture.

J. Mack Robinson had started out as a car salesman and moved into life insurance (Delta Life) and real estate. After meeting Bergé, he flew to Paris and was introduced to Yves, who valiantly tried his school English. "I'm completely ignorant of fashion," *Time* quoted Robinson as saying when it leaked the story in 1963 that Yankee dollars had been behind this particular burst of creativity in France's most hallowed national industry.

Robinson agreed to bankroll 80 percent of the new enterprise, and the moment his money was in escrow with First National City Bank on the Champs-Elysées, Yves and Pierre moved into high gear (while remaining more than vague about the origins of their capital lest Gaullist pride be offended). At 30 rue Spontini, a narrow but chic street in the sixteenth arrondissement, they rented space and began hiring people. "I hired the work crew one by one," Pierre was to remember. "Since I didn't know how to do a payroll, I phoned designer Madeleine de Rauch, who sent a bookkeeper over. I was almost alone on all that while Yves designed a collection."

The target date for the unveiling of the first Saint Laurent collection under Yves's own name was set for January 1962. Yves and Pierre were in no hurry to join the Chambre Syndicale, not because of its rules that to be a member a house must make its clothes in its own workrooms, and may not buy outside sketches or farm out work, but because of its blackout rules on publicity photos. The new partners needed all the publicity they could get, and if they had one fear in common, it was to come out looking like a cottage industry—small, rickety and amateurish.

During the fall of 1961, the staff grew to ninety. Among the specialists Pierre hired were several women who had worked with Yves at Dior and who were more than happy to work with him again. Seeing their chance to get even, the House of Dior bosses suddenly slapped Yves with a legal complaint, charging him with back-alley tactics in pirating two dozen key Dior workroom people for his new boutique. The theft of Dior craftspeople was nothing less than "reprehensible sabotage," asserted Bohan. Dior attorney Jacques Kam was more accusatory: "They have been corrupted. We admit that people change jobs, but we do not acknowledge such recruiting methods as sending people to Dior to persuade employees to leave."

Saint Laurent promptly denied complicity in the alleged plot. He had refused to interview any Dior employe, he said, until he or she had already left Dior, in accordance with Chambre Syndicale rules. Said Bergé, "There's no difference in salaries here, so if the staff wishes to follow Saint Laurent it's merely because they are happier working for him. Dior should learn that legal process is no substitute for talent." Several months later, Yves told *France Soir* that the House of Dior had tried to buy him off by offering him a huge sum if he would sign a written statement promising not to become a competitor. He refused, as he had refused an earlier offer to become the head of Dior–New York.

Things weren't going too well for the big house. Bohan's first collection had been a smashing success—clothes in the Dior tradition of desirable, wearable dresses—but his subsequent collections were criticized as ready-to-wear lines and fashion circles were atwitter with rumors that the House of Dior might abandon haute couture altogether and become a small, deluxe department store. Noting that the house had branched out into cosmetics, lingerie and menswear, *WWD* took a swipe at the new designs: "Because Dior already sells so many good things, people might even be tempted to buy some dresses while they're in the store."

On January 29, 1962, press and buyers gathered in the salon at rue Spontini for the unveiling of the first independent Yves Saint Laurent show. Charles and Lucienne were in the audience and Michèle and Brigitte peered from the staircase, looking a lot like their brother, a columnist said. J. Mack Robinson was there, too. Behind the curtain, Yves was ready. His face was extraordinarily pale, Pierre was to remember. "Let's go," Yves whispered to the models, and the ritual was under way.

The collection was 101 items long. The applause came in little bursts as he unveiled his sailor look—middylike tunics and pear-shaped, draped skirts—followed by circus-pony headdresses. The clapping became continuous when a black ciré satin jacket cuffed in black mink was modeled. At the end, the new couturier was mobbed by an emotional crowd of friends. Susanne Luling, Yves's "chum" at Dior's, held him in a happy hammerlock, while *Vogue* editor-in-chief Diana Vreeland fired off a verbal salute: "It was simply superbly, fabulously du-vine." Helena Rubinstein, who had sat impassively through the show, let a smile of approval light up her face (Helena Rubinstein, Inc., was rumored to have financed this debut). Zizi Jeanmaire shot off her chair like a rocket and hurled herself into his arms when he was brought out for a bow. He smiled, then broke down and sobbed on her shoulder. A second later, a potted palm fell on them.

The morning-after reviews were mixed. Eugenia Sheppard delivered her verdict with crisp incisiveness: "Saint Laurent holds Paris in the palm of his hand today," but the rest of the press called his fashion serious and even severe, and *Le Figaro*'s Augustin Dabadie allowed himself to wish that the young designer would be more in tune with his generation next year.

Yves was not discouraged—nor were Bergé and Robinson. The designs were consistent, if not spectacular, and orders were coming in. More important, perhaps, the word-of-mouth was favorable. Yves felt he might have been a bit too prudent, that perhaps Dabadie was right. The future, he felt instinctively, had less and less to do with rich women, who mostly wanted to go on dressing as they had before, and more and more with "fun" clothes. During the spring, he worked on designs that were lean, tubular and young, but he also pulled out a couple of old sketches. The beatnik look that had been the last straw at Dior's was now the Left Bank look and a *succès fou* for Marc Bohan! Perhaps other things he had sketched a year or two ago were right for now. The whole thing was a question of acute timing. He decided that from now on, he would keep extensive notes and all his sketches.

Why not a cowboy look after the nautical breeze? Why not a Robin Hood look, or rajah coats and slim dresses to be worn with turbans and dark stockings? Or long, pulled-down tops and barrel skirts accessorized with rich dark jewelry, or plain white dresses with cutout backs?

At the second collection—presented a week after the Algerians had voted for separation from France—hyperbole rose in the summer air and Saint Laurent was declared the sensation of Fashion Week. At show's end, he crept down from the head of the stairs where he had taken cover, to be smothered in the embraces of Zizi, Rubinstein and Jacqueline de Ribes. His trend for winter was fur and more fur—on cuffs, collars, scarves and hoods, combined with jewellike shades of color, flower tones and opulent fabrics. Now he was catapulted to stardom and, with Balenciaga and Givenchy, called one of the Big Three. "The little boy look is out," cried *Women's Wear Daily*, "the Big Three have rediscovered Eve."

A very young Eve in Saint Laurent's case. As the Beatles became a household word and Mary Quant launched her Ginger Group—a set of inexpensive clothes to be collected piece by piece and put together in endless variations—Yves put women in boots, boots and more boots, and, said British *Vogue*, made "brass studs smarter than rubies." He made alligator boots that went on and on to the thighs. When legs did show, they were covered in cables, paisley, knee socks, diamonds and tartans. To go with the thigh-high boots, he created a black ciré smock topped with a hood and a domed hat that conjured up a look midway between the new astronauts' uniform and the villainous lady spies James Bond had to battle. Less spacy were his bias shift dresses, his peasant shirts and painter's smocks, his bulky and loose tunics worn with wool stockings and flat pumps. For the second time in a row, he scored a smash hit.

Newsweek sent its reporters to Paris to do a four-page spread on Yves and the Rites of New Fashion, and managed a theatrical description of him as he gave the signal to start the fall collection ritual at rue Spontini. "There was an almost macabre air about the pale, gawky young man with the luminous eyes and the slim hands; they were fragile hands, as delicate as stalks of white iris, and his long, lank hair, carefully tinted in a flat russet, fell down in the back over his starched white collar, and over the templates of his heavy, wide-lensed eyeglasses," read the opening sentence in the August 12, 1962, issue, which called him the high priest of French couture and said that the most dominant influence on him might be his conviction that women were becoming less self-consciously feminine, more active and less cloistered. Said *WWD*'s John Fairchild when asked to contribute a quote, "This guy is the only designer in Paris who really belongs to the Sixties."

9

WHAT'S IN
A NAME?

*E*very November 25, the couture houses are closed and there is champagne and dancing in the workrooms, the corridors and the salons. To celebrate the feast day of Saint Catherine is a tradition: women who have had their twenty-fifth birthday during the year and are not yet married are given presents and wear lace caps with green and yellow ribbons. It is only in the couture world that the "Catherinettes" are feted; no other business or factory is closed on this day. The Catherinettes on avenue Marceau get to dance with the boss, and everybody shouts and laughs. Sometimes one of the tunes they dance to is one of the hits about a *mademoiselle de Paris* who, like the young girls being feted, was a junior seamstress in a famous house. Songwriters used to come up with these ditties every year, knowing the tremendous popularity of these working-girl heroines in Parisian folklore, but of late, the beat they dance to is more likely to be disco than three-quarter musette waltz time.

The corporate Yves Saint Laurent can afford this once-a-year homage to the *esprit de corps* of a unique trade because the house, as most of the rest of the business, is very much a modern enterprise. Today the House of YSL earns millions and millions through a worldwide web of agreements that cover 58 licensees who have the right to manufacture and sell 130 Saint Laurent–copyrighted products.

There are different licensing formulas, but the contracts are all basically the same. As a binder when the contract is signed, the designer is either paid "front money" from the distributor-manufacturer, ranging from $5,000 to $500,000 depending on the clout of his name, or a percentage of the projected first-year royalties. From then on, royalty contracts pay the designer from 5 to 15 percent of net wholesale sales, and there is usually a guaranteed annual minimum. Royalties, says Bergé, are all gravy, although he is reticent to disclose actual figures.

Fashion is an industry that doesn't mind touting its sales figures but is very shy when it comes to profits. Retailers are reluctant to discuss comparisons between designer and regular merchandise, but industry sources say consumers can pay as much as a 33 percent premium for designer-labeled goods. Manufacturers say a name doesn't necessarily mean instant profits. A spokesman for Max Factor in Los Angeles, which makes Halston's perfume, says, "A name certainly has an impact at first. People hear about him, read about him and he is always in the news. But an item doesn't sell very long if it is something people don't like." Michael Lichtenstein of Halston Enterprises, a division of Norton Simon, Inc., says consumers know the difference between good and bad, although some people confusedly believe a name adds a mysterious quality.

Pierre and Yves make a sharp distinction between products that demand permanent creativity and products that do not, such as perfumes, hosiery, eye wear and scarves (the latter are totally entrusted to Gustav Zumsteg of Abraham Fabrics). In the second category, the House of Saint Laurent will grant licenses to qualified manufacturers. In the first category, there are no YSL licensees.

"You never really control a licensee; contractually yes,

but not when it really comes down to style, prototypes and quality," says Pierre. "We must be prudent because you can put your name in jeopardy here, which is why we refuse licenses for clothes, lingerie, sweaters, handbags, etc."

The licensees return fees of over $10 million a year—enough for ample profits, says Bergé, while declining to disclose specifics. Franchising is not an area Saint Laurent is particularly eager to talk about himself, because he considers it beyond his moral responsibility. His input here is basically one of choosing. Prototypes are produced at 5 avenue Marceau, where there are a hatmaker's workroom and a shoe studio. Yves doesn't get involved in the structural design, but the workrooms do come up with stylistic alternatives for him to select. Sometimes he adds his own interpretations of detail, color, volume and other stylistic touches. His press secretary, Gabrielle Busschaert, says he takes pride in the fact that each of the products bearing his initials, from sunglasses to watches and cigarette lighters, has received his personal scrutiny and approval. Still, the road to easy fortune is not without potholes. Quality control is the constant nightmare. Also he will only do things he understands or relates to. Together with Bill Blass, Emilio Pucci, Givenchy and Ralph Destine of Cartier's, he was approached by the Ford Motor Company to lend his name to the designed lines of the Lincoln Continental Mark V, but he backed off, saying he was totally incompetent in automotive styling.

How does he do it?

What he creates is often absurdly simple, he says. When YSL went into bed linen, he did so by picking what is popular. "White is my favorite color for bed linens, freshly washed and country aired. But you can't go wrong with flowers. Stripes are always popular. Abstractions, particularly if small, seem to please. I like statements, things that say something. But the best critics, invariably, are overnight guests who say they have slept well and when may they come and visit again."

Cardin is the king of franchising, lending his designing ways, or at least his logo, to just about every wearable, digestible, drinkable and disposable product (although not the Continental Mark V). Since 1960 the House of Cardin has signed 400 licensees, of which nearly 370 are still active and sold in 40 countries. The Cardin-labeled items include wines, bikes, rugs, chocolates and the interiors of executive jets. "Pierre has made no claims to 'designing' a chocolate," says his license director, Jacques Manusardi. Cardin himself says he is too nervous, too crazy, not to create constantly. When asked if he has any new projects, he says, "Certainly. I would like to dress the Pope. I would also like to change the taste of China."

The runner-up in Paris is the House of Dior, with 150 Dior products that today represent 80 percent of the Dior turnover. But at least Cardin exists. Dior and the booming Anne Klein label are totally "ghosted," since the founders are dead and the name products are being designed by anonymous stylists.

It was George Bryant ("Beau") Brummell who, in the early nineteenth century, discovered the chic of discrimination when he decreed that a diamond solitaire cravat pin and a modest signet ring were all the accessories a gentleman needed. Before the famous English fop, men had displayed their riches with garish watch chains, diamond-studded shoe buckles, multicolored hose, scent bottles, snuff boxes and buttons that could be walking picture galleries, with painted miniatures of a favorite belle, a pretty shepherdess or more risqué subjects inspired by Pietro Aretino, the most energetic pornographer of the Renaissance. If Brummell, whose decrees in fashion were law in Paris, too, introduced the notion that chic doesn't have to be more, it was Christian Dior who realized he could put his own name on discrimination.

"There is a tendency to overcompensate by buying the biggest car or the biggest house," says Bergé. "People want to identify with prestige and status, to break into the circle of those who are 'in.' " The universality of fashion is both cause and effect of the success of famous logos. In an age of instant communication and the global village, any traveler can see that styles in the world's big cities differ more from those of their hinterlands than they do from fashion in other metropolises. It is hard to see the difference between a

Roman, a Parisian, a Montrealer; and, even if there are still sartorial clues to national differences, chic residents of Rio, Stockholm, Singapore, Houston and Teheran wear the same basic body covering and the same accessories, from glasses to shopping bags.

The export-minded Giscard d'Estaing administration came up with half a million dollars in 1976, through its Institute for Industrial Development, to keep the House of Balmain alive. "I discovered an extraordinarily fragile house," said Claude Potier, a former banker who joined Balmain to organize the rescue operation. "Sales were almost entirely from haute couture." With the infusion of government funds—banks and private investors put up $2 million—Balmain diversified with a vengeance, although the founder himself is no longer considered a trend setter. In 1978, the House of Chanel tiptoed into ready-to-wear, a step that must have had Mademoiselle spinning in her grave.

The first of the chain of Yves Saint Laurent boutiques opened in 1966 in a former bakery in rue de Tournon, off Boulevard Saint-Germain on the Left Bank. Since then, over 170 boutiques have been opened in Europe, the Americas and the Near and Far East. The Rive Gauche stores, with their distinct typeface, are slightly more pedestrian than the Yves Saint Laurent boutiques, the first of which is at 5 avenue Marceau. Besides the boutiques, YSL has a lucrative working contract with the Seibu chain in Japan, covering 39 products and 9 Japanese Rive Gauche stores. Since 1972, worldwide sales have increased by 30 percent a year and are approaching half a billion dollars annually.

Menswear is its own gold mine. For the first time in two hundred years, the male is assuming a colored, patterned, perfumed if not powdered appearance. The male as a peacock is the newest phenomenon in fashion, and for YSL, menswear brings in more profit, proportionately to volume, than women's fashion. Minor twists leave many men unmoved and major changes make them downright fearful, thereby depriving makers of three-piece suits for men of the hefty profits that a red-hot ladies' line can bring. Also, men's clothes cost more to make, but the squeeze is on the manufacturer, not on the designer.

Bidermann–Prouvost Crepy makes the YSL-labeled menswear, exporting 45 percent of it, but it *has* occurred to Bergé to follow the example of Dior, whose menswear for America is made by Hart Schaffner & Marx of Chicago, or Cardin, whose American menswear is made by New York's Intercontinental Apparel. It has even occurred to him to follow Ralph Lauren, the first designer to successfully cross over and buy *his* manufacturer, Lanham Clothing.

Cardin was the first women's designer to invade the menswear field, and in recent years, department stores have pressured manufacturers to come up with designer labels (as the department stores have lost credibility with their customers, say some manufacturers). Stanley Glanzrock of B. Glanzrock, which, in 1977, signed twenty-four-year-old Coty Award–winner Jeffrey Banks to design a men's line, says designer labels often work out well for manufacturers. Designer labels don't add anything to the value of the clothing, but they offer security, status and assurance.

Saint Laurent and Bidermann have had to interpret for American men—soften the Parisian look and switch to the lighter-weight materials Americans prefer. Frenchmen, says Yves, are slimmer, less muscular and have flatter stomachs, but the YSL menswear is still made in France (shirts are made in Hongkong), whereas Cardin's made-in-France originals are no longer available in the United States.

"Like Chanel made her suits, I make my menswear for myself," says Yves. With his menswear assistant and technical adviser Philippe Arnoux, Yves doesn't actually *invent*, he says. "We're an antenna; we observe and appreciate, maybe a little ahead of others, the beat of our times. In fact, I don't believe in a definitive masculine fashion but in expanded freedom. It's like the length of women's hemlines— *you* decide what's right for you. Why hang on to conventions of another era? Why is it more correct to work in an office in gray flannel than in velvet? Why is a tie more serious than a knotted scarf? Why can men only wear cotton in the summer?" As he told Hélène de Turckheim once, "Men's fashion isn't made with details, like women's fashion." Men's clothes, he feels, demand logic, a rigorous cut and utilitarian forms, and menswear should give the impression that tried and tested forms have simply been given new visual expression. "Even the choice of fabrics is difficult. Jersey, which a few years ago was being pushed in menswear, is good on a feminine silhouette. On a man it looks soft and sloppy."

Whether he is working in women's or menswear, he uses the shotgun approach, proclaiming his statements through a barrage of themes and subthemes. Then manufacturers leap on selected pellets and pass them along to retailers, who try to sell consumers on each idea. A lot of this "passing along" is unauthorized and takes place within weeks of the collection shows.

Ohrbach's vice-president and fashion director Irene Satz admits to attending the Paris unveilings, buying the originals and having them copied for sale in Ohrbach's New York and California stores within three weeks. Giant mass-marketer Sears, Roebuck and Company usually takes an unauthorized flier at YSL's latest look. Even his choice of fabrics sends rustles of hope—or dejection—along New York's Seventh Avenue. In 1977, his choice of Zumsteg's taffetas—in recent years equated with linings in men's suits and of coffins rather than high fashion—as underpinnings for his tiered skirts and opulent ball dresses rang a bell. Bonwit Teller took out full-page newspaper ads the Sunday following the Paris showing to announce that it already had a $500 taffeta-and-velvet ball dress by Oscar de la Renta, thereby jumping on a bandwagon that hadn't existed four days earlier. A month later, the peasantry part of the Saint Laurent collections was "integrated" into dress-pattern catalogs, and six weeks later, Burlington Industries was churning out miles of crisp, taffeta-looking Santora, a new hard-finish polyester-and-Dacron fabric in bright peasantry prints.

The Chambre Syndicale is powerless beyond France's borders and, even within them, stays out of all esthetic judgments. "We're not a select club but a professional organization representing everybody from the lowliest seamstress to the grand couturier," says Jacques Mouclier, the president of the Chambre. "Among other things, we examine candidates for the grand couturier title according to fixed standards: a minimum number of workers and workrooms, the compulsory two-a-year collection shows.

No subjective criteria. Women decide who's more 'in' than somebody else. In any case, if a couturier has no talent, he won't last long." The latest approved "grand couturiers" are Per Spook, a Norwegian-born former modelist for YSL and Louis Féraud, and Hanae Mori, a successful Japanese designer best known for her poetic caftans.

The first law protecting fashion creation was passed in 1920, under which couture designs registered with the Chambre are accorded legal protection inside France. Every design created by every member of the Chambre is registered in the Chambre files, with an exact sketch, photograph and swatch of fabric, before the official showings to media and buyers. French courts prosecute the high-fashion ripoff artists as severely as counterfeit painters, but plagiarism is often hard to define. An altered collar, a pocket moved from here to there or different buttons or trimmings can quickly turn a registered design into something else. And the ripoff entrepreneur often makes infinitely more money from the stolen design than the victimized couturier.

The sweetest smell of success comes from perfumes and cosmetics, that bruisingly competitive business that mixes strange ingredients with imaginative advertising and promotions and winds up selling some $10 billion worth of narcissism, hopes and dreams every year.

Yves likes to quote Proust's painter friend (and visionary forerunner of surrealism) Odilon Redon, who said that "the essence of mystery is to remain perpetually ambiguous." Scents are seduction and hype, but they are the only area of the YSL empire where Yves and Pierre aren't in charge, the only division not wholly owned by them. Since 1965, when J. Mack Robinson sold his 80 percent interest to Lanvin–Charles of the Ritz, YSL Perfumes has been a division of that company, which itself is a division of Squibb Corporation, the diversified pharmaceutical giant of New York City which, besides drugs, surgical instruments, household products and confections, fragrances and cosmetics, also owns a restaurant chain and provides catering services to airlines, has research facilities in Argentina, Brazil, France,

Britain and West Germany and plants in eighteen other countries.

The world's best-selling fragrance is not Chanel No. 5 but the mass-marketed Charlie from Revlon, Inc. Dior, Chanel and Nina Ricci no longer dominate world production; the bell-ringing folks from Avon Products do. The main reason is that American marketers didn't so much convince women to switch as go after new customers. Since the early 1970s, Revlon, Estée Lauder and others have pushed perfumes in the same way that they sell soap—with market research and with fragrances women can almost afford, backed by seductive advertising (Charlie was introduced in 1973 with a $10-million campaign). Says Revlon's vice-president of marketing, Annette Golden, "A woman will wake up and say, 'What do I feel like wearing today?' And she means fragrance as well as clothing. A woman now uses perfume like ready-to-wear or makeup coloring." Says Chairman Michel Bergerac, who has doubled Revlon's advertising budget to $135 million a year, "When things get rough, women tend to be a little depressed, and somewhere along the line it is nice to go get some cosmetics and feel good."

Americans can buy the same extracts, the same flower oils, sulfides, acids and other sometimes unglamorous ingredients as the French perfumers, and the toll has been heavy. Only Guerlain, Chanel, Deprez and Jean Patou are still responsible for their own formulas. The others work with aromatic wholesalers in Grasse, in southern France, where nearly all natural flower extracts come from, or invent nonorganic perfume bases. They can also hire the same "noses," those mysterious alchemists who, in their laboratories, compose a perfume from up to three hundred scents and keep the combinations in only one other head besides their own—usually their wives'—or locked away in secret safes. André Fraysse, who composed My Sin for Lanvin in 1925, and Edmond Roundnitska, who started with Femme and Moustache for Rochas in 1944, are the elder statesmen of the supersecretive trade. Jean-Louis Sieuzac is the boy wonder who, at thirty-two, made Opium for Saint Laurent.

The life span of name scents is getting shorter every year,

and the made-in-Paris labels no longer mean automatic leadership. A belated French counteroffensive began in 1978, after François Coty had become a subsidiary of Pfizer Inc., Balmain and Raphael had been swallowed up by Revlon, Cardin by American Cyanamid, Rochas by the German chemical multinational corporation Hoescht and Jean Patou by Borden. In near-desperation, Dior, which had already closed its money-losing plant in Stamford, Connecticut, Chanel and Guerlain began a general mobilization, while L'Oréal tried to impose the Guy Laroche line and Sanofi (a subsidiary of the French oil giant Elf-Aquitaine) pushed First, Stendhal, Molineux and Lubin. The battle was for floor space in the world's top department stores, the scramble was for new scents—and the casualties weren't all French. Helena Rubinstein and Max Factor also were absorbed by conglomerates after stumbling with the wrong perfumes in the wrong market.

Saint Laurent has been in perfumes since 1964, the year before Robinson sold out for a very handsome profit. The first perfume was Y, which brought in a profit of over $2 million a year from the start, allowing Yves and Pierre to begin buying into their own success. Y was followed by men's toiletries. Pour Homme was launched with an advertising campaign that features Yves wearing nothing but his glasses—and, presumably, his eau de toilette. For someone whose shyness is legendary, the photo was its own publicity, with Yves telling inquiring journalists that he knew he was not pretty but that since he had a good body, he had "decided to go the whole hog."

Saint Laurent Perfumes is a separate division of Lanvin–Charles of the Ritz (which also owns Lanvin, Arpege and My Sin), headed by Mark Laracy. Since Y, Saint Laurent has come out with four fragrances. Opium was the first to come with a line of makeup, including twenty-two eye shadows, nineteen shades of lipstick and six foundation bases, all in a deluxe kit that could be fitted into a black, enameled square box with a silk cord and tassel.

"I started with the name," Yves says. "It was the only name I wanted. I wanted a lush, heavy, indolent fragrance. I wanted Opium to be captivating, and it's a fragrance which evokes all the things I love—the refined Orient, imperial China, exoticism. The emperor of China smoked opium. The nineteenth-century esthetes, poets, writers knew and understood the very release of imagination, dreams and mystery it evokes. For me, the perfume evokes all that is romantic, sensuous and mysterious. Byron and Delacroix, Rimbaud, Baudelaire—they all understood the exotic beauty of the Orient without having to travel there. Opium doesn't have the same echo for me as perhaps it may have for those who associate it only as a drug."

Like other franchises, Opium is artistically controlled from avenue Marceau. Bergé will not give figures, and the perfume license fee is the best-kept secret of the house. Yet *Stern* could report that Opium brought in $3.5 million during its first three months on European department-store counters. Once Yves had sensed that women were ready for a new, smoky look that would reflect a new hunger for mystery and allure, Jean-Louis Sieuzac was borrowed from the perfume raw materials firm of Roure Bertrand-Dupont, for which he had worked since he was nineteen. It took Sieuzac two years to translate Yves's demand for a lush, heavy, indolent fragrance into a chemical formula. He only saw YSL twice and never received a thank you (but was paid $10,000 a month).

The psychology for the makeup was produced at Squibb's Manhattan headquarters on Fifty-seventh Street and the packaging at avenue Marceau. Juliette Maubras was given a series of samples of Yves's favorite colors—"red-red" and a hot, Indian pink. From these, she started building a lipstick and nail-polish palette. As for eye shadow, he sent her fabrics—greens, blues, browns and golds. "But the most Saint Laurent color is a khaki-green, which I combined with a turquoise blue for the most unusual effect," she said. "Saint Laurent really has his own colors that nobody can copy."

Opium was premiered in Paris at Maxim's in February 1978 and sold more in one month—at $100 an ounce—than Chanel No. 5 did in one year. The success was repeated throughout Europe, and reports came back to Yves that men loved to smell it on women and that some men loved to wear it. The line was only introduced to American consumers nine months later, making a midyear issue of *Vogue* coo that "Opium is being sneaked into the States." In Australia, it was banned in the state of New South Wales as having a name that might entice innocents to hard drugs, which prompted Charles Aznavour to cut short a Down Under concert tour in protest.

When Opium was launched in the United States (where one third of all cosmetics sales are rung up between Thanksgiving and Christmas), Squibb went all-out with a premiere party for nine hundred aboard a four-masted bark named *Peking* berthed at Manhattan's South Street Seaport Museum. Celebrities were packed stem to stern under Chinese lanterns, hundreds of fresh orchids and gold, purple and sienna streamers strung from the masts. The Beautiful People included everyone from Squibb chairman Richard Furlaud and organizer Marina Schiano to a gargantuan bouncer from Studio 54. For three hours, Yves himself trod the decks, trailed by geishalike models in Opium Fantasy clothes. He tried to evade the TV crews and, turning away after an interview with NBC's Chauncey Howell, confessed, "I didn't understand a thing I said." He greeted his peers, from Halston, escorting Cher, to Mary McFadden, with shy pecks.

The press wanted to know what the celebrities thought of the new scent. Patriotically, McFadden said she thought she preferred American designers' perfumes; Diana Vreeland diplomatically said, "I like the smell of money"; while Estée Lauder acidly noted, "It's only my Youth Dew with tassels." Dawn Mello was thrilled when Yves thanked her for wearing one of his dresses, while Furlaud thought it was wonderful that Yves had the stamina to stand for three hours and talk to all those people. What *WWD* called the Fashion Pack and the Highest Chic New York consumed 30 cases of Bollinger champagne; 3,000 mussels, oysters and clams; 160 pounds of veal and steak tartare and 50 pounds of strawberries. Hard-core party people wondered where the real action was—rumor falsely had it, *WWD* reported, that an actual opium den existed in the bowels of the ship. At the end, everybody watched $30,000 worth of fireworks inflame the East River sky and, in the finale, spell out *YSL*.

10

RIVE GAUCHE /
LEFT BANK

*I*n 1963, America's beautiful First Lady Jacqueline Kennedy and her sister Lee Radziwill became Saint Laurent clients. It was the year he showed women how to dress for their boots and told the world that designers were just beginning to catch up with the enormous social changes.

"The old balance between young women who partially set the style in the street and the elegant ladies who ruled it from the salon has been completely upset," he told fashion writers at the July unveiling of his winter 1963–64 collection. "The older generation goes to New Jimmy's to twist and find themselves completely *dépassé*. I know of clients of thirty and forty who've come to me and said their daughters call them out of date.

"Personally I don't believe a collection should be a revolution. The fashion press always wants revolution. But I don't think it's possible anymore, in the old sense. What is important is evolution, a smooth line development that moves from one collection to another. Above all I want to set out my own recognizable personal style and not something that flip-flops back and forth every six months just to make news."

He was being interviewed at his cluttered studio in rue Spontini. His desk was a mess of paper, sketches, buttons, pencils and bits of fabric, all dominated by the big brass bowl of hard candies that he sucked on when the strain of creation began to tell. The world was looking for a young solution, and his previous fall collection had brought the Left Bank look into couture with total success. The House of Saint Laurent had sold $250,000 worth of clothes to professional buyers, and Yves, Pierre and J. Mack Robinson were turning their first profits.

Fashion seers liked the twenty-six-year-old YSL, who looked like a teen-age seminarian. Overseas buyers were beginning to think patronizingly of Paris as an out-of-touch place, good for flashes of inspiration rather than line-by-line copying. Dior's massive commercialism was judged too crass—the avenue Montaigne headquarters now featured a tea room, and its latest license was Diorette baby clothes. Balenciaga's aloofness was found to be irrelevant and Chanel to be—well, uniquely Chanel.

A combination of enthusiasm, energy and iconoclasm of the kind Yves liked was making London the city of and for the young. The Beatles, Mary Quant, Jean Shrimpton, Michael Caine, Vidal Sassoon, Harold Pinter and David Frost were all very much under-thirty pop stars, designers, models, actors, hairdressers, writers and sharp-tongued TV wits concerned with being themselves and being inventive. A million young designers were spilling out of art schools, bursting with new ideas and practical expertise. As British *Vogue* said in 1962, "For the first time the young people who work in the rag trade are making and promoting the clothes they naturally like, clothes which are relevant to the way they live . . . ours is the first generation that can express itself on its own terms."

In New York, it was the London look; in Paris, it was *Le style anglais*. The French *nouvelle vague* meant Francois Truffaut's *Jules and Jim*, which inspired a knickerbockers-and-Jackie-Coogan-cap look and allowed Emmanuelle Khanh to make her debut in ready-to-wear. The youth of France was singing along with pop stars Johnny Halliday and Sylvie Vartan, falling in love with Jeanne Moreau and Catherine Deneuve on the screen and becoming sentimental listening to Jacques Brel's soul-searching ballads about better times that never came. *The Umbrellas of Cherbourg* had half of France forming lines in front of cinemas and, together with Françoise Hardy singing *Tous les garçons* and the seventy-six-year-old Marc Chagall climbing up to paint the ceiling of the Opéra, Yves was also reaching pop stardom. "I take our times as they come," he could say while the media were proclaiming that his collections were influencing women and other designers all over the world. In November, he was the most photographed young person at Cocteau's funeral.

The lesson he was learning, he said, was to get out—and stay out—of the couture ivory tower. "I know now that you can't take your clothes out of life, away from reality, and have them mean anything. A designer must get out and look at life around him. As soon as I went twisting at Régine's, I understood the problem older women have in a place like that."

He was realizing that fashion-conscious women were becoming less self-consciously feminine, more active and more restless. Younger, too, demographically. His winter 1963–64 show opener had been a black outfit that looked like a cross between a space suit and a James Bond antagonist's sexy uniform, which he simply called a Robin Hood inspiration. This set the theme of the relaxed fall and winter fashions, in which he gave up his usual austere Buffet colors and combined bright contrasts with easy elegance. "Others had tried to replace the old gussied-up couture with an easy, boyish look," *Newsweek* hummed. "But it is Saint Laurent who carried the boyish look through everything he showed—from daytime wear to evening clothes. The shirt, the jerkin, the sailor's jacket, the farm boy's smock, the fisherman's oilskins appeared first in tweeds, then reappeared in satins, all transformed by Saint Laurent's genius into clothes designed to catch what Saint Laurent calls the elusive mood of 1963."

Among the journalists crammed around Yves for the postoperative quotes was Princess Lee Radziwill. Jackie Kennedy's sister had taken on the "fun assignment" of covering the collections for *McCall's*. In haughty displeasure, Givenchy had declared that that made her a member of the working press and barred her from his showing. Radziwill stalked off in a huff. "It couldn't matter less," she said. "I haven't been buying his clothes; I've been wearing Saint Laurent's." She wasn't telling Givenchy anything new.

Questioned by the newswomen, YSL said he didn't think he had found himself yet—or a new look. "My collection is part of my evolution. I'm not yet where I want to go. I'm still on my way."

What he didn't tell the fashion writers was that the explosive "youthquake" was undermining the whole garment industry by making it impossible to foresee fashion a year in advance. As he and Bergé were realizing, the whole edifice was crumbling.

A corollary to something being in fashion is something else being out of fashion. If an article of fashion only lasts one season, then, by implication, the fabric it is made of is equally short-lived. When a fashion is over, its fabrics and remaining stock have almost no cash value, meaning that everything must be sold out all the time at all levels of the industry.

Haute couture was traditionally the undisputed fashion leader, and the ready-to-wear "stylists" were anonymous nine-to-five garment manufacturers' employes, whose job it was to soften couture eccentricities for the mass market. To be able to work smoothly, communications up and down the production lines of the garment industry must be open and fast, with a continuous process of identifying, defining, understanding, transforming and innovating. Each season, this "future knowledge" has to be redefined—which fabrics for what clothes, for what fashions at what prices, for what clientele? For everything to flow in an orderly manner, an eighteen-month lead time is necessary. Since it is a year and a half before any rtw clothes go on sale, the yarn mills must know what fibers and colors the textile factories will want to use (in the case of shoes, which require the longest manufacturing process of anything in the fashion industry, the lead time is even longer). When the textile manufacturers get the yarns, they make up sample fabrics, which they submit to the rtw stylists. With his selection from these samples, the stylist makes a collection, which his house shows to its retailers, who choose the clothes they think their clients will go for next summer or next winter. Since the consumer doesn't order in advance but buys—or refuses to buy—what is in the store, the retailer must order six months in advance so the clothes can be made. Six months earlier, the stylist must order fabrics from the textile manufacturer who, in turn, must order six months earlier from the yarn mills.

As long as haute couture is the fashion leader and ready-to-wear manufacturers can trust its lead and have enough lead time to adapt the novelties to "the street," yarn mills, textile manufacturers and rtw houses can live. But what happens, Yves, Pierre and a lot of others were asking themselves, if ready-to-wear doesn't follow the couture lead? What happens if couture is out of touch?

Ready-to-wear could accommodate a small youth market if certain retailers, manufacturers, textile and yarn mills specialized in fast-turnover rtw clothes, but Yves had heard society women saying they wanted to look like their daughters. During the fall of 1963, the industry grapevine confirmed this. Retailers were beginning to cut back their orders to rtw houses, saying they could no longer order in October for the spring, since no one could foretell what the fad would be in April. What if I order clothes in pastels, and browns and blacks invade the street? they asked. Worse, some of them said that if they ordered somewhat romantic styles and leather became the uniform of the young, even older women stopped buying. Adult women may not have the guts to dress like the kids but they refuse to buy what their daughters say is out-of-date and keep wearing what they have and end up buying nothing!

It happened sooner than anyone expected. Three months after Yves had warned that the balance—between young women setting the style in the street and elegant women from the salons—was becoming unsettled, retailers refused to order the 1964 rtw spring line. And no wonder. Youth was openly displaying its strength, allure and power, and the media were talking about nothing else, it seemed, than the exalted beauty and genius of the young—fashion magazines were the most craven—and the garment industry reacted the wrong way. Instead of joining what it couldn't lick, it tried to impose fashion by converting to the set ways of the designers who appealed most to the young. The attempt was doomed in advance. How could they expect Saint Laurent, Courrèges and Cardin, whose personalities and originality had guaranteed their success, to close ranks with the losers? All right, then, the industry pleaded, just *tell* us what you're going to do. Disarmingly, the designers answered that they couldn't know now what would be born of events that haven't yet taken place.

Nineteen sixty-four was the year of Courrèges. With his spring collection, the former Balenciaga trainee, who had been producing his own collections since 1961, made headlines with a smashing show. To the throb of tom-toms in his chalk-white showroom on avenue Kléber, Courrèges introduced the new space age to fashion. Everything was white, silver—and short; and from then on, the 1960s would revolve around bare knees, pantsuits, outsized sunglasses and white leather boots. "Courrèges' clothes are so beautiful," enthused Andy Warhol, "everyone should look the same." Six months later, Mary Quant and the British Fashion House Group introduced the miniskirt to America. The models in their thigh-high dresses stopped traffic on Times Square, and Americans squealed with pleasure and surprise when the Mary Quant girls modeled the clothes on television to a nonstop dance routine of pop music.

It wasn't Yves's year, it seemed. He was so annoyed with the unfavorable coverage of his summer collection that he resolved not to let the press have the first chance to pass judgment on his designs ahead of the store buyers. In November, he caused something of a stir by having the

Chambre Syndicale endorse the idea of separate shows for media and buyers. In a dramatic midnight announcement, Chambre Syndicale president Jacques Heim said the houses of Saint Laurent and Maggy Rouff would not admit journalists to their next couture collections; that a special showing for the press would be held one month later. He intimated that others would follow.

Six months later, Yves's Mondrian Look was a worldwide hit, and all bitterness was drowned in the euphoria of rave reviews. It was his mother who had given him an art book on Piet Mondrian (1872–1944), the Dutch painter who developed a distinctive style of nonobjective painting based on the reduction of pictorial elements and the elimination of curved lines and even of the sensuous appeal of color. Mondrian, who lived most of his adult life in Paris and died in New York, had a profound influence on modern architecture, furniture design, advertising art and now—fashion.

Mondrian was a last-minute inspiration. "In July I'd already finished a good part of my collection," Yves told *France Dimanche*. "At the second rehearsal, I was miserable. I watched my coats and dresses pass by without an ounce of pleasure. It was no longer possible for me to continue dressing women like that. Nothing was alive, nothing was modern in my mind except an evening gown which I had had embroidered with paillettes like a Poliakoff painting. It wasn't until I opened a Mondrian book my mother had given me for Christmas that I hit on the key idea."

The idea was simplicity itself—a plain white jersey shift and lines and blocks of blacks and primary colors. As he scrubbed a third of the already-finished line, rue Spontini went into overtime to produce the Mondrian line. Not that it was easy. The various rectangles had to be harmonious sizes and, to look like anything, they had to be sewn together with near-invisible seams. The final lineup included twenty-five Mondrian creations, plus the scintillating multicolored evening gown inspired by Serge Poliakoff. "There are still a number of coats and dresses of my ancient syle," he said, "I simply haven't had the time to redo a hundred and fifty garments. Oh well."

The twenty-five Mondrian dresses were a triumph. Store

buyers loved the clothes, and the media said that not since the summer of 1963 had anyone cut such a winning figure. French papers called it a new art, a new fashion full of simple lines; American fashion writers hailed it as a turning point; and British *Vogue* soberly cautioned that it would be the easiest thing in the world for the ready-to-wear market to copy. Indeed, among the front-row watchers, next to Jane Fonda, sat Elsa Martinelli in a Mondrian checkerboard dress that wasn't Yves's.

By the time British *Vogue* was in print, its prediction was almost anticlimactic. In rag-trade back rooms, pattern makers and machine operators turned out millions of cut-rate Saint Laurents that were in shops around the world before the Paris originals were hemmed. Pop- and op-art fabrics followed. Yves was more baffled than appalled—as they said, what bigger compliment could he wish for?—but Pierre and J. Mack Robinson saw it differently. If the world was going to wear Saint Laurent ripoffs, why didn't the corporate Saint Laurent do the copying? Why didn't they make their own ready-to-wear?

Their three-year-old company was a considerable achievement. Not only was Yves on the artistic pinnacle, they were also making money. It was hard to say which success astonished the trade more. Many designers were obviously out of touch, and couture, as a whole, was losing $3 million a year. Many of the older, wealthy customers were dead or dispossessed (said Jean Dessès in closing his house in 1963, "Every time I read about a South American revolution, I knew I'd lost another set of good clients"). Worst, said Pierre, haute couture was not adapting itself to the new world. Dresses were mercilessly copied and given worldwide distribution, but all Paris got—even legitimately—was the price of the originals.

Yves was all for going into ready-to-wear. He loved to design for his contemporaries, but few young women could aspire to a Saint Laurent creation. And the very rich and the very chic who bought his clothes were often a pain in the neck, although unlike buyers, they were less affected by what the press wrote and remained pretty independent and pretty good at making up their own minds. But creating

Seventeen-year-old Yves Saint Laurent tightens the bow on the crepe dress executed by Hubert de Givenchy from Yves's design (seen in background) that won first prize in a national design contest in 1954. (ADP)

Christian Dior, whose sudden death in 1957 catapulted YSL, his young protégé, to the top of the most influential fashion house in the world. (Keystone)

Hubert de Givenchy in 1948. (Roger–Viollet)

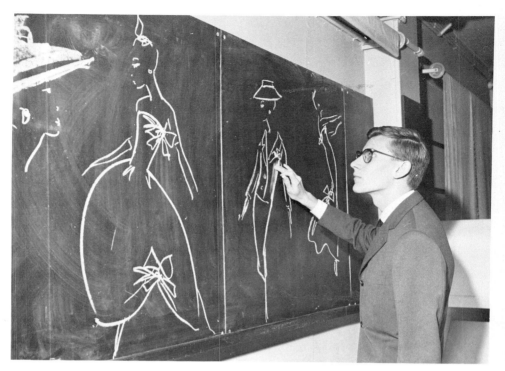

YSL with his sketches for Dior's 1957 line. (AGIP)

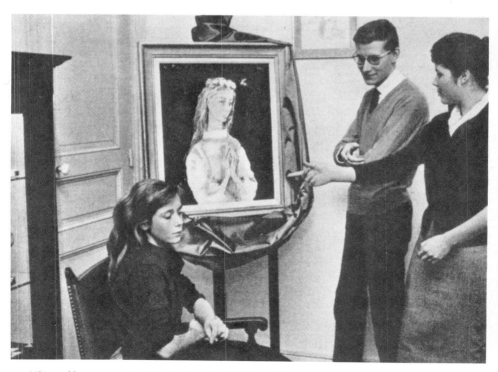

YSL and his sisters Brigitte *(left)* and Michèle and his portrait of Brigitte. (Marie Claire)

From YSL's 1958–59 winter
collection—the "puffball" look.
(International Wool Secretariat)

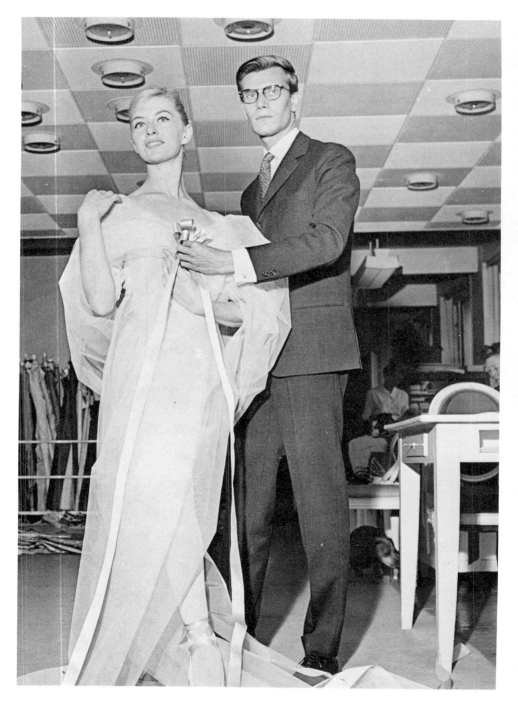

YSL's first ballet costume—for ballerina Tessa Beaumont in 1959. (Roger–Viollet)

YSL recuperating in the Balearic Islands after his ordeal as a conscript in the French army in 1961. (Elle)

After the showing of
YSL's first collection under his own
name on January 29, 1962, Zizi
Jeanmaire rushed to congratulate
him, and a minute later *(left)* he
broke down and cried on her
shoulder with emotion and joy.
(Keystone)

Two YSL designs for Claudia Cardinale in the film *The Pink Panther.* (UPI)

Opening day at the first YSL
Rive Gauche boutique in Paris,
September 1966. (AGIP)

Inspired by pop art, a trompe
l'oeil painting of Yves dominates
the bloodred walls and steel and
glass decor of Rive Gauche. (International Wool Secretariat)

YSL's pop dresses in positive-negative contrast, inspired by Andy Warhol in 1966 when miniskirts were at their highest. (International Wool Secretariat)

Modeling the summer fashion, 1969. (Elle-Scoop)

Mother and son, 1970. (Elle-Scoop)

YSL wearing nothing but his glasses—and presumably his new eau de toilette for men, "Pour Homme." This picture was the main feature of the publicity campaign. (Keystone)

Three styles from YSL's "Left Bank" fall-winter collection, 1971. (UPI)

Bathing suits appeared for the
first time in YSL's spring 1974
ready-to-wear collection. (UPI)

From the spring-summer 1976
collection. (UPI)

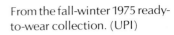
From the fall-winter 1975 ready-to-wear collection. (UPI)

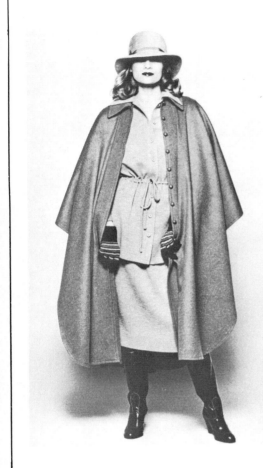

From the haute couture collection, July 1976—YSL's Cossack-gypsy-Turkish fantasy look. (UPI)

A 19th-century dress with picture hat—from the 1977 spring-summer haute couture collection. (UPI)

The fantasy look continued into the 1977 spring-summer haute couture collection. (UPI)

For the spring-summer ready-to-wear fashions presented in October 1977, fantasy was out and the casual, sporty look was in. (UPI)

A see-through dress from the 1977 spring-summer collection. (UPI)

A return to traditional sportswear in April 1978. (UPI)

YSL sketching his SportYves
mix for evening, with his model
Mounia Orhozemane. (Guy
Marineau/W)

Adding the final touches before the July 1978 unveiling. (Jean-Luce Hure/NYT Pictures)

The haute couture collection in July 1978 was called YSL's most wearable collection. (Agence France Presse)

One of the hits of the July 1978 collection—Mounia in a simple two-piece black dress with a handbag in the shape of a heart. (Jean-Luce Hure/NYT Pictures)

Front office at Yves Saint Laurent S.A. Sitting under Warhol's YSL is Pierre Bergé, and standing from left, Jean Sebastien Szwarc, Marc Vincent, and Yves Faro. (Le Point-Scoop)

Workroom at Yves Saint Laurent S.A. From left, Anne-Marie Muñoz, Jean-Pierre Derbord, Mounia Orhozemane, YSL, and Ida Fayoll. (Le Point-Scoop)

YSL at home. (Patrice Habans/Sygma)

Yves and the muses—Loulou Klossowski *(left)* and Betty Catroux. (Guy Marineau/W)

Paloma Picasso Lopez and her husband, Rafael Lopez-Sanchez. (W)

High Seas Chic —YSL's ready-to-wear summer line—November 1978. (W)

Plucking flowers from the past—YSL's sailor look, 1978 edition. (W)

YSL with Loulou (*seated*) and his "jeunes filles," models of the House of Saint Laurent. (Patrice Habans/Sygma)

for celebrities produced its own headaches. Dame Margot Fonteyn was now his most devoted customer and Lee Radziwill his most constant VIP. After a ball that Radziwill gave in New York in 1965, she was so annoyed at the advance publicity about the lime-green silk crepe YSL creation she wore that she cabled rue Spontini, telling Saint Laurent and Gabrielle Busschaert that information on her wardrobe was not in the public domain. Yves and his publicity chief were innocent, but Radziwill had to be placated.

And it was neither Dame Margot nor Princess Radziwill who kept Yves Saint Laurent, S.A., in business. For 1966, Yves was toying with pop-art clothes, and ready-to-wear, he felt, would give him the first spectacular possibility to reflect the times. The social and economic changes made people want new forms and new expressions—the first pop-playing boutiques, packed with clothes ideas for the young, were opening on Boulevard Saint-Germain—and even the idea of fashion dictatorship by designers, buyers, fashion editors or women of taste was beginning to look stale. As Brigitte Bardot said, to dress in couture, *"Ça fait mémé"* ("That's for grannies").

Yves dreamed of a future in which his generation would get a big play. "I have dreamed of opening a big department store called Yves Saint Laurent," he would say in 1979. "It would be a place where everything I make is sold together. The cheapest cotton dress would be in the basement while couture would be sold on the top level. And I would design the building, the interior, the furnishings for the store, the logos, everything. That's what I've been dreaming about since the mid-1960s when it became obvious to me that the old division between women who can afford to have their clothes designed for them by some great couturier and women who have to be content with inadequate, deliberately delayed copies was dying out."

The year before the Mondrian triumph, he had played Balenciaga. Deliberately, he had tried to go for high elegance and conjured up designs for blasé millionaires. The press had hated it and caused him to lash out with the ban on journalists. He had been wrong—it was to remain the only defeat he would admit to. Most of his influential ideas—the pea jacket, the styled-up beatnik look, the shirt-waist, the Mondrian and pop-art styles—had not been unusually original, but his perceptive timing was beginning to set a huge fashion ball rolling.

In July 1965, Robinson sold his interest in Yves Saint Laurent, S.A., for a cool million dollars to Lanvin–Charles of the Ritz (which was also acquiring Vidal Sassoon). Bergé felt obliged to tell the world that becoming part of an American conglomerate didn't mean Yves and he were giving in to megalomania. "We're not changing anything in the house," Pierre emphatically told a news conference. "We're not moving into a larger building. We have six workrooms and we will not expand. We're not planning to have more licensees or to bring out new products with Saint Laurent's name."

Richard Salomon, the president of Lanvin–Charles of the Ritz, was an enthusiastic conglomerateur who even spoke French. A fourth-generation New Yorker, he had been a philosophy major at Brown University and had spent his junior year at the Sorbonne. He got into the perfume business through an uncle who had also introduced Coty to the United States and owned a piece of Charles of the Ritz. At fifty-eight, the husky, dark, enormously assured Salomon headed a $70-million empire that included Jean Naté toiletries, Hermès and Dior perfume in England. The only string he attached to the corporate takeover was that Yves would come to the United States to publicize a new scent that Lanvin–Charles of the Ritz would bring out.

In December, Yves, Pierre and Yves's muse and friend Betty Catroux were in America, Yves and Betty to tour with Y, Pierre to stay put in New York and talk Salomon into bankrolling YSL ready-to-wear. For some couture houses, Yves told reporters, ready-to-wear was a financial story. "For me," he blushed as he produced his rehearsed English, "it's a love story.

"The young lead very different lives from the lives of the women who wear couture fashion," he explained. "Not all of the young would want couture even if they could afford the price. Sometimes elegance builds a wall between people. Many young people don't want that."

His definition of youth was elastic: "Anyone from the age of fifteen to the young at heart." He conceded that even if the youth wave wouldn't spell the end of high fashion, couture would no doubt never be the same. "I don't know how but it will be different." When *Business Week* did a story on the YSL–Lanvin–Charles of the Ritz marriage, it pointed out that it was Yves's proclivity in design for the young that Salomon counted as the biggest asset, and quoted a company official as saying, "We want to associate ourselves with the young look."

The publicity tour took Yves and Betty to the wilds of Kansas City and beyond to submit to cocktail parties, golf-club weekends, business associates and interviews. Yves hated it, and whenever he and Betty could, they slipped away, to stroll the streets of strange cities and discover their own night spots. The only experience he was to remember was meeting Hollywood designer Edith Head and, in a Los Angeles street, seeing a poodle wearing a Mondrian dog sweater.

As Yves and Betty flew back to Paris, he decided that the outlet for the new ready-to-wear for which Pierre had negotiated startup capital would have to be located where the young were, on Saint-Germain-des-Prés or the Latin Quarter, in any case on the Left Bank. Before the two of them landed at Orly, they also had the name for the new endeavor—Saint Laurent Rive Gauche. And, yes, the boutique would stay open every night till midnight, like so many stores did in California.

11

SHIFTS

The rag trade is, like Heraclitus's universe, in constant flux, and no one ever steps twice into the same stream. The tension between efficiency and competition, which has accelerated fashion beyond the public's willingness to absorb it, constantly dislocates the business. So far, says Maurice Bidermann, the French garment industry has been leaderless (intimating that he may be its first leader), and the future doesn't lie in more labels but in a rational concentration of efforts. Women's wear manufacturers are crazy when they totally refuse to consider prices, he says. "They still say fashionable clothes must be expensive, that if they are too cheap, women won't buy them. To keep women's ready-to-wear a luxury preserve is certainly one way of never getting anywhere." The only way to keep factories running, he adds, is to do what he does in menswear—strive to make sure YSL's men's suits can retail for no more than $200. In America, creative leadership is in New

York, but the garment industry is fast regionalizing, with apparel marts in Dallas, Atlanta, Chicago and Los Angeles cutting into Seventh Avenue's traditional dominance. New York is still firmly entrenched as the key marketplace, and its annual sales of $7.5 billion are more than double those of California, its chief and fastest-growing rival, but Seventh Avenue has lost 20 percent of its jobs since 1970.

Today, the great Boussac empire lies in ruin, the textile industry lives off advances in petrochemicals and Saint Laurent believes more and more in style and less and less in fashion. To make clothes that are timeless is neither heresy nor a contradiction of terms, he says.

Although France is still a sizeable supplier of high-fashion textiles, the conglomerate that Marcel Boussac built has become a victim of the same ruthless advances in technology and overcapacity in third-world mills that have crippled American, Japanese and European textile groups. After selling off its Dior perfumes to the Moët Hennessy champagne interests and trying to diversify into washing machines, newspaper publishing and race-horse breeding, the Boussac empire remained on the skids. With monthly losses of $2 million, an outstanding debt of over $100 million and $33 million owed in taxes and social security payments, and with stubborn, ninety-year-old Boussac a barely retired backseat driver to his nephew's management, the company was, in 1978, one enterprise that the government of President Valéry Giscard d'Estaing decided *not* to rescue with massive public funds, even if it would have meant salvaging eleven thousand jobs. Eventually, the government allowed the Boussac interests to be taken over by Willot Frères, the textile–pharmaceutical–real estate–department store conglomerate, which promised to keep up employment at least until January 1, 1980.

Polyester may be a tacky joke to the fashion-conscious, but man-made fibers now account for 70 percent of all textiles in the industrialized world, and much modern fashion wouldn't be possible without synthetics. Nylon, Orlon, Fortrel, Arnel, Qiana and all those acetates, rayons, acrylics, triacetates and aramids have allowed all the permanently pressed, uncrushable, drip-dry, shrink-proof clothes no one would want to live without. Any wardrobe, rich or poor, is made up more of by-products of unpronounceable chemical formulas than of the historic foursome of linen and cotton (both derived from plants), wool (from an animal's fleece) and silk (from a worm's cocoon).

And more are coming. DuPont has invented "spun-bound" fabrics that aren't woven or knitted but sheet-constructed like plywood. Kayser-Roth is experimenting with lingerie synthetics that will reflect the light of the outer garment and take on its hue, and other innovations are in the making in the labs of Eastman, Monsanto, ICI, Hoescht and the other multinationals, who have annual sales beyond the gross national productivity of many countries. DuPont is working on a crepe-type nylon with built-in resistance to clinging, and British and Japanese manufacturers have come out with superfine filaments that may enable knitters to make fabrics with a "natural handle" resembling silk but with the easy care of synthetics. Major American and Japanese mills try to match all the qualities of natural polymers like silk and cotton, and, if they cannot beat nature, to exploit it by finding new natural polymers. The word is that one could be in production in the 1980s. In the meantime, the emphasis is on "big brain"–designed fabrics. A computer comes up with hundreds of variations of a print and creates its own design from mathematical abstractions. "It's perfect," says Janice Lourie, a tapestry weaver and inventor for IBM, which holds most of the patents in this area.

Charles Worth was the first couturier to tell textile mills what materials and colors he wanted. When he became Empress Eugénie's couturier, Lyons was going through an early version of the Boussac shakedown, because the city's hand looms were threatened by new, steam-driven power machinery of English and German manufacture. Napoleon III was a protectionist and forced Eugénie, who preferred gowns of tulle and lace, to appear in magnificent crinoline confections of rich Lyons silks and brocades, which she called her *robes politiques*. Court and bourgeoisie followed, and during the 1860s, the crinoline grew in circumference, and the number of Lyons silk looms doubled. So did Worth's renown, influence and bank account. He got to hate the crinoline and wanted to replace it with the bustle (the inspiration for which came to him when he saw a washerwoman hoist her skirt on her thighs), but by his ascendancy and, more incidentally, by helping the Lyons silk industry, he became the first of the grand couturiers—individuals who, by proposing clothes in tune with the conscious and subconscious self-image of their times, become interpreters of feminine aspirations and, by the breath of their artistic command, the intimates rather than the tradesmen of the social elite. Manufacturers of textiles, fabrics and accessories seek their advice and bring them the newest information about their research and novelties.

Saint Laurent is inevitably in the middle of contemporary battles, solicited by DuPont de Nemours ("Qiana is sensuous, luxurious and addictive"), Dow Chemical, Badiche and countersolicited by the International Wool Secretariat, which will remind others, if not him, of the prize he won when he was seventeen. At collection time, the fabric suppliers buy flattering color spreads in French *Vogue* and trade magazines of YSL's most gorgeous creations and only discreetly mention themselves at the bottom of the ads.

Yves is very sensitive to fabrics. For him, a garment and its fabric must interact, the "hand" and movement of the cloth, the mood, the scale and spirit of patterns must be characteristic not only of the fabric but of the finished dress. He is saddened by the fast disappearance of natural fibers. "It's not even certain that the basic linen, cotton, wool and silk will be around much longer," he lamented in 1976 when, as a reaction, he deliberately chose opulent satins and silks. Duplicated, he said of the fantasy-look opulence, "it will look cheap, and that's precisely the point."

The fantasy look was also a reaction against the long-popular, pared-down styles of limp rayon dresses and against the sportswear look that seemed to go on forever. YSL felt that women again wanted glamour and detail—*he* certainly needed to work with satin, silver lamé, velvet, taffeta, chiffon, chenille, muslin and moiré. To bring off blouses with billowing sleeves, bouffant skirts and soft petticoats, wasp waistlines defined by cummerbunds, corselets and cinched belts, he needed braided and tasseled cords, floral scarves and satin ribbons; and he finished by setting the whole thing afire with violet, emerald, scarlet, tangerine, sapphire, turquoise, lime, azure and royal purple.

Over the following years, he continued working in velvet, wool, serge, satin and taffeta until these fabrics became identified as exaggerated-chic materials, and *Vogue* editor-in-chief Grace Mirabella wondered how long this could go on. "You knew you couldn't see anything like it anywhere else in the world," she wrote about the winter 1978–79 haute couture collection. "There was faille, gazar, ciréd taffeta, sequined fabrics, brocades, cloqués and—over and over—colored embroidery."

Like Worth's silk crinolines, Yves's late-1970s high-chic look did more than just help manufacturers of marginal lines of tasseled cords and brocades. In 1976, the women's garment industry was in a worldwide slump after two disastrous years, and everybody embraced Yves's costume-ball fashion. Even Sears took a flier on the look, going outside its regular channels to get the clothes that its usual suppliers had not managed to get into production fast enough.

For years, the industry has lived off technological innovations in petrochemicals. Saint Laurent cannot do the same thing, he says. All he can do is react—and react to reactions. His "weakness" for the 1920s and 1930s is a predilection for what he considers the century's artistic peak and for a spirit, an elegance and a shape. In 1974, his "weakness" dominated everything he did. He was more than happy to do the thirties costumes for his friend Alain Resnais's new picture, *Stavisky.* Visually, the picture, starring Jean-Paul Belmondo, Anny Duperey and Charles Boyer, was a gem, with every surface perfectly cut and polished, and Yves's swan-song dresses were an echo almost of Resnais's *Last Year at Marienbad* and contributed as much as Stephen Sondheim's score to the glittering evocation of 1930s elegance. The inspiration carried over into his ready-to-wear, where he made a big effort to bring back the suit. Worn by a model with curly, shoulder-length hair, the suit was in hairline flannel, with tailored lapels, and featured a carnation at the buttonhole and rows of pearls over a softly tied blouse.

With *The Great Gatsby, The Sting* and *Stavisky* on the

screen, 1974 was a year of transition from pants to skirts and away from the long-lived unisex silhouette. In Paris, it was *la mode rétro;* in London and New York, it was the nostalgia wave. Young Parisiennes flocked to flea markets to discover quality materials, embroidery and pure silk crepe de chine in period prints. The summer colors were shades of shell pink, peach and coral. By fall, the thirties craze had spilled over into cosmetics and hairstyles. Girls in fluttering clothes tried to look pale and pretty like Daisy in *The Great Gatsby,* with frizzed hair, plum-berry lips and smoky eyes. Helena Rubinstein proposed "Jazz Age" mascara, Elizabeth Arden suggested plum-berry crayon lines, Estée Lauder had new browns and blacks, Charles of the Ritz had "Pearly Pewter" and Revlon "Misty Gray."

Yves was appalled by the dimension of the ripoff, so much so that when it came to decorating the new avenue Marceau headquarters, he turned from a planned thirties decor to Napoleon III's Victoriana. Economically, the opening of the opulent town house couldn't have come at a worse time. Like most of the world, France was suffering from the economic fallout of the quadrupling of oil prices, and Saint Laurent was reduced to quoting Cocteau's *mot:* "Wisdom is to be crazy when circumstances allow it."

Not to indispose the gods who had been so favorable during the twelve years in rue Spontini, he brought with him to avenue Marceau a playing card, a ten of clubs that he had found in the basement the first day he and Pierre had set up shop at 30 rue Spontini. The kissing friends were there for the new opening, from Zizi Jeanmaire to Catherine Deneuve and Yul Brynner, and success seemed assured with Yves's naive chemise a dazzling overnight hit and, for evening wear, Edwardian gowns to go with the new Second Empire decor.

With the exception of Laura Ashley's prim Victorian look, everything was either blue denim or of *The Great Gatsby* repertoire. When Yves was interviewed by *GAP*, the Paris trade paper, he confessed he was confused. "I feel totally alienated from what's going on," he said. When he was asked if he wasn't touched by the thirties craze, he patiently explained that he had collected lamps and furniture by Jean

Dunand and Emile Jacques Ruhlmann for years, but couldn't see what interest a couturier had in copying once more what anyone could find at a flea market.

"After twenty years in the business, it's hard to rediscover your own naiveté," he added. "To do a haute couture collection is to let yourself go. If you love luxury, it's the time to forget about cost. It's also the right place to ask questions, to have the guts to try and translate an atmosphere. That's what I did in 1965 when I brought out my Mondrian dresses, and in 'seventy-one with my 'scandalous' forties look. It's the opposite in ready-to-wear because there you must come up with solutions, you must eliminate everything that isn't absolutely certain, even when you're proud of what you've invented."

He felt it was time to try and combine tradition and modernity, even if the two were always in conflict in his own mind, and in November, he took his couture collection to New York to see if there were enough wealthy consumers to save made-to-measure. "It would have been easier to bring my ready-to-wear," he told a Manhattan news conference, "but that's a different image—alive, dynamic, full of life, boys and girls. Americans know that kind of show; they created it. Couture is tradition, couture is perfection. It is something of the past but something that must be kept alive to maintain the traditions of workmanship and beauty."

It was the first time he had shown his couture collection in America, and over six hundred YSL followers turned out for the occasion in the grand ballroom of the Hotel Pierre. He had brought six mannequins with him from Paris, and his flowered chemises, black-velvet dinner suits and taffeta ball gowns drew repeated applause. When the final model of the collection, the traditional bride in white, curtsied to the crowd, Yves's devotees dissolved in praise. "Ravishing," cooed Lauren Bacall. "Sublime," echoed Bianca Jagger. "He is totally a chap of this generation—unique, brilliant," intoned Diana Vreeland.

John Fairchild wasn't thrilled. The publisher of WWD complained they were all the same clothes Yves had shown in Paris four months earlier. "To spend all that money to rent the Pierre ballroom and drag in all those painted society warhorses in the middle of an economic crisis is just ludicrous," *Newsweek* quoted him as saying.

Ethics and energy were on American minds as the country reeled under Richard Nixon's downfall and the Arab oil boycott. After a week in New York, Yves felt the full extent of the somber mood. New Yorkers, he felt, were more preoccupied with the economic crisis than Parisians, perhaps because they were less prepared for the situation. He was even sure the crisis would affect the spring couture collection he was to start upon his return. Even if he didn't think about it, he said, unconsciously the crisis would influence his work.

But it all brought into focus an idea that had been germinating in his mind for some time: maybe fashion should stop. The very last thing the industry wanted was to tell a woman to be herself, but maybe this was the time to follow Cocteau's crazy advice and somehow shift the whole emphasis from novelty to quality. A lot of things pointed in this direction. The inflationary spiral kept pushing fashion out of reach for most people. Feminism, especially strong in New York, was telling women to express their individuality. It was considered in to be casual and unconcerned about fashion, but, in fact, most women were, as always, fascinated with appearance. Only they wanted clothes on their own terms. Also, this was the "me" decade, with people turning from most outside authority to the creation of an independent authority within themselves. People were concerned with the personal. Physical health, therapy, personal growth, running, the home, ecology and "creative relationships" were the new priorities.

He tried out his idea on the media, saying the economic crisis made him think that this was the time for a basic wardrobe. What he meant by that, he explained, was "good clothes that are well made and timeless, basic things that don't change so that a woman can be more confident about her clothes."

"Women have not been educated to have style and confidence in themselves," he told *WWD*. "They are confused by new things, by new excitement, by new design. They must have individuality with basic clothes. . . . More and more I believe that chic is not in the dress. Elegance is in the spirit. I know women who have nothing to do with fashion—fashion is not important to them—but they have great chic." As an afterthought, he added that he liked people who lived their lives their own way, without restrictions, people who made an art of living. "I don't like people who are playing with their lives."

The basic wardrobe became the theme of other interviews that crystallized his thinking. A basic wardrobe, he said, should be like a man's suit, blazer and pants. It should give women the freedom to impose their own identity onto a classic wardrobe; it should give stability and a sense of self-confidence. Presaging the romantic peasant look that was still two years in the future, he said he would rather look to the beauty of yesterday than to the uncertainty of tomorrow. The future was behind us, not in a straight line, perhaps, but in the middle of a knot, like a pretzel. He felt very adaptable and knew he would never regret anything. He also knew it was impossible to discipline the forces that were changing the world.

12
THE
OPPOSITION

Y ves is the most influential designer I've ever seen—
the complete innovator," said John Fairchild in
1974, in the same breath with which he complained
about Saint Laurent's haute couture splurge for those
"painted society warhorses." If YSL is on the proverbially
lonesome summit, the field is crowded by designers clawing
their way up, as it is, on the opposite slope of the metaphor,
by those slipping to also-ran and has-been irrelevance. No
top-ten or beautiful-twenty ranking is fair or even interesting. The fashion business is not lonely, silent or secret, but
when Saint Laurent is contrasted, or simply juxtaposed, to
his rivals, the whole tantalizing subject of fashion gains in
clarity and relief.

The number of Parisian houses remains remarkably constant, at around twenty-five. For the designer, ready-to-
wear may demand a sense of concept and rigor, while haute
couture, as YSL says, can be a tonic plunge into inspiration,

when it is not self-indulgence. But for ninety-nine point nine percent of consumers and even industryites, fashion is ready-to-wear, and not even the Chambre Syndicale tries to maintain a distinction between Dior and Ted Lapidus, Balmain and Sonia Rykiel.

The Young Turks nipping at Yves's heels have never known what made-to-measure is and, as a group, have nothing but contempt for the caste and class system that haute couture implies. "Clothes reflect the social and economic convictions of the wearer," says Jean-Charles de Castelbajac. "The way a person dresses tells you everything he or she wants you to know, either in a conscious or unconscious way—how rich he is, how free or not free, his social aspirations or lack of them. A woman who wears a two-thousand-dollar dress has to assume the responsibility of wearing a two-thousand-dollar dress and must be careful where and how she wears it."

Born in Casablanca in 1950, Castelbajac uses such fantasy labels as Co & Co, saying his name is too private to put on clothes. Like many bright young Frenchmen, he has a hang-up about his own bourgeois background. Instead of an apartment, he lives permanently in a hotel and gets around Paris on a motorcycle. He is hot and hotly contested; no one is indifferent to his clothes, which are the most recognizable of the young designers' creations. His bright rainbow stripes continue in collection after collection, and his blankets and tweedy rib-knit "dishrag" clothes are legend. In 1978, he took Technicolor maps from *National Geographic* magazines and printed them on waterproof ski parkas. When asked about the future, he says that by the year 2000, wool will be a luxury as expensive as mink is today, but that designers will make marvelous things in prescented acrylic fibers that will smell nice. When he made his transition from tough-tailored worker's clothes and athletic sweat shirts to soft, all-girl spectator clothes in 1977, he opened his collection with an electronic music interlude that kept repeating the words "It's so strange" in English, interspersed with sounds that resembled a computer gone berserk.

Together with Thierry Mugler and Claude Montana, Castelbajac thinks the status cult of dressing is on its way out, that the way clothes are designed and shown, the way they are sold and worn, must change. Clothes should be collected and mixed, he believes, and they should even wear out from being worn.

Thierry Mugler, whose boutique is on place des Victoires, is a former dancer with a very individual feeling for shape and color. His friend and collaborator is Russian-born Zulaika, a girl who, with Grace Jones and Edwidge, is the queen of Paris nightlife. Mugler designed the sci-fi, Flash Gordon uniforms for the waiters at the Palace disco, and he uses his sense of theater and ballet to work out the themes of his collections.

Claude Montana is a tall, taciturn blond with a walrus mustache and piercing blue eyes who has designed for half a dozen rtw manufacturers. His "thing" is soft, crayon-colored leather, and he has perfected his leather styles over half a dozen seasons. His shows have turned into brawls—purposely, cynics say—when he has shown storm-trooper, leather-and-chain fashions. His punk and neo-Nazi themes and bold, tough look have commanded attention. In 1978, he was hailed as the new Saint Laurent.

Jean-Claude de Luca wants his clothes to be worn alone—or mixed with other designers' clothes. A movie-star-handsome ex-assistant to Givenchy, de Luca is of mixed French and Italian background and designed for Dorothée Bis and a half-dozen other rtw houses before making it big in 1977 with what *Vogue* called his "non-fantasy super style." He believes in a strong, aggressive woman without frills and fuss, and has offered giant blousons with rugby-player shoulders, and always has a pair of jeans in mind to go with his shirts or wide, rough linen or wool coats. He admires Saint Laurent but thinks Yves is trapped in a couture versus ready-to-wear schizophrenia.

There is a camaraderie among these young designers that is unlike the bitchiness that characterized their elders. When he is not roaming India or Africa, Mugler talks to Montana every day, although they never discuss collections. Castelbajac has asked Montana to model a couple of things in his show, and his friend and fellow designer Issey Miyake has given up morning jogging in the Salle Wagram so Jean-Claude could have a place to rehearse a show.

Anne-Marie Beretta is, with Sonia Rykiel, the most exciting of the women designers and the designer most young Parisiennes find interesting—and within their budgets. The granddaughter of a shepherd, Beretta is, together with her husband, in close contact with the women who buy her clothes, helping them relate to her things. She feels the anonymity of the department store makes shopping difficult, and in the late afternoon, she is always available in her boutique in rue Saint-Sulpice. She thinks Saint Laurent is now nothing more than a commercial operation, that he no longer invents anything new, but admits to a certain bitterness because of the hard times young designers have making their breakthrough. She thinks fashion is going through a purge and is heading toward a period of neatness, that women are longing for cleanliness and tidiness. Together with Anne Beranger, Castelbajac, de Luca, Montana and Mugler, Beretta made up "the six from Paris" who were brought to Japan in 1978 for a special promotion of rtw that proved to be highly successful.

Sonia Rykiel is the current high priestess of ready-to-wear. Four years older than Saint Laurent, she made her first impact in 1968, with her "poor boy" knitwear—tight, body-hugging little sweaters that were a completely original departure from the classic, formless Chanel knits. She never went to a design school and hasn't undergone the rigors of traditional training—to her advantage, she says. Like Castelbajac, Mugler, Montana and de Luca, she believes the real modern trend is to mix clothes. Like Yves, she thinks the fashion press is going to be the death of fashion, "if it doesn't stop rushing to kill off clothes ideas before their time."

Geraldine Stutz, the president of Henri Bendel and one of fashion's savviest (and most quoted) seers, thinks the fiery redhead is the Chanel of our time. Rykiel, who drives a black Honda in Paris and is the divorced mother of two grown children, can talk fashion for hours. The toughest thing about the big time is the perpetual pressure to produce original, fresh designs, she says, and what keeps her going isn't so much inspiration as shock of living. Her work begins with colors instead of fabrics, and she will spend up to two months looking for colors that please her.

"Space and time are the most important things now," she says. "Women must take up more space, both physically and spiritually. When I try to make clothes with four arms, it is to take more space." She thinks fashion has nothing to do with a woman's allure; that a woman who has both masculine and feminine traits is very much a woman; that force, aggressiveness and mystery add up to modern femininity. "What is true half-and-half impresses me in both sexes," she says. "This is a very important concept of our epoch. The men I like most have a feminine side, yet they are strong, they have manly characteristics."

Of the theoreticians speculating why all post–World War II fashion has been made by men, Rykiel has the most down-to-earth explanation: "Men won't be wearing the clothes, therefore practical considerations are secondary and they can create magnificent designs. Women designers define things with a more practical eye because of the limitations of their body. A collar that looks attractive on the drawing board might be difficult to pull over the head. And pants that appear elegant can be constricting."

Jacques Lenoir, the elegant owner of Chloe (and Karl Lagerfeld's boss), has the most Freudian explanation for the modern predominance of male couturiers. Most designers, he says, from Dior on, are repressed transvestites, and even those who are married have kinky marriages. "Designing is a sublimation of the urge to put on women's clothes," says Lenoir. "They neither love nor hate women. They are rarely in love, especially the most successful among them, like Freud who stopped making love at forty-one when he became totally caught up in his work."

Lagerfeld, who spent four years as an apprentice with Pierre Balmain, has designed for Chloe since 1964 and freelanced for Rome's Fendi sisters since 1972. He thinks homosexuals are no longer a fashion influence. "They used to be," he says. "Now they all have the same mustaches, the same clothes. Very conventional, very boring."

Heir to the Glucksklee fortune (Germany's equivalent of the Carnation conglomerate), Lagerfeld thinks of himself as an eighteenth-century personage who has stepped into the twentieth and decided to stay. He says the modern world makes him feel like people must have felt getting up on the fourteenth of July 1789. "A new revolution must be coming any day. One has a feeling that a new fashion is coming, different, strange, both for women and men." In the meantime, most things are a bore; especially, today's rich are far less stimulating than those who lived in the century of his choice. "They're all tanned, have blond hair, are terribly body conscious and not very inspiring. They're not creative with their money—just boring. They're the same all over the world. They own the same boats, the same planes and even their houses look the same—white canopies. Very often they divorce to marry a similar person."

He thinks rich women are lazy and unimaginative, that the surfeit of choice is a poor excuse and that a woman can be fashionable with very little money. "Every woman must be her own stylist. Not only for her clothes but in makeup, hairstyles, accessories. The same dress with different accessories can give you another silhouette."

Lagerfeld's influence is recent but widespread. Dominated by a ravishing mother during a difficult childhood, he started designing clothes in 1969, made unconstructed silk dresses in 1972 and unfinished hemlines a year later. He has turned furs inside out and the fur industry upside down, and the Chloe boutique on avenue Franklin Roosevelt is visited by designers and manufacturers from around the world, who buy his dresses and jackets to copy. Lagerfeld's collections often brim with ideas and lay down trends for several seasons. But that, too, is a bore. "I have no opinion whatsoever about my influence," he told W in 1978. "Who cares?" Which doesn't mean he doesn't like to point out that he did short, close-fitting spencer jackets three months before YSL, and that Chantal Thomass copied his use of lace-embroidered cotton tulle. His "crowd" includes Paloma Picaso, Anna Piaggi, Suzy Dyson and Anouk Aimée, and he would like to become a movie producer and make sophisticated but mean, bitchy Marx Brothers–type comedies.

Kenzo Takada is, like Karl Lagerfeld, a designer who has outgrown the label he designs for. The name of his place des Victoires boutique is Jungle Jap, but Kenzo moved out of Asia long ago and through Disney World, Fellini's Rome and tin-soldier militarism. The originator of Mao-now peasant chic, the Japanese-born designer, who is only three years younger than YSL, is a poet with a rare sense of humor. He pokes fun at establishments—churches, armies, the courts—and is the darling of the very young, although Kenzo can be safe for any age. His clientele includes at least one woman in her sixties. Once, when Kenzo saw her in the boutique, he danced about, saying, "You wear this, and this, and this," and his choices were perfect for her.

Kenzo's designs are the most copied and/or modified by others, and his fireworks collection shows have even caused Saint Laurent and Bergé to jazz up the YSL presentations. In Milan, some of the biggest designers have made fortunes adapting Kenzo's witty spoofs in beautiful, expensive fabrics, thereby trading them up to an age and taste level that broadens their audience far beyond the Jungle Jap cult.

His clothes have suggested rollicking pirates, swashbuckling naval officers, the Indians of the Raj, naughty seminarians and Edwardian toy soldiers in a riot of colors. Surrounded by a staff whose median age must be under twenty-five, the little man with the toothy grin makes a lot of very good fashion. Comes showtime, and he provides the joie de vivre and the childlike fun in dressing up. For a romantic taffeta finale one year, he had a red carpet rolled out for his models to mince down and throw gold dust ahead of the bride, who wore black velvet, and the bridegroom, in burgundy. All wore tacky tiaras and crazy crystal jewelry, even two models who roller-skated down the runway wearing big, balloon ivory dresses. In 1977, Bloomingdale's was elated about gaining exclusive rights to Kenzo in New York.

Kenzo thinks Californians and Brazilians are the sexiest, and politicians everywhere the ugliest, people. Jungle Jap's owner, Gilles Raysse, is considered an eccentric in the industry. The brother of a painter of whom he is excessively jealous, Raysse sits in on interviews with Kenzo and practically shuts up his star designer for fear he will say something wrong.

Joining the big league from the opposite direction is Jean-Louis Scherrer, an exact contemporary of YSL and also a Dior graduate. Bankrolled by Orlane and, more recently, by Harriet Hubbard Ayer, Scherrer has set up shop at 51 avenue Montaigne, almost directly across the avenue from his former employer. When Anne Giscard d'Estaing chose him as her favorite couturier, his fortunes took off, and he is doing everything he can "to make the dream go on," as he says, by trying to combine elegance with trendiness. The image that this former ballet student puts across is one of sophistication, an image that goes with the French First Lady, who is one of the best-groomed women in the world. Lately, Saks, Nieman-Marcus and Martha of Palm Beach have jumped on the Scherrer bandwagon.

What the rising stars have in common is an awareness of the broader implications of fashion, of the social functions of objects. Realizing that clothes are really the expression of a culture's attitude toward itself, the new designers are very critical and feel they must perform a useful social function. Among them is a perception that complex social, economic and environmental problems are interrelated, and that young designers, architects and urban planners should take a more integrated approach to the quality of life. The question to ask, they feel, is not only whether an object is in good or bad taste but what its sociocultural meaning is. This attitude is a good part of what makes their clothes fresh and vital and sometimes unpretentious, and what makes them look and feel right.

To the right of Saint Laurent—in more ways than one— Marc Bohan is the man who dresses some of the most famous women in the world, but whose fortune is linked to the resolution of Dior's future. The House of Dior is still the General Motors of the industry and has developed into an international company, with more than a thousand employes and sales running ahead of YSL's. It is Bohan who has expanded Dior's ready-to-wear to include a children's and men's line, and today the Dior signature is on stockings, ties, lingerie, lighters, sheets, skiwear and 125 other products. In recent years, Jacques Rouet, now in his sixties, has tightened control over the licensees and demanded that each Dior article conform to the current look, as conceptualized and defined by Bohan each season.

A typical Bohan-designed dress for Barbra Streisand, Sophia Loren, the queen of Sweden, or Grace of Monaco sells for between $3,000 and $6,000, but the label says Dior, not Bohan. That is what the reclusive and sometimes snappish widower must live with. Told that many people don't know he is the designer behind the famous logo, his reactions have ranged from a snipped "Too bad" to a subdued "Staying behind the name Dior is perhaps my search for security."

With the exception of his former assistant Philippe Guilbourgé, Bohan has no close friends in the industry. His wife died in a car accident in 1962, and his grown daughter lives in England. Home is a small, art-filled apartment one block from avenue Montaigne, and a comfortable converted farmhouse near Fontainebleau. Without being exactly chums, Saint Laurent and Bohan have kind of made up. The forgive-and-forget reconciliation came in 1965, when they were both witnesses at the marriage of designer Maurice Renomma and Anne-Marie Joyon. Bohan is defensive when talking about Saint Laurent, claiming that his old rival invents clothes that are spectacular and theatrical while his own are more private. YSL's runaway success with the 1976 fantasy look had Bohan saying, "Overdressing is vulgar," but a year later, his own motif was late-Victorian opulence.

Emanuel Ungaro's idea of perfect bliss is a quiet Sunday with his longtime companion Sonya Knapp, reading Proust and listening to Beethoven string quartets. Born in Aix-en-Provence, the son of a tailor, Ungaro has been on his own since 1965, but he is the proprietor of only two of the fifty Ungaro boutiques in the world. He learned tailoring from his father, trained with Balenciaga and Courrèges, and owes a lot of his success to Sonya, the former wife of Peter Knapp, ex-Courrèges photographer and *Elle* editor.

Ungaro has retained his enthusiasm for haute couture. "The kind I do is stripped down—without toiles and unnecessary fittings, but also without concessions," says the pint-sized designer. "This streamlined couture goes three times faster than the couture we used to do at Balenciaga's."

Surrounded by a tightly knit and interchangeable crew at his avenue Montaigne headquarters, Ungaro spends two months a year in a Turin ready-to-wear plant where two hundred employes tool up his designs.

Pierre Cardin is the man for all seasons who has difficulty remaining meaningful to young women. Known from the beginning as a designer of the avant-garde, Cardin has paid the penalty of being a pioneer. His timing has been terrible, and although he has been first with many looks and his intuition has been flint sharp, he has come out with them the wrong year—or the wrong decade. In 1966, he was showing the tweed pinafores with polo-necked sweaters that girls adopted in the seventies; his incredibly ingeniously cut space-age fashions keep reverberating; and he startled his audiences with what later proved to be a smash hit—a maxi coat over a mini dress.

"I believe in simplicity," he says. "Over the years, I've honed my style. I continue to filter and to subtract." Born in 1922, in Venice, of French parents, Cardin has grown increasingly haughty and moody, and on more than one occasion, he has managed to antagonize the fashion press. His turnover in the mid-1960s was second only to Dior's. He set up separate studios for men's and women's clothes, signed up hundreds of licensees and saw his menswear bring in 60 percent of his profits. Unlike others dabbling in menswear, he dedicated himself to it with passion and became a world leader in the field. He has exceptional contracts with his menswear manufacturers: he has the right to insist that they do a certain style even if it is not among the one hundred commercially viable models they have themselves selected.

He has gone into children's wear, and invented cutout clothes that mothers stitch together themselves.

Cardin is the only one to franchise his label in the Soviet Union, and in early 1979, the Chinese government named him fashion consultant to its textile-trade agency. He has made clothes for movies and ballets, designed packaging for industry, furniture and interior "environments." He once resigned from the Chambre Syndicale because he was too impatient to wait for biannual showings to get public reaction and, to calm his nerves, even straightens the shelves in his avenue de Marigny boutique himself.

Cardin's work mania and ever-thrusting curiosity have made him extend himself more than any other designer. As a lasting value, his diversity may supersede his designs in women's clothing, although here his big innovations are genuine creations insofar as they owe nothing to the past.

André Courrèges is another original who is having a hard time remaining relevant. Fifty percent owned by L'Oréal, the House of Courrèges is today considered "classical bourgeois," although the balding designer continues to soften and lighten his already-streamlined fashion. He deliberately turned his back on the *rétro* and folklore looks. "When the girls are through exploring the fifties and sixties and are ready to espouse their time, I'll be waiting for them," he says, guessing that the encounter will take place in 1980. In the meantime, he has built a plant in his native Pau, in the foothills of the Pyrenees, expanded his sure-winner knitwear and his perfumes and relentlessly cracked down on waste. "Even in haute couture, you don't use two and a half meters of fabric when only two point three meters are necessary, and when a coat takes forty hours, nobody can spend more than fifty hours on it."

A year younger than Cardin, Courrèges spent eleven years with Balenciaga before opening his own house in 1962 and, three years later, made history with his space-age projections, which featured skirts above the knees, pure colors and characteristic accessories. Mercilessly, his designs were knocked off the world over and became the uniform of the late sixties.

Alix Czereskow wanted to be a sculptor, became an illustrator instead and, when she first showed her sketches to Michel de Brunhoff, was told to forget couture and continue drawing and sculpting. She opened her first boutique in Faubourg Saint-Honoré in 1934 under her first name, Alix. Since 1941, she has been at 1 rue de la Paix as Madame Grès, unswayed by passing events.

Grès is the doyenne of the Parisians, a frail old woman whose day clothes seem dated now but whose gracious evening dresses a faithful clientele still swear by. Respected by everybody and still fabulous in her draping, Madame cuts the fabric herself, and her technique is so much a part of her style that no one has really tried to copy her. Her draped dresses often use twenty yards of clinging silk jersey and may take a month to drape, mold and sew into their myriad folds that follow the human form. "It's a business that kills you," she said in 1978, "but I'm surrounded by great people who never say no to technical difficulties."

Pierre Balmain is the elder statesman, the most eloquent of gentlemen, an exquisite draftsman who prefers crayons to felt tips when sketching evening dresses and calls fabrics "the vehicles of our dreams." A tall, heavy man with powerful shoulders but an impish nature, Balmain is a man for whom fashion is a happy adventure.

Born in 1914 in southeastern France, Balmain studied to be an architect. For fun, he made fashion sketches, which, when submitted to Edward Molineux, so impressed the Anglo-Irish designer that Balmain was offered a job and stayed nine years. Working alongside Dior, he supplemented his training at Lelong's. "Christian was a boy who had one thing—taste," he remembers. "Dior knew how to express taste although he didn't know how to put in a needle, and models were always scared of his pinpricks."

Mobilized in 1939 and sent to his native Savoy on the Italian border, Balmain met and made friends with Gertrude Stein, a vast black-clad woman in sandals. He won her affection, making for her and for Alice B. Toklas "nice warm suits," and when he opened his boutique after the war, she wrote a charming piece about him in *Vogue*.

Responding to feminine desires to forget the nightmare years, Balmain offered the security of a subtle elegance that renewed tradition, and he has remained the favorite of women who want to project a self-image discreet enough to defy recognition. Balmain was the last word in elegance in the 1950s and 1960s, and today thinks of himself as one of the last defenders of haute couture. He says Saint Laurent "desecrates" haute couture with his buggy-before-the-horse reversal of rtw and couture emphasis, calls Ricci a small-town seamstress, and on a television talkshow where Courrèges showed up in a canary jumpsuit, told his *confrère* (and neighbor in rue François Premier) that he nearly mistook him for the corner Shell station attendant. He thinks young women in Milan dress with more chic than Parisians, and thinks the Paris hegemony is fading because Parisian couturiers resemble each other less and less and because bestsellerdom is everything now. He has found his style and his clientele, but he is not afraid of going into new things. Recently, he launched a Balmain furniture line.

Hubert James Marcel Taffin de Givenchy is the master of the last house founded on aristocratic chic rather than youth. As obsessed with the metier as Cardin, Givenchy starts his new collection the day the previous one is shown. He loves to work in high-voltage excitement and with improvisation, and says if he isn't keyed up, how can he expect his 170 employes to show enthusiasm. His greatest happiness is to arrive at his avenue George V studio early in the morning and to sit among his beautiful fabrics and hear the personnel arrive, the phones begin to ring. "For me, it's like a heart beating. My day always ends too soon."

The escort of elegant women—Bunny Mellon, Capucine, Audrey Hepburn—Givenchy was born in northern France in 1927 and opened his own couture house when he was twenty-five. He calls his ready-to-wear *haut prêt à porter*, since he says he makes no differentiation between his couture and his ready-to-wear in terms of elegance or style. His lasting friendship with Balenciaga, who died in 1968, greatly influenced him, and his orbit still floats around the last *éminence grise* of haute couture. Like Saint Laurent, Givenchy feels he must carry on because, if couture ever stops, it will never exist again. When asked about creating luxury in an economically and politically troubled world, he says that every era has its crises. "If I start thinking about wars, about recessions, my enthusiasm is gone. And once you lose your enthusiasm for your work, everything goes."

Philippe Guilbourgé, Jules-François Crahay, Serge Lepage and Gérard Pipart are in charge of houses whose founding mothers are no more but whose magic they must try to live up to. Since the House of Chanel eased itself into ready-to-wear, Guilbourgé has tried to bring Mademoiselle's tried and true suits up to date, but the atmosphere in rue Cambon remains sedate and experimentation is not encouraged. Crahay, who was the ghost behind the aging Nina Ricci, has had more luck keeping the name Lanvin alive in couture and, under the tag Lanvin II, in ready-to-wear. Lepage gets joint billing at the House of Schiaparelli, which the Chambre Syndicale now lists as Schiaparelli–Serge Lepage, but the clientele remains small. Nina Ricci turned to ready-to-wear and boutiques early, and Pipart, who was one of the first stars of Parisian *prêt à porter* for Chloe, has designed the Ricci label for the dozen years of its existence. With Sophie de Wurtemberg as his muse and Robert Ricci, the son of the late founder, as the administrator, Pipart is a creator of realistic fashion.

Guy Laroche, Ted Lapidus and Paco Rabanne are the also-rans of Saint Laurent's generation, designers who hang in there but rarely blaze new trails. Partially owned by Baron Bic of the ballpoint fortune, Laroche has his ready-to-wear designed by Guy Douvier, who used to work for Dior–New York and, as a pro, is expected to pull the label up to significance. Born in 1924, Laroche started with a bang when he opened his boutique in 1956, and if he has never equaled his initial triumph, he has husbanded his name, which, besides the traditional lines of clothes and perfumes, appears on shoes, baggage and eye wear. In Paris, a lot of women who find YSL ready-to-wear too expensive go to Laroche.

Ted Lapidus is as much for men as for women, and his clientele of lawyers, doctors, journalists and celebrities like Adamo and Charles Aznavour is faithful to the Lapidus cut—for men, suits fitted close to the body, for women, a romantic *flou* "with a little something extra" that makes his clothes recognizable. Lapidus himself is a top technician who likes to say he could earn a living as a seamstress anywhere.

Paco Rabanne is better known for his perfumes than his clothes but, like Cardin and Courrèges, he has made original experiments with materials, from aluminum to plastics linked together by small chains, and his hideaway Saint Germain-des-Prés headquarters in the rue du Cherche-Midi (a casual stroll from Rykiel's rue de Grenelle haunts) is a hangout for smart people in the know. This former engineer who is never short of ideas is something of a Left Bank character and is to be found at the Café de Flore every day at lunchtime.

Commercial fashion doesn't *originate* in many places, but the importance of Milan is very real. The Milano Alta Moda Pronta, Milano Vende Moda and Modit are biannual affairs where fifty designers and manufacturers show ready-to-wear collections to a thousand buyers—60 percent of them German and American—who spend around $2.4 billion a year on Italian fashion and increase their orders by 30 percent every year. The week-long events are held in March and September, before the Paris collections, giving buyers and journalists a leisure week to recuperate and cross the Alps.

Nationalism is not a Milanese hang-up, and Parisians like Lagerfeld, Muriel Grateau and Jean-Baptiste Caumont have designed for Fendi, Basile and other Italian manufacturers, and the vitality of the Lombard scene is contagious despite the added pressures of life in Italy today, with the threat of terrorism making entering a fashion show the equivalent of getting through airport security, frequent and unpredictable strikes and erratic deliveries.

"Of course we buy more in Paris," says Bergdorf Goodman's Ira Niemark. "But it's different in Milan. For one thing, the clothes are more understandable to the average American woman. For another, they're more colorful. Dollar for dollar, Italian ready-to-wear is also of a higher quality, even if the French can claim a stronger creative lead."

Italy is still producing the most advanced modern designs—from cars to couches, typewriters to tables—but the breakthrough in clothes was delayed by regional rivalries—not only Milan versus Rome but Milan versus Florence—which, until 1975, staged the most important fashion fair. The reasons for the split between Milan and Florence are many, but rooted in money. Top designers were increasingly dissatisfied with the group shows at Florence's Palazzo Pitti, and they resented being mixed with the good, bad and indifferent and having to pay stiff fees on top of it. Florence is still an active artisans' center to which some foreign buyers go for leather, gift items and lingerie.

The leading Milanese are Armani, Versace, Krizia, Missoni, Basile, Schoen and Fendi for furs, and what they have in common is an extraordinary mix of fabrics and a dedication to hard work. Fashion in Italy is a very responsible business.

Giorgio Armani, who is the master of layering, is called "a designer's designer." In menswear, he is out front, year after year, and his name, mark and ideas are the symbol of the latest and best in Italian fashion. Operating out of a Renaissance palace with frescoed walls, Armani is the best known of the new Italians—for sheer volume alone. His hallmark is a soft, unlined jacket for either sex, and three-quarters of his turnover is in menswear. In *American Gigolo,* the male lead wears no fewer than thirty Armani suits.

Gianni Versace is a bearded classicist who, like Armani, designs for a host of other houses besides his own label, and Krizia is Milan's answer to Kenzo, although the label's creator, Mariuccia Mandelli, is more Rykiel than Kenzo. Today dubbed the godmother of Milanese fashion, Mandelli is a former schoolteacher who opened for business with $400 and a name from Plato's unfinished dialogues. "Krizia was a rich man who ruined himself by spending too much on women," she explains. "When I started I was hoping I'd run into someone like him." It was she who gave Basile's Aldo Ferrante his start. Ferrante, whose house is one of the most dynamic in Milan, has had Muriel Grateau and scores of others design for him.

Missoni is a family affair divided between Rosita and Tai Missoni, and, by popular demand, Missoni has gone into menswear with the same knitted sweaters, tops and jackets that made their women's wear the most inventive in knits.

Fendi is a five-sister act comprising the world's most exclusive furriers and leather artisans. Since mother Adela Fendi died in 1978, the daughters Carla, Franca, Paola, Anna and Alda—with eleven members of the *next* generation waiting to carry on—have made furs into some of the most innovative of the new Italian offerings. The Fendis are unquestionably Roman, but their cautious iconoclasm is in line with the down-to-earth business sense of the Milanese. A combination of meticulous craftsmanship and Lagerfeld's glamorous designs have made their furs into radical high chic and expanded their clientele to include Barbra Streisand, Diana Ross, Jacqueline Bisset and Carly Simon, with price tags ranging up to $85,000. Says Bergdorf Goodman fashion director Dawn Mello, "You don't just own a Fendi. You collect them."

Valentino Garavani is the most famous and international of the Italians, a handsome overachiever and perpetual jetsetter who wears his shirt unbuttoned to the navel and loafers without socks. Four years older than YSL, Valentino was a school dropout at seventeen and left his little town near Milan for Paris. Within six months, he had a job with Jean Dessès. He stayed for six years, left with Dessès's chief designer, Guy Laroche, and after two years, ditched Laroche and Paris and opened his own couture house on Rome's via Gregoriana. In recent years, however, he has been back in Paris, showing his collections in the Chambre Syndicale fashion weeks. His Beautiful People clientele has included Jacqueline Onassis, Gloria Guinness, Elizabeth Taylor and Jacqueline de Ribes, but he has also designed uniforms for TWA flight attendants.

Oscar de la Renta is the closest thing New York has to Valentino, but his influence—as that of the rest of the American designing community—is hard to assess, since New Yorkers rarely export. Like much of American industry, Manhattan's Seventh Avenue is parochial, with little inclination or incentive to measure itself on the world market. The distinctively American style of free and frisky clothes with an emphasis on casual comfort has won worldwide respect—and imitation—but the emergence of American designers is very recent. Less than a decade ago, only a handful were known. Most American clothes bore the labels of large manufacturing firms—Jonathan Logan, Sue Brett, Junior Sophisticates, Levi-Strauss—employing thousands of stylists. The change is due, in part, to the recognized talent and success of Calvin Klein, Halston Frowlick, Ralph Lauren, Mary McFadden, Stephen Burrows and, in de la Renta's generation, Geoffrey Beene and Bill Blass. On the global marketplace, however, it is not so much their ideas translated into fabric as American merchandising techniques that impress. "Now, take Halston, he could sell the emperor's new clothes," says Zandra Rhodes. "He has a gift for putting things over, and that's not a criticism. You can design the best clothes in the world, but if you can't sell them, what's the point?"

Seen from Paris, Calvin Klein is *l'enfant prodige* grown up and become sophisticated, going from nothing to a $100-million-a-year business in ten years. Klein has been in and out of therapy for fifteen years, but his success is all hard drive and, he says, an almost religious certainty about what women want and what will sell. Paris admires his "colorless" clean clothes and his concept of casual sportswear that is soft yet imbued with a rare style. With Bill Blass, Klein is the only New Yorker to really sell abroad (the Isetan chain of Tokyo carries a Japanese-made Calvin Klein line). Klein is no great admirer of YSL. When *Newsweek* did a cover story on him in 1978, he said the Saint Laurent *paisana* princess collection of two years earlier was an ego trip that gave him nightmares.

As a native New Yorker, Klein is, with Ralph Lauren (né

Lifshitz), something of an exception. Most New York designers are either from the Midwest or foreign-born. Halston is from Des Moines, Bill Blass from Fort Wayne (Indiana also gave the world the late Norman Norell). De la Renta is from the Dominican Republic, Diane von Furstenberg (née Halfin) from Belgium, Cathy Hardwick from Korea, Adolfo Sardina from Cuba and L.A.'s Rudi Gernreich from Berlin. Giorgio di Sant'Angelo, who became plain Giorgio Sant'Angelo in 1977, was born in Italy and raised in Argentina.

In the view of French *Vogue,* Adolfo knows the secret of flattery and very feminine styles; Geoffrey Beene, who once studied medicine at Tulane University in New Orleans, is the designer who constantly evolves and, in many ways, is perhaps the most prestigious of the New Yorkers. Perry Ellis is considered an imaginative newcomer who may be important in the 1980s, and Stephen Burrows an imaginative designer with a great eye for mixing colors. Halston carries authority and is a provocative merchandiser whose soft, tactile sportswear is the basis of his immense success. He, too, is less than kind in public when it comes to YSL. "Name me one original thing St. Laurent [sic] actually invented?" he asked *People* when the magazine did a cover story on him in 1977.

Mary McFadden is a perfectionist and the most exotic of the New Yorkers. Long Island–bred and educated at Columbia University and the Sorbonne, she started making clothes in South Africa and likes Indonesian batiks, Japanese pongee and Indian tussah, and seeks to "revitalize the past in terms of modern technology, to produce through our screening techniques the aura of ancient robes." Her own best model, she boasts that she cuts all her clothes on herself.

Reversing the usual trend, Ralph Lauren began with menswear, then entered the women's field. He is seen as the designer of the most indigenous-looking American styles, a masterful tailor who brought out such classics as the Gatsby look and the Annie Hall look and may be the most pervasive influence of the New York school.

Sant'Angelo, who came to the United States to do animated cartoons for Walt Disney in Hollywood and entered fashion via jewelry design, has a wild, baroque talent. He made his first impact with elaborately draped gypsy clothes. One of his first models was Marina Schiano, now a vice-president of Yves Saint Laurent in New York.

Bill Kaiserman, whose name first appeared on men's hats and whose label on all his clothes says Rafael, knows what comfort and ease of movement mean, says Paris *Vogue*. His wife Milly was an actress who appeared as the body-paint girl on *Laugh-In*. The Kaisermans consider themselves health freaks, and as an amateur weight lifter, Bill says that if he can't be the biggest women's designer, he can be the strongest.

The dynamics of American clothes affect the way people dress everywhere. No single designer speaks for the American look (New York fashion editors use words that are strictly Californian—*comfort, ease, relaxed, informal*). As *Time* put it in 1976, "None of the Americans divine as cunningly and consistently what women crave as France's Yves Saint Laurent; none show the innovative brilliance of such younger Parisian stars as Japanese-born Kenzo Takada. Fashion historians will probably look back not on any individual but on American designer-entrepreneurs in general as the School of the 1970s—and a very savvy school at that." The genius of American clothes lies in how the parts can be put together; how they are mobile, versatile, harmonious in proportions, fabrics and color; how they are clothes for "live" people. Koko Hashim of Neiman-Marcus says American designers are concerned first with life-styles, and that this preoccupation is no less creative. "Even Europe is fascinated with the American way of dressing," she says, calling New York the center of all the fashion. "California is casual. It is the easy pieces that work, and Harriet Selwyn of Fragments represents that best. It's almost throwaway casualness which began two years ago with the trend of bigger and softer clothes. Californians are going to hate me for saying this, but they still have homework to do."

13

THE
LAST
CRISIS
OF ADOLESCENCE

A month and a half after YSL's thirtieth birthday, he and Pierre opened the first Rive Gauche boutique at 21 rue de Tournon, one block up rue de Seine from boulevard Saint-Germain. Pop art was the great way of being new, and a huge trompe l'oeil painting of Yves dominated the blood-red walls and steel-and-glass decor. "Before conquering Europe, Yves Saint Laurent strides across the Seine," said the caption of one wire-service photo showing the designer and a miniskirted model in front of the store on opening day, September 26, 1966. "Henceforth, elegant ladies wearing less than size 15/16 can wear his label at prices ranging from 250 to 650 francs [$50 to $130 in weighty 1966 dollars]." In interviews, Yves said he was interested in dressing the woman in the street, the woman who could not—and would not, if she could—pay a thousand dollars for a coat and who was unlikely ever to set foot on his particularly hallowed ground at 30 rue Spontini. "I hate couturiers who confuse their world with art," he said. "Couturiers, haute couture, *la mode*—they're all terms that are outdated. It's horrible to say, but all the designers I admire have disappeared—Dior, Balenciaga, Chanel. If I were one of the couturiers left today, I'd take a walk in the street and look at the way girls dress and probably come away telling myself, 'But this is awful; I have no influence whatsoever.' It would be like a slap in the face."

The stride across the Seine, which was to prove momentous, was both cause and effect of another inner crisis for Yves. He and Pierre had realized that "the girl in the street" wasn't waiting for them, that she was becoming her own force in fashion and threatening to upset the whole apple cart.

As Bergé was to explain later, the speed with which society was becoming kinetic, fickle and impermanent was only dimly understood in 1966 in the fashion industry. In haute couture, the focus of creative attention was the rich woman of thirty. The ripple effect spread the fashion novelty to all ages among the rich—with the exception of over-sixty matrons—and progressively influenced the wealthier classes without actually going much beyond the higher end of the middle-income bracket. Since the 1950s, rtw had allowed the splash to radiate further without actually changing the focus. The target of creative attention remained the thirty-year-old woman, even if the ripple trickled further down toward very young women and girls in their teens and eventually reached the less-than-average-income categories.

The new tremor, which Yves, Pierre and the industry had first felt in 1963, had created a third force, simply called *style*. Young people had style, as thousands of newspaper and magazine articles kept telling them. To be young was, in itself, to be fashionable. The postwar baby boom was the demographic reason behind the mass of fifteen- to twenty-year-olds who were not only a new economic market but a whole new social order. Youth itself was becoming the stone thrown into the pond that was sending waves in all directions. Youth was threatening to engulf the entire age spectrum.

What made the sixties revolutionary, says Bergé today,

was that fashion waves were becoming supersonic. Instead of an accelerated-wave effect from a focus of creative attention that could indeed be a girl of eighteen, the influence of style was immediate among all the young, regardless of social position. What was new was the *way* things became fashionable, in the largest sense of the word. Instead of the classical totem pole according to class, the new stratification was according to age. Money was being superseded by age.

With the exception of Cardin (Courrèges had closed down his boutique in anger at his designs being knocked off the world over), the high-fashion industry preferred to stick its collective head in the sand. Many of the name couturiers had boutiques on their premises, but these were merely extensions of the couture salons where their clients could shop for accessories, perfume and, in the case of Dior, especially, for such items as shirts and negligees that didn't demand interminable fittings. Bergé was determined to strike out. Richard Salomon was all for it. So was Yves, but he was far from sure he wasn't over the hill.

He had just crossed the barrier of thirty—beyond which, the young said, no one should be trusted. In the streets, he saw so many currents and influences that had so little to do with what he wanted to do that the faces getting slapped included his own. And if that wasn't enough, the youth cult had brought about a veritable *antifashion*. The point was not only to create a style in opposition to adult modes and manners, because as soon as an older woman (anyone over twenty-five) adopted a youth craze, this fad was immediately abandoned in favor of still newer forms of opposition. Whereas the businessman was smartly or conventionally dressed, the rock star simply was not. Whereas the businessman wanted a white shirt, his son wanted a colorful one. As soon as the father wore a colorful shirt, the son looked for a garish shirt, or didn't wear any at all. On the sidewalks of boulevard Saint-Germain, longhaired artists sold jewelry. Feathers, leaves and seeds were threaded on pieces of string and patterns were created with bits of wire. The momentary value was not the point; imagination was.

"It was a horrible crisis for me," Yves would say later. "I had that anguish of not being alive. I began to realize that fashion can come from anywhere, that daily life is where the clothes designer belongs today. You've got to have your eyes everywhere."

It was odd to see fashion filter *upward*. The first subculture group to wear leather was motorcycle hoods; the first people to wear denim were construction workers. Yves realized not only that the young were shaking off old taboos in clothes, in outlook and in behavior, but also that a lot of "flower power" wasn't as spontaneous as it liked to think it was. The pop revolution was fabricated and merchandised, and showed up most insistently in those places where what's new is what sells—art, records and advertising. He agreed with Eugenia Sheppard that a very thin line divided "a little touch of the chic new vulgarity" from the absolute dead end of kitsch.

For 1966, which was to be called the craziest fashion year of the decade, he wasn't doing too badly. Everywhere—from couture to rtw—the favorite dress was the briefest triangle taking account of the waist, and worn with the shortest hair, silver stockings and silver shoes laced up the leg and bangles of clear plastic and chrome. Yves's gypsy-print shifts or shirt-and-skirts with kerchiefs covering the hair were as well received as his shifts in sheer organza, transparent except where they were striped or chevroned with silver sequins. His fall collection had included a few jokes—pop dresses inspired by Warhol, with vivid profiles of a face or a body scrawled over them in positive-negative contrast—but he was insecure, suspicious of the success and sensing that the current aggressiveness in fashion would soon yield to a gentleness, if not a new romanticism. Unisex was also in the air, he felt, because miniskirts were at their highest, making the knee and the thigh the new erogenous zones, to the detriment of the bust, hip and waist, which were understated to the point of dismissal. "In London especially," Yves said, "girls were taking to pantsuits in classic checks, close-fitting pea jackets, peaked yachting caps, while longhaired men wore flowered shirts, extravagant ties and very definite stitch and seam details. I thought why not go the other way and dress everybody alike. I thought that would be the ultimate in suppressing sexual and class differences."

Cardin was perfecting his space-age look, and everybody was talking about Paco Rabanne and his "neon kite coat" made of plastic diamonds on white crepe. Makeup was pure decoration, with "wet looks" and body painting, and the Paris event was the Cinderella wedding of Johnny Halliday and Sylvie Vartan. In the spring of 1967, when Olivier Mourgue opened his basement boutique prophetically called Djinns, and Sonia Rykiel introduced her poor-boy knits, Yves came up with the nude look.

Credit for the undressed look was evenly divided between YSL and a Berliner settled in far-off Los Angeles, Rudi Gernreich. It was indeed Gernreich who made headlines in 1964, with the topless bathing suit, but Yves was always to consider himself the originator of the nude look. "I didn't have bare breasts," he was to say. "I had the illusion of nudity."

By April, Ohrbach's in New York was selling copies of the sheer dress, banded strategically at the neck, cuffs, hemline, bust and lower torso, at $200 apiece. Cardin also tried the undressed look by poking holes in the midriff of a linen dress and calling it refined nudity, "more cerebral than tangible"—which meant the navel didn't show. Body clothes were created by every designer, exploited by every store, insinuatingly promoted and publicized by magazines, in newspapers, on television. Cutouts appeared on pajamas, gloves and raincoats, umbrellas and bags made partly of see-through vinyl. Shoe manufacturers tried see-through vinyl boots, but they had the tendency to fog up like windshields after a few minutes of just standing around. Plastic was the new material in anything but rainwear, and in the Paris fall collection, silver was the color of the season—silver dresses, trimmings, accessories. Yves went one better by getting the weaver Malhia to come up with a gleaming silver sequined material. Her fabric allowed him to fashion the trend-setting "mermaid" sheath.

He was bored, but was accorded a distraction when Catherine Deneuve asked him to do her wardrobe for *Belle du*

Jour, a study under microscope of feminine masochism directed by Luis Buñuel. It was Yves's first movie wardrobe. The film turned out to be a French box-office success despite a generally thumbs-down critical reception. Said one critic, "Didn't like the film but came out humming the clothes."

Deneuve and her photographer husband David Bailey joined Zizi Jeanmaire, Françoise Sagan and three hundred other partygoers at Régine's New Jimmy on boulevard Montparnasse to launch Yves's wicked little book, *La Vilaine Lulu*. No partygoers could read their copies during the party, since New Jimmy's was pitch black as usual except for strobe lights, but the decor was different. There were cut-outs of Nasty Lulu and her white rat, Lulu dolls, Lulu balloons, Lulu sketches and Lulu placemats.

Lulu was a perverse little girl with no neck and no waist whom he had been doodling since his first year at Dior's. Nasty Lulu, in Yves's sketches and text, is a ghastly ten-year-old with a horrid vocabulary, whose confidant is an English-speaking white rat. Published by Claude Tchou with a price of $5 (and $40 for a deluxe edition), the book came with a disclaimer by the author saying he was *not* Lulu. "I've warned everybody not to try and psychoanalyze Lulu," he told his guests. "It's useless." The wonderfully perverse cartoon character hangs out in the Café de Flore, dresses badly, takes hallucinatory drugs, goes to a dance carrying a cactus for her bouquet. She sets fire to houses and gorges babies with red wine, makes patients scream for mercy by giving them ten injections an hour. She takes newborn babies out of their cribs by their mothers' beds and substitutes little white rats. When Yves showed the drawings to Sagan, she persuaded him to have *La Vilaine Lulu* published. Today, the Tchou publishing house no longer exists, and the coffee-table book is a collector's item.

Yet another pleasant distraction from the haute couture chore ahead of him was the standing-room-only success of the Rive Gauche boutique. There were days when it was impossible to get in and buy one of those vinyl raincoats at $90 that were the hit of 1966–67. Pierre was in rue de Tournon daily, and Yves tooled to rue d'Aboukir to attend to the thousand and one details of the ready-to-wear that C. Mendes, S.A., was manufacturing on overtime. YSL wanted his rtw to be original, not a knockoff of the couture sold in rue Spontini. Others were content with adapting their haute couture; he tried to rethink everything, from shortcuts to shapes and elaborate cuttings. "I adore it," he told *Life* magazine four years later, when there were forty-six Rive Gauche boutiques in Europe and America, turning an annual profit of $6 million. "It's alive, it's quick, it's daring. The challenge is to make a raincoat which looks just as good on a girl of fifteen as on a woman of sixty."

He had never liked the leaps into space, and thought Courrèges and Cardin served themselves, not women, with their aerospace fashions. If the youth revolution had an obvious aspiration, it was toward equality and dignity for all. The space fashion, he felt, showed contempt for women by making them look grotesque. If the youth revolution had anything to tell fashion designers, it was that the person they were designing for, not the design itself, was important.

A seventeen-year-old from North London who called herself Twiggy made looking seventeen and starved the fashion image of 1967, and the industry was jumping on the teen-age bandwagon in earnest. Teen-age girls made up 11 percent of the United States population, *Seventeen* magazine revealed, and purchased 20 percent of the apparel and 23 percent of the cosmetics sold in the United States. *Women's Wear Daily* said half the women of America were under twenty-five.

With Guy Laroche, Saint Laurent was out front as a presenter of youthful concepts. Yves believed in pantsuits, turtleneck pullovers, sleeveless shifts with side slits, classic raincoats, and said the young and the less young could wear his clothes. "All you need is the right frame of mind—think of seduction before elegance." He ushered in a new romantic slant in 1967, showing black-velvet evening suits with gently tailored silk shirts, and his fall collection featured pantsuits in a color that had been taboo for years—black.

When the rest of Paris went on a short-lived African safari with robelike "African Queen," "Boubou" and "Kaftan" dresses and with bold silk and chiffon prints featuring jungle designs and zebra stripes, Yves's pantsuits were an overnight success. In his fall collection, he developed his masculine romanticism further. Egged on by his new friend Betty Saint (soon to be Betty Catroux), he launched an evening breeches suit, again in velvet and again in black, to be worn with highly swathed white silk neckcloths and buckled shoes.

Suddenly, the romantic look was everywhere. Women wanted to dress up and put geometrics and creaking plastics behind them. Young girls were romantic in Indian leather fringes, headbands and color mixtures in layers of crepe and brocade, while jet-setters dressed like wealthy gypsies in Afghan coats made of sheepskin with gold embroidery, and in art-nouveau inspirations. Yves contributed to the mood by designing the wardrobe for Claude Lelouch's *Live for Life*, an unabashed followup to *A Man and a Woman*. The movie was of the kind where men must wander and ladies must weep, alone, and it starred Yves Montand as a world-weary TV reporter, Annie Girardot as his musing wife and Candice Bergen as the beautiful but blank American model with whom the wayward husband falls in love for a while. For social significance, *Vivre pour vivre* showed the Vietnam War and said the United States had no business fighting it.

France had soothed its own neocolonial conscience by granting Algeria independence in 1962. Like the million other *colons* who had left with what they could carry in their suitcases, Charles Saint Laurent had lost the property in Oran, but the family had otherwise escaped unscathed. Now Yves's father lived in Cannes, which looks very much like Oran and in fact contains a sizeable colony of *pieds noirs*. The Saint Laurents had been living apart for a while, Charles in Cannes and Lucienne in Paris, where both their daughters, now married, lived. Charles came to Paris once a month, and they all got together for family occasions, such as cousin Catherine Saint Laurent's marriage to Alain Castil. As he had done for his sisters, Yves designed Catherine's wedding dress.

Yves lived on place Vauban, behind L'Hôtel des Invalides, in the discreetly opulent seventh arrondissement. His small, elegant apartment, rented from the Duke of Sabran, was becoming a treasure trove of art. Yves's furniture was a mixture of antiques, velvet sofas and contemporary Eames and Mies van der Rohe chairs. The library contained his growing art collection—a Miró, a Braque lithograph, a drawing by the hero of his adolescence, Christian Bérard. There was also an Alexander Lieberman, an egg-shaped bar designed by Lalanne and shelves crammed with books. Besides a manservant, the household included Hazel, a wheezing Chihuahua. "I don't like little dogs," Yves said in 1970, "but somebody gave her to me and now she's getting old and I'm fond of her." On one wall was a Buffet painting of a rat which Yves maintained was a portrait of Hazel. "It's the only Buffet I love. I'm not crazy about his work. All the other ones here belong to Pierre."

The two partners, who were fast becoming millionaires, bought themselves a hideaway in Marrakesh during the summer. Morocco was not Algeria, where the first President, Ahmed ben Bella, had been eliminated by Colonel Houari Boumedienne, a gaunt, chain-smoking ascetic who was launching the country toward strident, Third World socialism. The two-story Arabic house Pierre and Yves purchased was of yellow stone and contained a balustrade, two patios and chalk-walled interiors. To begin the remodeling, they had workers scrub years of patina from the yellow sandstone walls with soap and water and, as Pierre would remember, were rewarded with a display of vivid colors.

The year 1968 started out propitiously, with Gabrielle Chanel telling a TV audience in February that her heir was obviously Yves Saint Laurent. In his spring collection, Yves had a wedding gown that was nothing more than two garlands of lilies-of-the-valley slung around bust and waist. The gag nearly backfired when *France Soir* huffed that it was an assault on decency and Yves had to explain that his matrimonial creation was intended as nothing more than a show-stopper. The summer collection included wide-legged pantsuits and featured loosely belted tunic tops and clinging jackets that went some way toward reconciling the twin demands of practical comfort and femininity in this "anything goes" year.

But in May, France was suddenly on the brink of revolution. What began as demonstrations against student lock-outs in parts of the sprawling and overcrowded University of Paris system grew to full-scale revolt in the Latin Quarter, when authorities refused to release arrested students. On May 10, students built street barricades on boulevard Saint-Germain, and when the smoke cleared and police had brought down the barricades, the streets were littered with three hundred wounded and the wrecks of fire-bombed cars; five hundred people had been arrested. The de Gaulle government tried to defuse the situation by denouncing police brutality and freeing most of those arrested, but student leaders had already escalated the confrontation by persuading organized labor to call a one-day general strike. Young workers occupied plants, and the giant Renault works were disrupted by militants. By May 17, the movement had spread to hundreds of businesses, and the country seemed to be sliding toward anarchy. What really frightened the government was that the events were not controlled by the Communist Party or big labor, but were the result of a spontaneous grass-roots movement.

Yves wasn't on the barricades on Saint-Germain-des-Prés or boulevard Saint-Michel, but he was close enough to get a whiff of police tear gas and to look at the kids—and at what they were wearing: pants, shirts and huge scarves (to wrap around the mouth and protect against tear gas). The rue de Tournon boutique came through the riots unscathed (but six months later, the avenue Victor Hugo outlet was robbed by thieves who knew what they were after, since they left winter shirts and concentrated on spring-collection pantsuits).

Yves felt more than ever on the side of youth and of the jolting energy of social convulsion. What André Malraux called "an immense lyrical illusion" showed that Gaullist France had remained a "blocked nation," as the students said, a country not yet decolonized at home. For the first time, Yves felt acutely that he was a prisoner of his own success. Deeper down, he felt robbed of his own youth. He let his beard grow, made disparaging remarks about fashion and entered what he was to call "my last crisis of adolescence."

The Latin Quarter was seething with ideas, and Yves began to hang out in student cafés and to listen to the interminable arguing about why the revolution had failed. The consensus was that the revolutionary force had been betrayed by hesitant leaders and by the Communist chiefs who had been overtaken by the events. Student militants, who dominated every faculty, were miles to the left of anything Yves had thought possible. The notion of power in a modern industrial society was more important to them than ownership, and they demanded that the individual be defined in other ways than the objects he or she produces or the functions he or she fulfills. They dreamed angrily about masses and spontaneity, criticized the very notion of a party—especially the Communist Party—as a political, structured organization. The consumer society was a rightwing plot, and fashion, with its planned obsolescence and calculated, addictlike dependence, was the squalid opium of a society dancing on its own grave. The changes that fashion constantly imposed prevented the individual from expressing his or her own permanence.

Authenticity was the big word. Clothes were a means of expressing oneself, and if all *contestataires* looked alike in jeans, shirts and those huge scarves, the reason was that they wanted to tell each other who they were. Jeans were not only clothes; they were clothes-language, instant and eloquent symbols of brotherhood; unity-in-protest clothes that talked body language. Yves thought the argument a little specious. Either clothes expressed the self or the group; you couldn't have it both ways—an "antiestablishment uniform" was a contradiction in terms—but he liked the idea that clothes should express the wearer as authentically as possible. He thought a lot about this and decided that there was perhaps a niche for someone like him between the ideas gushing forth in the street and the widest possible expansion of these ideas.

In September 1968, he was in New York with Betty and Pierre to open the first overseas Rive Gauche store. America was in turmoil, reeling from the assassinations of Robert Kennedy and Martin Luther King, a war that wouldn't end, student unrest and street riots, and gearing up for a presidential election that opposed Hubert Humphrey and Richard Nixon. Yves had shaved off the beard, but his new radicalism seeped through in interviews. As he told *The New York Times*'s Bernardine Morris, the girls and boys at the barricades in May had looked beautiful because they *were* beautiful. "Fashion is not haute couture although many people think so. Events are more important."

He was impatient with the chichi crowd who came to the avant-premiere of the 855 Madison Avenue boutique, which had orange carpeting climbing right up the walls. Eight thousand garments had been shipped over for the opening, and Yves's Citypants, at $145 to $175, were instant best-sellers. Betty wore a black satin sequined jump suit opened to below the rib cage, and when Yves himself arrived, sporting an outsized tie, paisley shirt and multiple chains worn hip-hugger style, the scene, said *Time*, "was pandemonium." When he was interviewed, he said unisex was coming, that to design for haute couture and ready-to-wear was the same thing, that, in fact, he would like to turn his back on the very rich. "People on the streets have more impact," he told *Time*. In other interviews, he mused at how far the world had come in the twelve short years since he had started with Dior. "That was the time everybody wanted to look very rich. Now I think it's the contrary. Fashion is no longer a fete, a carnival. It can be very serious."

During the first day of business, the Madison Avenue Rive Gauche store grossed $25,000 and was out of so many sizes that rue Spontini was cabled to air-freight more clothes. A year later, Yves, Betty and Pierre repeated the New York formula in opening the first London boutique in New Bond Street. By the end of 1969, there were eighteen Rive Gauche outlets in Europe alone, while such revered houses as Balenciaga and Castillo closed their doors for good.

Yves said he was appalled by the Vietnam War, a statement some fashion writers managed to twist into the idea that he had designed his 1968 rtw as "a mourning for Vietnam." He talked about a need to get "out of the straightjacket," and for 1969, designed fitted hussar coats and caped highwaymen's coats to wear with pants, a collection that the

London *Times* called "the leanest, hungriest, blackest and most devastating yet."

But there was no escape from success. The public wanted casual clothes with character, and his pantsuits were everywhere in 1969, even if skirted legs were still the norm among young women. Unisex was in the air, with Jacques Esterel stealing the publicity thunder by saying that to identify the sexes by their clothes was a thing of the past and designing identical tunics and pants outfits "for father, mother and child." YSL had everybody's attention when he announced he was through with haute couture. "My true public are young women, working women. If I keep certain private clients, it's in order to keep my seamstresses, not the other way around!"

He agreed to star in a short but sumptuous documentary about himself, *Woman Is Sweeter,* produced by Lanvin–Charles of the Ritz, for showing, in collaboration with *Seventeen,* on American campuses. Directed by Martine Barrat, a vivacious Parisienne who had studied in New York, the thirty-five-minute film avoided the habitual runway parades and concentrated instead on Yves creating a dress on a model while confiding to the camera that he is thinking of a client of his—"young, pretty, very rich and very leftist, which sure doesn't hurt." With electrifying music by *Hair* composer Galt MacDermot, the movie featured offbeat views of London, New York, Paris and Marrakesh and Yves saying that he didn't want to make new things to excite buyers because he hated that concept of fashion. The movie's biggest fan was Lucienne, who, after the first screening, embraced Barrat and said, "You have understood my son, Madame."

For the Pour Homme publicity, he posed in the nude—with the beard back on—and called fashion an outdated and often stupid business. He was thirty-three and had never stopped working since he was eighteen, he said. "Maybe I shouldn't take the whole thing too seriously."

14

WHY PARIS?

As fashion leaders of the world, the Parisians nearly lost the ball twice. The German occupation in 1940 was a blow, although twelve houses managed to show abbreviated collections in 1941 and 1942 and to sell their creations, mostly to recently moneyed black marketeers, German wives and those French mistresses of Wehrmacht officers who dared to wear them. As president of the Chambre Syndicale, Lucien Lelong successfully resisted German efforts to move the couture business, lock, stock and barrel, to Berlin and Vienna, and in delicate negotiations, managed to keep 80 percent of the work force despite ever-increasing demands for labor for German war industries.

The war actually created an uncommon solidarity among industryites. When Madame Grès and Balenciaga were ordered to close for two weeks for exceeding the authorized yardage in some of their dresses, other houses joined forces to finish their collections for them. The Liberation, in 1944, found the industry as intact as Paris itself, but why should the triumphant Allies again fall in the thrall of a fashion capital that for four years they had managed very well without? Talent and a pool of artisan know-how did it for Paris. Lelong's first postwar collection in 1946—designed by his assistants Pierre Balmain and Christian Dior—was an unprecedented success and made British and American women feel dated in their wartime Utility suits. A year later, Dior reestablished the hegemony with the New Look.

The second fumble came with the 1960s "youthquake," which made fashion "Anglo-Saxon." London became the most inventive fashion leader, Carnaby Street a household word and America's ubiquitous blue jeans the uniform of the young the world over, France included. In 1967, England's Mary Quant exported thirty thousand dresses to France alone, and in three years, Barbara Hulanicki's Biba boutique (named after her sister) was a multinational success.

Saint Laurent's explanation for London's fashion fadeout since then is that there was not so much a lack of designer talent as of backup coordination. The Parisians and the Milanese managed to leap into collective ready-to-wear marketing, but the Londoners were the last to organize their rtw into one fashion event, and the excitement of London fashion has remained amateurish in the flair and flavor of vibrant shops and boutiques on Kensington High Street and its tributaries. Citing uneven quality both in construction and design, big-time buyers treat the British capital on an item-by-item basis, picking from shows rather than buying entire collections. Generally, however, they regret that London has lost its grip.

Yves has five Rive Gauche stores in London, under the management of Lady Clare Rendlesham, who is, in her own right, a legend in retailing. He thinks the Big Four are Jean Muir ("a classicist"), John Bates, Marissa Martin and Zandra Rhodes, but wonders if they aren't shortchanging themselves by spending so much time in the United States and by constantly worrying about what New York thinks about them. "These designers have always been remote from the fashion scene but very good at being themselves," he says. "London has a tailors' tradition, but no women's wear background. *Les petites mains,* the nimble hands of the garment industry, were never there, and the boutiques remained cottage industry. Paris has the Mimi Pinson, the midinette, tradition. Seamstresses used to be the mistresses of wealthy men, which may explain why they're still so underpaid. It's absolutely terrible." The House of Saint Laurent pays the highest hourly wages in the industry, in 1978 $3.85 an hour for workroom technicians.

The French luxury trade is based on centuries of expert craftsmanship. The Renaissance marked the beginning of fashion—that is, of styles that change and become personalized—and of inventive artisans who knew how to influence their noble clientele. By the time of Louis XIV, ostentatious clothes were essential at Versailles, and courtiers felt obliged to copy every whim and fancy that derived from some innovation by one of the Sun King's mistresses. And Versailles was imitated throughout Europe and beyond. Louis XIV also had a great statesman in Jean Colbert, who encouraged a luxury textile industry and laid the foundations for it. Better still, Parisian artisans and merchants realized that by anticipating the tastes of their noble patrons and by using them as live billboards and mannequins for their concoctions, they could sell their inventions to the increasingly wealthy and commanding bourgeoisie.

Rose Bertin was the first name in fashion history, the daughter of poor but respectable parents from Abbéville, who became Marie Antoinette's dressmaker when she was still in her twenties. Bertin set herself up in rue Saint-Honoré and bought a house in suburban Épernay. She survived the French Revolution—and Marie Antoinette's beheading—by leaving Paris with four employes and fifteen cases filled with "spangled finery," which she sold at high prices in Frankfurt. Later she moved to London, where many of her old clients had settled, but they were now penniless émigrés, and it was with the wealthy English that she did her successful business. Rose visited Russia, where the czarina patronized her, and when she returned to France, managed to extricate herself from political trouble by stating that she, an honest, hard-working woman, had not been paid by many of her aristocratic clients and had been obliged to go abroad to sell her wares and talents. She lived to sell her business and to retire to her beloved Épernay.

Louis Leroy was the trend setter of the revolution and of Napoleon's parvenus. Initially a royalist, Leroy's allegiance changed overnight when he realized that the Republican war profiteers and Napoleon's nouveaux riches were unsure of their taste and would willingly follow his suggestions. The Directoire period brought Greco-Roman forms into fashion, and women appeared in all-revealing, clinging muslin gowns that fell from beneath the breasts and demanded figures as shapely as those of Madame Récamier and Thérèse Tallien, who was so lovely that she was compared to the Capitoline Venus. Leroy bribed his way to Empress Joséphine's attention, and saw himself as the sole creator of fashion—his delicious empire muslin dresses worn over blue, yellow or pale pink taffeta were the craze of 1800—but Napoleon commissioned a painter, Jean-Baptiste Isabey, to design the coronation robes. Isabey's stiff drawings showed no understanding of fabrics and, at Joséphine's insistence, Leroy transformed the dull sketches into sumptuous garments of satins and velvets.

Leroy had the intuition of what a house of couture could be, but Napoleon wrecked Europe and France before the dress designer could execute his ideas. After the fall of Napoleon, Leroy found himself working again with members of the old aristocracy, but he didn't know how to renew his style and, after handing over his business to a niece, died a forgotten man in 1829.

Fashion became current events in the 1840s with the appearance of ladies' journals, but there were few top fashion figures between Leroy's retirement and the Victorian rise of Charles Frederick Worth, whose sons and grandsons continued the house until 1956. Worth was the first to use live models, first using his wife. Their son Gaston was a man of exquisite taste. He had wanted to be a painter, and when he took over from his father, his coloring was dominated by soft pastels. He knew how to deploy the large-patterned

Lyons silks with a precision that enhanced the sweeping lines of a garment. By 1900, the House of Worth had branches in all the major European capitals, dressed most of the courts of Europe and was known for the dignity and splendor of its designers.

Jacques Doucet, whose grandfather had opened a men's shop in rue de la Paix in 1824, branched into women's dresses in 1871, with immediate success, and lived long enough to be a wealthy patron of Cézanne, Picasso, Matisse and Braque, whose canvases he bought when they were still unknown. Picasso's famous *Demoiselles d'Avignon,* now in the Museum of Modern Art in New York, once hung in his hallway, and Henri Douanier Rousseau's *Charmeuse des Serpents,* which he willed to the Louvre, graced his study. Doucet created both the stage and street wardrobe for the actress Réjane (who figures in Proust's *Remembrance of Things Past* under her own name), and sought his inspiration in eighteenth-century fashion, but his name didn't survive his death in 1929.

During the Gay Nineties, Madame Paquin was the first woman since Rose Bertin to achieve a top position in fashion. Actually named Jeanne Becker, she was a woman of obscure Levantine origins who designed for the queens of Belgium, Spain and Portugal and the queens of the demimonde. With her banker husband, she founded her house in 1892 and was an immediate success. For the 1900 Universal Exhibition, she had a beautifully dressed wax figure of herself on display. She was the first designer to create publicity for herself, sending ten models wearing identical dresses to the races at Longchamps.

Four other women designers made their mark on the first decades of the century. Jeanne Lanvin and Madeleine Vionnet both started from the bottom, Lanvin in millinery, and both opened modest houses before World War I. Both carried on the long tradition of native French elegance, both catered to a clientele of exceptional taste and both refrained from ostentatious advertising of themselves. Vionnet was a sorceress with a pair of scissors. She began sewing at the age of eleven, was apprenticed to Kate Reilly in London and worked in fashion houses in Paris until she opened her own boutique in rue de Rivoli in 1912. She invented the bias cut as a dressmaking technique, and her success in the 1920s allowed her to purchase a town house on avenue Montaigne, thereby making that cross-avenue of the Champs Elysées the new couture street. Like Chanel, she didn't know how to draw and created all her fashions by draping on a wooden dummy. "Actually, I never did fashion, I did harmonies, things that were pretty together," she said in 1940. "They resembled nothing I'd seen." If Poiret took women out of corsets, her bias dresses increased the intimacy between the dress and the body.

Lanvin's love for Botticelli, stained glass windows—her famous *bleu Lanvin* was derived from the heavenly blue of medieval church glass—impressionist painting and embroidery was reflected in her romantic and slightly theatrical clothes. A tiny woman, she was orphaned young and widowed young. She dressed her only daughter, Marie-Blanche, so exquisitely that mothers of her classmates asked her to make dresses for their daughters. When Lanvin was twenty-three, she rented a loft at 22 rue Faubourg Saint-Honoré and, with nothing more than three months' credit from her suppliers, set herself up in business. Her clientele was youthful and elegant, and the romantic styles for which she became known in 1915 continued in popularity throughout the 1920s. The House of Lanvin grew in the twin image of mother and daughter, and Lanvin's inspiration remained Marie-Blanche, who became Comtesse de Polignac and a patron of Igor Stravinsky. Like Doucet, Jeanne Lanvin collected an incomparable number of paintings, particularly Renoirs, and had Vuillard decorate her salon. She died in 1946, and her house, still at 22 rue Faubourg Saint-Honoré but occupying five buildings, is now the oldest in Paris.

Paul Poiret was the first conscious artist of dress. He was the sartorial genius of the 1910s, a megalomaniac and a dazzling designer of theatrical costumes, an inconsistent fashion dictator and a native Parisian who, with the exception of one delirious decade, was always magnificently out of step. He was a sharp-tongued bon vivant who left his mark on every aspect of life, didn't make it into the Reckless Twenties, was fleeced out of his despotic dressmaking business by bankers and died, penniless, on the Riviera in 1944.

An apprentice of Doucet and—less happily—of Worth, Poiret set himself up in business with a tiny amount of capital that his mother gave him. The year was 1904, and everything in his rue Auber shop was totally unlike anything seen elsewhere, including the windows, for which he created the display himself. Though married to a rich wife and the father of a large family—for his children, he made the most delightful designs both in decoration and dress, and he named his perfumes after his daughters—he was always a public rather than a private man.

After his first, easy success with straight dresses that fell in graceful folds to women's feet, Poiret lived in the theater, boulevards and restaurants, where his eccentricities made him famous. He created a simplified form of fashion and caught the updraft of the era, exemplified by the emancipation of women and the intense interest in modern art. He was inspired by Serge Diaghilev's Ballet Russe and its electrifying fantasy, Léon Bakst sets and costumes and Vaslav Nijinsky's dancing, and by the *fauves* painters.

Poiret soon had *le tout Paris* dressed like Asiatic princesses, in the vivid colors of Kees van Dongen, Henri Matisse, André Derain and Raoul Dufy. He forbade his clients to wear corsets, and on travels, had his models wear uniforms with a *P* embroidered in their hats. His clients included Ida Rubinstein, Sarah Bernhardt and Isadora Duncan, for whom he created a room without windows. He attended first nights in capes and flannel evening clothes, and in summer, affected white. Bearded, dark-skinned, a man with virile eyes and small feet, he trod the Parisian summer avenues in the Indian silk bush jacket of a visiting lion hunter.

In 1919, Poiret made a spectacular comeback after the disastrous war, but he was never quite able to translate what was successful on the stage into clothes in which postwar women felt comfortable. A new element in fashion was sports, and two ballets appeared which were the synthesis of the postwar mode—*Le Train Bleu* (scenario by Cocteau, choreography by Nijinsky, music by Milhaud, costumes by Chanel and curtain by Picasso) and *Les Matelots* (postcard painting, sets and costumes by Pruna), which both dealt with the new chic of beach and casual wear. Poiret opened a palatial house at the Rond Point des Champs-Elysées, where the zodiac painted on the foyer ceiling indicated the stars at the moment of his birth. He gave splendiferous garden parties—recorded on canvases by van Dongen—and egotistically designed clothes that pleased himself and into which he could bully many of his clients for a while. For the 1925 Exposition des Arts Décoratifs, he had his models parade on the decks of three launches moored in the Seine, but, unlike Chanel's unerring sense of the twenties, his taste was no longer avant-garde, although his work bore the stamp of a true artist. He outlived his financial ruin by nearly twenty years, earning a living as a painter and a sometime stage and movie decorator, exhibiting his poverty as he had once vaunted his wealth.

Only four years younger than Poiret, Gabrielle Chanel seems to belong to another period in fashion. The daughter of a scrappy small-town family whose sticky dependence she was to endure most of her life, she loved to surround her origins with mystery. Every anecdote about this extraordinary woman is unique, if not always true. She owed her first success to her intelligence and her pretty face, to a short career as a cabaret singer (her cooing singsong style earned her the clucking "Coco" nickname), and to successive lovers with culture, influence and money. From one of them, she obtained the means of opening a small millinery shop in Deauville, the fashionable summer resort. She opened in rue Cambon in 1914, and said she almost believed the war broke out to spite her, but her modest couture house soon acquired the notoriety of its owner. One legend has it that she invented the short jersey dress, but what she really created was a new way of wearing clothes. Time and again she came up with just the thing women wanted, and her name came to mean a total look, from sailor hat to beige-and-black sling-back shoes, even to the scent in the air. Her flair was instinctive, and the fashion house in rue Cambon soon employed three thousand people. As a rule, artistic temperament rarely goes hand in hand with financial acumen, but Chanel was the exception. Her horror of being dependent on anyone gave her a shrewd and provident approach to money.

She was often quoted as saying that she alone created the flapper. In reality, women had for some time shortened their skirts and thrown away tassels and trains, laces and loops, but she was the first to make clothes for the young— until the twenties, youth was a preparatory step, not life itself. In 1920, she made the first chemise dress, and five years later, she introduced the collarless, braid-trimmed cardigan jacket. She turned sports clothes into everyday clothes, made pants elegant and gave costume jewelry an intrinsic value of its own. As young designers would do after her, she adapted men's styles for women, and at the height of her prewar career, she controlled a fashion empire that included the rue Cambon complex and textile and jewelry factories, but not, to her grief, the Chanel No. 5 perfume which Ernest Beaux, the most famous "nose" of his time, had invented for her.

Paul and Pierre Wertheimer were intelligent, rich and aggressive. When, in 1924, they suggested that she and they incorporate as Parfums Chanel, saying, "And you, dear Coco, will be president of the company," she agreed and turned over the rights to all brands so far marketed under the Chanel label, as well as Beaux's formula for the legendary No. 5. She soon realized that she had been cheated, and for the next forty years, fought with the guile and stubbornness of a peasant woman, with the great lawyer René de Chambrun as her counsel, before she managed to wrest better terms from the Wertheimer brothers. It was after Pierre Wertheimer died that she tried to lure Bergé away from Yves to manage the perfume division, which had made her a millionaire many times over.

Chanel is the only couturier to retire and, after an absence of sixteen years, to return successfully with her offerings of the cardigan suit, the lace and chiffon dresses, the pleated skirts and masses of junk jewelry that had made her rich and famous thirty years earlier.

The two top Frenchmen of the interwar years were Lucien

Lelong, who is remembered for being the first to launch a ready-to-wear department and the first to make a collection show a private theater play, and Jean Patou, who became famous for his easy sportswear and for importing American girls to model for him.

Lelong dressed the Duchess of Windsor and Marlene Dietrich, and married the niece of the last czar, Princess Natalie, who left him for Hollywood and a starring role in *Les Folies Bergères*. Lelong was never a creator, but, as Jacqueline Delubac put it, "What art in his choices! To wear his clothes is to feel utterly secure." When his two top collaborators, Pierre Balmain and Christian Dior, left him within a month of each other after World War II, he closed his house and retired to the Riviera to grow roses and play golf.

Patou realized early that to live in the shadow of such arresting self-promoters as Poiret and Chanel was to be condemned to a slow death, and from the moment he opened his house when he was twenty-five, he became a society lion and a perpetual gossip item. When he returned from the States with six American mannequins, paying them the unheard-of salary of ten thousand francs a month, newspapers all over the world carried the story. If a woman was pretty, Patou didn't care whether she was a nightclub dancer or a duchess. In his crusade for a return to femininity, he launched his first attack against low waists in 1925, but his big revolt came four years later, when he suddenly lengthened the skirt. He was excessively jealous of Chanel, to the point of counting the pages of *Vogue* illustrating Chanel and comparing them to the number of pages devoted to his own collections. If Chanel's outnumbered his, he wrote furious protests to the editor, Edna Wooman Chase. Patou and Chanel would never sit down in the same room. Whoever spotted the other first always left as ostentatiously as possible. Patou died very young, in 1936, leaving his house to his sister and brother-in-law, who developed Joy, "the most expensive perfume in the world."

Chanel's arch-enemy was "the Italian artist who makes dresses," Elsa Schiaparelli. Twelve years younger than Chanel—and therefore all the more hated—Scap, as she was always known in Paris, was a descendant of Giovanni

Schiaparelli, the Italian astronomer who, in 1877, threw science into a fifty-year tiff by declaring that he had observed canals on Mars. She had a difficult beginning in life, which included an unfortunate marriage to a Polish dreamer who took her to America, spent her dowry and left her with a child. She began making a living in Paris by designing sweaters patterned with African art, which she persuaded Armenian refugees to knit for her. She leased rooms on the top floor of a building in the rue de la Paix, and was soon turning out eight thousand dresses a year and designing Greta Garbo's wardrobe.

Schiaparelli claimed she didn't know how to sew a button (and, in fact, she was the first to use zippers in haute couture). Of the couturiers of her time, she is the one whose creations are the most recognizable, but they were never for the timid. A friend of Cocteau and Salvador Dali, Schiaparelli asked for their inspiration and introduced surrealist touches to her collections. Tyrian purple was her favorite color and, renaming it "shocking pink," she created her most famous perfume. Her collections were built around themes—the circus, butterflies, music, Botticelli—and she had the manufacturers of her fabrics, embroideries and accessories echo her motifs. Her openings were as eagerly awaited as a first night and attended by as many of high society as could be accommodated in her new premises in place Vendôme, next to the Ritz (Chanel's rue Cambon salon was the "backside" of the Ritz, which allowed Scap to say, "Poor Chanel, I use the front door of the Ritz, she must use the back").

Scap spent the early war years in America, trying to work in that "expensive and clumsy business called Hollywood"—Chanel had been the first to be invited, by Samuel Goldwyn—but was back in place Vendôme in 1944. Three years later, she saw Dior dethrone her square-shouldered elegance with the New Look, and in 1950, she closed her house. The last woman designer until the emergence of Sonia Rykiel nearly two decades later, she died in 1973.

Edward Molineux was the first Irishman and Mainbocher the first American to become Parisian couturiers and owners of their own houses. Molineux was a former painter who, with the backing of a London press lord, opened a house at 5 rue de la Paix in 1919, and through the twenties, created a disciplined yet sumptuous fashion. He dressed the beautiful and stylish Princess Marina of Greece, who became the Duchess of Kent and for whom he made the most flattering and understated clothes money could buy. With the outbreak of World War II, Molineux moved to London.

Mainbocher, whose name was originally Main Bocher, was a Chicagoan who came to Europe to study music, became a fashion writer for *Vogue*, opened a shop at avenue George V in 1931 and showed new, molded sheath dresses. He became famous for creating Wallis Simpson's dress for the wedding that made her the Duchess of Windsor. He dressed Gertrude Lawrence and Lynn Fontanne, and was a favorite of the American theatrical colony. With the war, he moved to New York, where he continued designing until he retired, at eighty, in 1971, and died five years later.

Marcel Rochas, who is given the credit for the first padded shoulders, became famous overnight in 1930, when eight women at a party came face to face wearing the same Rochas dress. A man about town who loved parties, people and pretty women and, together with his third wife, became associated with the very feminine line of clothes she liked to wear, Rochas was something of a film freak. He designed many costumes for movie stars, and in Jacques Becker's 1944 film *Falbalas*, played a Bluebeard couturier who hangs up in his shop window all the women he has loved, in the dresses he had made for them.

Couturiers and fashion have rarely been subjects of screen treatments. Besides *Falbalas*, only two other French films are habitually cited: Abel Gance's 1938 *Paradis perdu*, in which Fernand Gravey played a barely fictitious Poiret, and the Fernandel comedy *Le Couturier de ses dames* (*The Dressmaker*) of 1955, directed by Jean Boyer, with costumes by Cardin.

Between 1920 and 1940, the most influential houses were in the hands of women. Besides Lanvin, Vionnet, Chanel and Schiaparelli, Nina Ricci and Alix Czereskow—first as Alix, then as Madame Grès—opened and successfully directed their own houses, but the decades following World War II all belonged to men.

Cristóbal Balenciaga was the master. A Spanish *hidalgo* of icy courtesy and burning insolence, limitless generosity and deeply cultivated mystery, he alone of all the couturiers knew how to cut and stitch every part of a garment. The son of a captain of a fishing trawler, Balenciaga was born in Guetaria, near San Sebastian on the French border. At twenty, he opened his own dressmaking establishment in San Sebastian, later expanded to Madrid and Barcelona, and didn't move to Paris until he was forty-two and the Spanish Civil War had ruined him. He was a perfectionist in the true meaning of the word, and made absolutely no concessions, in his workrooms or to his clients.

Balenciaga was also alone in refusing all publicity. His friend Hector Escobosa, the director of I. Magnin in San Francisco, had a series of copies made of Balenciaga prototypes and took them to Paris to try to convince the couturier to let him launch a Balenciaga ready-to-wear line in America, saying, "You will sell thousands." Balenciaga agreed with an approving smile. Then, after a beat, he added, "On the condition that my name is never mentioned, of course."

In 1937, he set himself up on avenue George V, and in no time, imposed his nonchalantly structured suits on the fashion world. The "Balenciaga bias" remained a secret, but others imitated the "Balenciaga cut," which began under a loose collar. "The manner with which his jackets insinuate the body without propping it up created more than a passing fashion; it gave every woman a kind of sharp femininity, both willowy and fleshed-out," wrote Lucien François, who knew him. "Balenciaga seemed to think, 'I would look like this if I were a woman.' "

Few people ever saw Balenciaga. He never appeared in his own salons, never answered letters, never gave parties or interviews and barely allowed magazines to photograph his collections. Henri Cartier-Bresson dined with him once— without his camera. Balenciaga chose his models for their angular grace and for the way they bore down on the spectators at his collection shows, all too skinny, too tall and too rude. A creator of parade dresses for royalty and celebrities, clothes that were beautiful but austere in spite of their richness, he had a flair for guessing next season's silhouette. In 1957, he ended Dior's ten-year reign as the most influential designer with the chemise or sack look.

Like Chanel, Balenciaga was harried by his family—a sister ran the Madrid boutique, but it was his apprentice Givenchy who accomplished what all the onrushing Spanish clan members failed to do—to be his spiritual heir. After the student unrest of 1968, Balenciaga closed his house on an impulse, saying, "The life that supported culture is no more," but he came out of retirement shortly before his death, in 1972, to fashion the wedding gown of General Francisco Franco's granddaughter when she married Prince Alfonso de Bourbon, the grandson of Spain's last king.

Yves Saint Laurent was overwhelmed when he managed to hire Madame Felisa, Balenciaga's lifelong assistant, in 1977. "She has given me the thing I wished to know since my work began, and that is the true *flou*, the sensual *flou* which gives you the feeling that the dress may fall off a woman's back at any moment. *Flou* is seduction."

Yves thinks that Balenciaga was perhaps the greatest and Vionnet a close second. "One always has an image of austerity in relation to Balenciaga, but he was pure sensuousness when it came to making clothes. He was a great admirer of Vionnet. Long before he was a great couturier, he bought her patterns. Vionnet's *flou* of the thirties is the most beautiful. Her bias cut rivaled the Directoire in showing women's figures and her cut demanded perfect bodies since it offered no tricks to conceal defects."

When Vionnet died in 1975, a few months short of her hundredth birthday, YSL said that the modern feminine body begins with her, "in all its suppleness and seductiveness." Three years later, he predicted that Vionnet would soon be revived, that her 1926 line was "perfect."

Of his great predecessors, Chanel paid YSL the highest compliments. As much as she hated Cardin, and said so, and attacked Ungaro, Rabanne, Courrèges, Laroche and Patou's successive modelists, Michel Goma and Lagerfeld, she showed regard for Balmain and YSL, saying of Yves, "He'll go far. I know that he copies me, but that means he admires me and I like that. His designs look like mine, which proves he has taste." She said that, like her, Saint Laurent wanted to show a woman wearing his clothes to her advantage, not his, and commented, "That's rare among my *confrères* nowadays."

Yves easily gets sentimental when he thinks back over the fabulous hundred-odd years. Like Balenciaga and Balmain, he wishes he could continue haute couture. Not for his sake but for its own, because it is so terrible to see something so beautiful wither and die. "Since ready-to-wear makes it possible to maintain the bottomless pit of haute couture, I must continue," he says, while at the same time acknowledging that there is no longer any school for couture craftsmanship, that the only schools left are the couture designers' workshops. "As the individual couturiers disappear, there will be no more artisans. At this time, one can count the genuine couturiers on the fingers of one hand—perhaps one doesn't need the whole hand. There must be someone to transmit the craft. The moment there is no longer anyone to transmit it couture will disappear. You always want to exceed yourself in this business, which is inhuman and exhausting."

But why Paris?

He smiles and wonders if it has something to do with a collective climate, if it has to do with a special knack for giving luxury the dignity of taste, or if it has to do with women —that is, if it is a feminine predilection that sustains Paris, insofar as luxury is both coveted and made famous by women. "Or pure chance?" he wonders. "All I can say is that for some mysterious reason, fashion is made in Paris, and made by people coming from . . . well, anywhere."

15

FOLLOWING
INSTINCTS

*B*y 1970, Saint Laurent was so pared down to function and logic that it was impossible to go any further without self-destructing. He had wanted to freeze fashion with a basic wardrobe, to interiorize elegance to a kind of permanent chic; and, since the jarring May Events of 1968, he had begun to think of himself as merely the transmission gears between near-spontaneous street styles and their dissemination among aware young women, who wanted to show they were hip and were ready to challenge society.

To put on clothes had always meant to enhance one's appearance—physically and socially—which really meant that a garment's image was mostly in the eyes of its wearer, a bit in the eyes of the beholder and not at all in the dress itself. Yves could imagine a fashion that would lose its seasonal frenzy, a fashion where everyone would express personal preferences from a wealth of possibilities. But where was the designer in all this? And what was the collective climate?

The Parisians entered the uncertain seventies with apprehension. Some (Givenchy, Scherrer) wanted to retain their traditional role as creators of high-gloss wardrobes for an affluent and trend-setting clientele. Through discreet franchising and boutiques, they tried—often successfully—to amortize the huge cost of the creations that were their justification. Others (Cardin, Ungaro) moved with determination into ready-to-wear but had difficulty remaining aloof from "the street" and defining their own function and position in the scheme of things. Still others (Laroche, Lapidus) turned out the number of collections prescribed by the Chambre Syndicale only for the publicity it afforded, while concentrating their energies on the lucrative *produits griffés*, as Parisians call the ever-widening array of designer-labeled consumer goods.

Saint Laurent felt his way toward the future by trying to combine authentic high chic with a selective ready-to-wear, in which he tried to combine street inspirations with the wishes of increasingly independent women. His kind of fashion—the fashion that for the past century had come out of semiannual couture shows—was dying, he felt. The broadening of information and the rising standard of living had given all women the desire to be *à la mode*. Under the pressure of youth and revolution, the kind of fashion Yves had always worked in—the fashion that was *imposed*—was disappearing in favor of more varied inspirations and freer styles. Fashion was becoming repertoire. There was ethnic, tweedy, classic, Hollywood, nostalgia—and clothes were becoming casual. The concept of fashion was becoming the basic look. The fundamental change was that a T-shirt could be worn to the opera and sport suits could enhance a dinner table as easily as the driving range. The sixties might have been revolutionary, but in hindsight, the decade had had its own formalism, since being in and out of fashion had been a matter of skirt lengths and age groups. Perhaps the seventies would be more flexible, more versatile.

Of Saint Laurent's zeitgeist premonitions, the basic wardrobe was the first to win media attention. "Investment fashion," British *Vogue* said in 1974, "is really something that continues to give pleasure long after the novelty is over, and that means beautiful cloth, faultless cutting and making, and great discernment on the part of the designer and the buyers." A year later, Calvin Klein called his own high-priced low-keyed clothes investment dressing.

The decade certainly started out Saint Laurentian. The vogue for pants was his, as was the trend of knitwear with a lanky, hugging effect. He stayed away from the great Maxi debate by showing a spring collection in a range of lengths, from micromini to Maxi. "Length," he declared, "is no longer important. What is wonderful is the freedom to choose one's length." But with the fashion world undecided about the mini versus the Maxi, 1970 was a particularly difficult year for the fragmented garment industry, as everybody wondered whether the longer hemline was there to stay or whether it was a flash in the pan.

Paris, London, Rome and, more reluctantly, New York had voted for the Maxi, or ankle, length, and WWD publisher John Fairchild staked his reputation on the "longuette" with such fury that he created more resentment than acceptance among American women. Stores were intimidated. Many of them wanted to compromise between high fashion and sales and settled for just-below-the-knee hems. In September, they received the backing of the Italians, and for fall, Courrèges, the inventor of the mini, showed midi lengths. Not since Dior's New Look had the world been so caught up in fashion. Cover stories, talk shows and dinner conversations were devoted to the Maxi dictate and consumer revolts against what Gloria Steinem called those "Germanic, stick-and-carrot urgings" to fall in line. By the spring of 1971, however, hems fluctuated from mid-calf to knee level and ceased to be a point of controversy. Instead, Saint Laurent became a subject of contention.

But three weeks before the spring showings, Paris mourned the death of Chanel. Everybody attended the funeral at the Madeleine Church. Yves was pale and meditative, Balmain solemn and somber. They sat behind Marc Bohan, Guy Laroche, Michel Goma, Gérard Pipart, André Courrèges and Paco Rabanne, most of the Rothschilds, Luchino Visconti (Chanel had been a friend of the director's father), Salvador Dali, Serge Lifar, Jeanne Moreau, Lady Iya Adby and the famous hairdressers, Antoine, Guillaume and Alexandre. The only absentee was Pierre Cardin, who nevertheless sent someone to represent him.

Yves held his showing on the last day of Collection Week. His models came down the runway dressed in jackets with heavily padded shoulders over shortened, low-pleated skirts, artificial flowers at tightly draped hips, pulled sleeves, silver fox stoles, boxy coats, ankle straps and chunky wedge-soled shoes. As the girls clinked past the wide-eyed journalists and buyers, there were audible gasps, and when it was all over, faces were puzzled when they were not indignant. This was the 1940s all over again. The revival was roundly criticized as a poor-taste exercise in kitsch, an exercise that added up to a look variously described as raucous or harlotist.

Yves was stunned and hurt. When *WWD*'s Paris correspondent wanted to see him he told Gabrielle Busschaert he didn't want to see anybody. Why hadn't the press understood that his collection was a reaction against the turn fashion was taking?

The indignation *was* puzzling. What had convinced Fairchild to mount his crusade for the "longuette" was YSL's Citypants of a few seasons back, which Yves had said were the first step toward covering women's legs, and Visconti's *The Damned*, not so much for the film's Wagnerian plot line but for those slinky Nazi couture clothes Ingrid Thulin got to vamp around in. (Fairchild liked the clothes in the movie so much he arranged private screenings for Seventh Avenue designers and retailers.) Yves thought the Maxi looked awful, especially on older women, and that the only way out was toward a more tailored look.

Only years later could he talk about it. "The collection everybody called 'kitsch'—I hate that word—was a reaction against the 'longuette'—another word I hate; it isn't even French—the gypsies, all those long skirts and bangles on middle-aged women. So I did a collection as a kind of humorous protest, only everybody took it seriously. Large shoulders, high heels, black stockings—it was all too daring; lots of women left the show fuming. People thought it wasn't me, but it was; they don't know my reactions. I am quiet but inside there is an explosion. Only when I'm really fed up, but it happens. And that collection was one of my good reactions. It helped me find myself."

His first public announcement after the fiasco was that the upcoming couture collection would be his last. He would no longer exhibit a major haute couture collection to retailers and the press twice a year, but would concentrate on the ready-to-wear. To his private customers he would offer a pared-down, unpublicized couture collection, but the April and October ready-to-wear collections would be the only full-fledged shows. "What a relief," he sighed. "I always gave birth in pain. Now the agony will be only twice a year instead of four times."

The decision was not financially significant, since 80 percent of the revenue already came from rtw, but it was an indictment of haute couture's increasing dependency on hype. Were there no grand ladies anymore? Ten years earlier, made-to-measure customers had been haughty enough not to be put off by press reviews. Now there were fewer of them, and those that were still there seemed intimidated by the mass media, which, in any case, tended to blow up what was outlandish and headline-catching. "The press looks for one thing—gimmicks," Pierre said, "and unfortunately the private clients are influenced by the press." Yves was more irritated and more blunt: "Haute couture prices make haute couture clothes possible only for the sort of women no one wants to look like anymore." What neither of them said was that they were increasingly influenced by the fact that rtw could quickly carry new trends to the widest possible audience; indeed, that many of Yves's best recent ideas had already gone directly into his boutique collections.

The announcement nevertheless came as a surprise. Within a week, however, Cardin and Courrèges both hinted that they might actually follow suit.

Yves spent a fortnight in Italy. Visconti's *Death in Venice* made him read the original Thomas Mann novella and long for the enchanted and moody otherworldliness of Venice in 1911, if not identify with the character of Aschenbach, whose work, like Gustav Mahler's, is received with storms of abuse and whose image of Tadzio's rare, exquisite but unattainable beauty separates him from his art and from morality. Yves attended the Venice film festival, an event trying to find itself after flirting with far-left radicalism. Because Maoist dissidents believed prizes amounted to bourgeois elitism, the festival had gone noncompetitive and the 1971 edition was a crushing bore. But Yves stayed at the Hôtel des Bains and daydreamed about Venice at the time of Doucet and Paquin, Mahler and Mann. With a mixture of apprehension and exaltation, he learned that Visconti was going to make a film of *Remembrance of Things Past*, that negotiations with Nicole Stéphane, Proust's grandniece, had been going on for a few years.

By fall, Richard Salomon had convinced Yves and Pierre to continue in haute couture. Squibb Beech-Nut, Inc., as the conglomerate was presently called, and its Lanvin–Charles of the Ritz subsidiary insisted that YSL continue the made-to-measure collections for prestige reasons. More crassly, the New York headquarters felt that to give up haute couture might cause the influence of Yves—and Paris—to disintegrate. Yves and Pierre complied, but the order made them even more determined to become owners of Yves Saint Laurent, S.A. It didn't take long. On April 28, 1972, they signed the contract that, with the exception of the perfume division, bought out Squibb.

The couture collection Yves presented in January 1972 was an about-face, a return to classicism that the few journalists admitted to the show found remarkably reminiscent of Chanel. But if it failed to inspire dramatic headlines, it did start the cash registers ringing again. Yves was sure that consumers were coming down from a four-year high of revolutionary fervor. "I had a feeling of lassitude," he would say later. "The suit, that eminently bourgeois element of the feminine wardrobe, was back; hemlines were stabilized just above the knee. It was as if the young girls who had been everywhere—in movies, magazines, publicity—had fallen asleep and a young matron was taking her place. The new ideal was a woman who had kept her youthful slenderness yet was in full bloom. She was often the wife of a middle executive. She was a person with a sense of comfort, she was health-conscious, knew how to dress both for work and play. She was the perfect incarnation of society and felt totally at ease in it."

His summer look was a success, a combination of wide white gabardine pants with cutaway red and navy vests, worn with bright, rope-soled espadrilles. "All girls love a sailor suit," cooed *Vogue* as shops filled with sailor sweaters, anchor-print shirts, spotted and striped trousers and T-shirts with yachting motifs. Yves didn't particularly like the times, and welcomed the possibilities that the "Great Gatsby nostalgia" opened up for fashion.

For Parisians, 1972 was a year of return to calmer waters after the post-1968 upheavals, and Yves offered a spring fashion that was less rakish and more sober than any of his recent styles. "Try dressing like a lady," British *Vogue* proposed, saying that the greatest incentive to do so was YSL's long ribbed cardigans, bow-necked silk shirts and striped or spotted shirtwaisters. Reviewers said it was the first year that French rtw and couture met in the middle, indicating that the two might soon be unable to exist apart.

Yves's summer look was called blueprint Saint Laurent. To make everybody sparkle after dark, he experimented with the synthetic fabric Lurex, and for winter, came out with an extralong cabled cardigan with V neck and cuffs ruffed with fur. For the first time, he tried designing for the home—everything from bed linens, towels and blankets to wallpaper—saying he wanted to relate to "today's total environment."

Increasingly, he felt like an overcautious, if not very wise, magus, or like that most deadening of concepts, a *sensible* designer. He heard himself say he believed in investment clothes, in ready-to-wear and in flights of fantasy in couture. The basic wardrobe, he insisted, remained the "masculine" jacket-and-pants combination.

Was it a Freudian slip when he told one interviewer that a woman's worry wasn't so much to change but to find herself? "To find herself seems to me to be more interesting than to disguise herself as this or that, as the media keep telling her to do," he told *GAP*. "For designers—at least for me—the problem is to get to the point where you can make clothes that both make profits and make economic sense to the buyer. The way fabrics and labor are going up forces you to reduce the number of items and to limit as much as possible the choice of fabrics. Logic, too, compels you to do that. Why change the pattern of a trench coat or a pea jacket if you feel you've got it absolutely right?" When he was asked how he knew that he had a garment absolutely right, he said, "When I see it live in the street, on dozens of women of different size and different looks, and when I no longer have an urge to move a pocket from where it is or to change the size of a lapel."

Freudian slip or not, he was looking for himself and feeling totally out of it. "I had the impression I was choking, that I was out of fashion—not what I was doing, but I myself," he was to remember. A symptom, perhaps, was that he loved *Ludwig II*, the movie Visconti directed and his friend Helmut Berger starred in as the homosexual king of Bavaria who built mad medieval castles and was the patron of Richard Wagner.

His fashion certainly wasn't out of touch. He provided the freshest touch of the 1973 summer look. Reacting to swirling capes over crushed riding boots and back-flaring chemise coats, he came out with a perfectly tailored white linen jacket, worn over a multicolored print silk dress with pleated skirt. His shapes for after dark became more fluid and more sophisticated, and he made a big effort to bring back the suit in his haute couture, continuing what was becoming a kind of trademark. He would rather look to the beauty of the past, he said, than to the uncertainty of the future, and in early 1975, he intuitively grasped an idea that was to give him his greatest personal triumph. While he was in Marrakesh, he realized, at first only dimly, that the yearning for romanticism that he and other people experienced didn't have to find its satisfaction in the past, that nostalgia could also be found in exotic inspiration, in faraway lands.

The mood was changing. People wanted to look rich again, although rather nonchalantly so. For fall 1975, Yves presented a collection that was suave and terribly adult. The daytime clothes were in dark, muted colors, the evening wear had occasional glitter, but the overall silhouette was long and sleek and meant to be worn with extraordinary grace.

The crisis that sent him to the American Hospital in Neuilly was here, in his approaching fortieth birthday and in the vertigo of feeling at a dead end, to be terribly adult, terribly sophisticated, but standing still. To be forty, a millionaire, world-famous and at the peak of his profession meant nothing if he were in a cul-de-sac, if he had refined his craft to the limit, if he felt bored with its simplicity and guilty because he knew that all those attempts to make fashion useful and universal were hopeless. The dead end was a certain purity; a certain perfection that was rationalized, clever and terribly mature and cultivated, but in which all flight of fantasy was repressed. Was he a latter-day Ludwig of Bavaria, building self-glorifying castles belonging to another age? Was he, like Proust's Princess de Guermantes, so vain that he only repeated what he knew would throw his grace and wit into greater prominence?

To be a designer meant to address the senses and to go on from there. To advance was to impose new forms and new patterns, but social pressures imposed a code of clothing that constituted the current fashion. New forms didn't obey any logic of taste, any precepts of harmony or laws of contrast and complementariness. New forms didn't follow rules, they set them; yet to be successful, such rules had to please the individual woman's temperament and character and try to tell her something. Whatever fashion was, it was only adopted if it rang the right bells of recognition and anticipation in people's unconscious. The designer made his collection with these new impulses and thereby invented the next code of clothing. The elbow room was even narrower than he had imagined.

Partially sketched in the psychiatric clinic of the American Hospital, the fantasy look was a burst of renewal, a sudden release from guile and inhibition. For the first time, he was able to set it all down, at once and definitively, in drawings that had the assurance of dreams and the affection of his inner self. At once and definitively, he was free from the disappointments and corruptions of adulthood. Egotistically, he plunged into the world he loved—the world of Vermeer, Delacroix, Ingres, La Tour and Rembrandt, of his heroines Madame Bovary and Catherine of Russia, of *Tosca*, Bellini and Verdi—sketching the beguiling, all-purpose *paisana* princess image as if it were the swan song of fashion.

The Cossack-gypsy-Indian-Slavo-Circassian-Anatolian look was from an Asia of the mind. Yves's Orient was a mythical one, a vast picture book of springtime covering Mongolia with Tartarian roses, of *The Firebird* and Genghis Khan and of caravans of camels crossing the Pamirs. His Asia was a China full of scents and dreams, Nizhni Novgorod under the snow, the morning sun touching the mosque at Samarkand, Manchurian warlords and Afghan shepherds, temples and teahouses, the Far East of Maugham and Malraux, of *Lord Jim* and *Madame Butterfly*. "Fabulous boyards, grandiose samurais, wild Mongols, a whole epic poem of golden brocades, coarse-grained silks and grosgrains that are sharp-edged as scimitars," he would write in the book he started as postoperative therapy and self-exploration.

He tried it out in ready-to-wear, presenting full dirndl skirts cinched at the waist and soft, Russian peasant blouses with billowy sleeves and braid-edged jackets at the April showing (where Kenzo was the only other designer to score). Yves's fun peasants wore boots and babushkas, and over their long, full skirts and big sleeved blouses they slung big, flowered scarves or coats with toggles. At night, the skirts were hiked to show petticoats. The wedding-party finale had the audience rising to its feet, and *The New York Times*'s Bernardine Morris wrote that it was the intensity of his approach that gave his collection such impact. She predicted that the folklore of YSL and Kenzo would be the most widely copied novelties in the coming months.

Yves realized he needed the fully glory of haute couture to really pull it all off. Besides the theatrical abandon and deliberate assertion that made-to-measure afforded, he needed the luxurious and tactile qualities of satin, gold and silver lamé, velvet, taffeta, chiffon, faille and moiré. He needed tasseled cords, floral scarves, satin ribbons, hammered gold jewelry and passementerie. He needed turbans, babushkas and fezes. And he needed the workmanship that just wasn't in ready-to-wear. Once the drawings were finished, he repaired, exhausted, to the hospital, only to do a lot of the sketches over again. Anne-Marie Muñoz and the workrooms began putting together the parade that would be 106 outfits long. It was the costliest collection ever. When all the bills were added up, the tab was a half-million dollars.

His nerves were shattered, but he couldn't stay away from avenue Marceau. His doctors agreed to let him out in the afternoon, he confided to *Le Point*'s Barbara Schwamm. Heavily sedated, he worked until it was time to be taken back to Neuilly.

Mounia Orhozemane was a pale Nefertiti who, like himself, came from North Africa. She became his new inspiration. "Mounia possesses that innate black elegance; with her, I can transform an entire collection," he said, calling her one of those rare models who understood clothes. "It's all in her spirit, her movement. It comes from within, this silent communication, and for me, that's vital." Against doctors' orders, he left the hospital during the last week before the show and was on medication the day of the unveiling. Shattering tradition, Pierre and he decided not to show this couture collection in the salons at avenue Marceau but instead to rent the ballroom in the big new Hôtel Intercontinental.

Collection Day was July 28—four days before Yves's fortieth birthday. *France Dimanche* had been given a sneak glimpse and the previous Sunday had come out with a drawing by YSL and a teaser headline: LADIES, YOU WILL BE VERY FEMININE. A thousand people crammed the ballroom.

During the first half-hour of the show, the spectators were hushed, as if aware that they were in the presence of powerful ideas. The daytime clothes came down the runway to the sobbing strains of Puccini's *Tosca*, in an incendiary eruption of color and sumptuous, devastating forms. Mounia and the other models glided along in black blouses, bouffant skirts, velvet bodices and huge, all-enveloping coats topped with turbans, mink toques, knit caps and fezes, feathered and buttoned, with boots, boots, boots. During the second half, when the evening clothes came onstage and exploded in an extravagant assertion of coruscating color and jubilant femininity, the applause was continuous as it was for the magic of his theatrical ballgowns, billowing taffeta skirts, soft petticoats, wasp waistlines and gigantic puffed sleeves in brilliant hues of orange, fuchsia, emerald, violet and tangerine, and the Arabian Nights accessories in the form of gold turbans, lamé shawls and feathered headdresses.

At the end, some of the usually unflappable fashion pros had tears in their eyes. *Vogue* editor-in-chief Grace Mirabella felt history was being made. "I don't think any of us will see a presentation like that again," she said. "It's been a long time since we've had that sense of excitement about clothes. In fact, I'm not sure I've ever seen it."

When they rushed to the dressing room where Yves was waiting with his mother, he didn't have much to say. "Yesterday, I was afraid. I saw all the dresses, all the color, and I thought it was too much." He mentioned Vermeer's painting *Young Lady Adorning Herself with a Pearl Necklace*, saying that her turban, black bodice, pale rose skirt and Vermeer blue sleeves had provided the springboard for it all, and said that his heroines from the novels, the operas, the paintings were all in the clothes. "It was my heart. Everything I love I gave to this collection."

Someone couldn't help asking if his opulent array wasn't impractical. "Why should haute couture be practical?" was the only answer he could give. "That's for ready-to-wear. This is a dream, a spectacle." Those who cornered Bergé in the corridor were told that Yves had resurrected the frontier between rtw and couture. "For the last fifteen years or so, that frontier has ceased to exist," Pierre said.

The next day was Thursday, and *The New York Times* called the collection "revolutionary." The front-page dispatch from Bernardine Morris said, "It is as stunning in its impact as the collection Christian Dior showed in 1947, the one that came to be known as the New Look and affected the way women dressed everywhere." On Friday, however, the *Times* retreated somewhat by printing a series of sober reaction from American fashion purveyors and designers. Said Geraldine Stutz, president of Henri Bendel, "It will offer a marvelous way for women to look, but not the only way. It's another alternative." Others agreed that the fantasy peasant look would enhance, rather than replace, existing wardrobes. Oscar de la Renta said YSL was much more talented than Dior had been, "but we don't get carried away that way anymore." Geoffrey Beene called the collection "a great exercise in self-indulgence far beyond the realm of reality," and Halston said his reaction was "plain disappointment."

The Parisian reaction was also subdued. *Le Figaro*'s Viviane Graymour intimated that the collection was folklore and theater but not fashion, and *Le Monde*'s Nathalie Mont-Servan came out with a review that was more description than critique, which made *Time* wonder in a follow-up piece whether the raves of *The New York Times* and *Women's Wear Daily* didn't "reflect the yearning of the hard-pressed U.S. fashion industry for a replay of the late Christian Dior's New Look, the style that so profitably transfigured women and their wardrobes." By Saturday, however, the Rive Gauche store on Madison Avenue was mobbed as women scurried to snap up the toned-down rtw peasantries shown in Paris in April. "We're getting fantastic phone calls from customers asking us to hold things for them," manager Elvira Connery told the *Times*, which stayed on top of the story. Most popular items: the braid-edged gray flannel jacket selling for $470, the flowered challis skirt ($195) and the print shirt ($130).

Sunday was Yves's birthday, and he passed the milestone with yawning equanimity. Except for a small celebration—Pierre gave him a cake with four candles—he slept through most of the day.

The fantasy look didn't repeat the Dior coup. Perhaps because of a preference for durable jeans and the unstructured soft look, perhaps because of a faltering economy, or the feminist mood to defy dictates, women resisted the change—which didn't mean that the rtw versions that went on sale the same week in 111 YSL boutiques didn't sell as fast as at 855 Madison Avenue. By year's end, knockoffs were appearing in shopping centers and discount stores, again making Yves the most adapted, if not copied, designer.

It fell to Pierre Schneider, who twenty years earlier had

found Yves to be "a well-behaved, tremendously overgrown schoolboy sleepwalking his way through a world of grown-ups," to sort out the meaning of Saint Laurent's romantic burst. In an egalitarian age of comfort and convenience, wrote the art critic in *Vogue*, haute couture is not a vestige of the age of aristocracy that ought to have been discarded with royalty, but a reminder of the sacred. Insofar as it is totalitarian regimes that put their citizens in uniforms and ruthlessly erase ethnic and regional differences, haute couture is a hymn to democracy, the body mask of an industrialized society that created both denim and Poiret. "Haute couture is not better than ordinary garments: it is *other*. It is to the latter what the sacred is to the profane."

Yves was to agree with that assessment, saying that what he had reacted to was the moment when everybody was pronouncing haute couture dead. "My instinct was to go against the prevailing attitudes," he was to say three years later, adding that the fantasy look was so jarring that it gave a whole new vitality to couture. "I didn't calculate that effect in advance; I simply followed my instinct."

16

ART
AND
HOME

*F*riends call Yves Saint Laurent an artist and a dreamer, and his private world is indeed a reflection of art as transcendence, imagination and *raison d'être*. He has a graceful, persistent familiarity with all kinds of arts, and at home, he and Pierre live on separate floors cluttered with eclectic modernism, whimsical mementos and priceless possessions. At home, Yves's tight sentences seem to lose their formality and his vocal cords to relax enough to lower his voice toward the register of a mellifluous baritone.

The theater is the *grand amour*, his first love, and, if things were not what they are, the natural next metamorphosis. The four-collections-a-year grindstone prevents him from experiencing the artist's sense of "separateness" that, in his more private moments, he firmly believes in. Not being able to do more in the theater than he has is a nagging regret. "I'm too busy for that now because I can't just design the costumes. I must get involved with every detail, everything.

I cannot give part of myself, only all to a project." Yet giving part of himself is all he can do. At idle moments, he daydreams about leaving fashion and beginning a new romance with the theater.

Great couturiers have rarely been successful in creating theatrical costumes—Paul Poiret was the exception—but over the years, Yves's contributions to stage design have not been inconsiderable. He likes to quote Poiret, who said of a coat he created for the actress Réjane that it contained "all the sadness of the denouement of a love interest, all the bitterness of the fourth act" and that in seeing it, "the audience has a foreboding of the play's ending." Saint Laurent's involvement with the stage began with his friendship with Roland Petit and Zizi Jeanmaire and has passed through Cocteau revivals to costumes for Edward Albee's *A Delicate Balance* and Colin Higgins's *Harold and Maude*, the Hollywood movie that became a long-running stage play in Paris. In 1974, he exhibited a hundred gouaches of ballet costumes and stage models of sets created over the past decade at the Proscenium gallery in rue de Seine—*Cyrano de Bergerac* for the Petits, *Notre Dame de Paris* for the Opéra and *The Marriage of Figaro* for Jean-Louis Barrault, among others.

As a stage designer, he is no revolutionary. His 1966 designs for the revival of Cocteau's *Les Monstres sacrés*, starring Arletty and Yves Vincent, cleverly modernized the costumes but copied the original 1940 sets by Christian Bérard. The Saint Laurent style, as *France Soir* said in reviewing the Proscenium exhibition, has its origins in Léon Bakst and Bérard, "with a touch of the *fantastique* of Erté, the magician of the Casino de Paris revues of the 1930s." Yet his interests are not confined to the well-produced and well-acted *théâtre de boulevard* but extend to the experimental *théâtre de recherche* that largely grew out of the 1960s counterculture, and to the work of such companies and dramatists as Jerzy Grotowski's Polish Laboratory Theater, Fernando Arrabal and, most of all, the Living Theater. After seeing the Living's production of *Antigone* and its experiments with Antonin Artaud during the American troupe's self-imposed European exile, he said he would love to live and travel with the communal troupe to "work out visual ways of expressing

194   o   *Living for Design*

moral ideas." Now, he finds it exciting that eighty-eight-year-old Erté may design the costumes for a 1980 production of *Der Rosenkavalier* and that there's a new ballet for Roland Petit that Erté may do.

The walls of the library at 55 rue de Babylone are full of photographs and mementos of artists and actors, ballet dancers and directors. "These are the people I admire," Yves says, "artists like Nureyev, Bakst, Plisetskaya, Diaghilev." He is not astonished that several Hollywood producers are in a dead heat to come out with a film about Nijinsky and the Ballet Russe. "It was a phenomenal era," he says, and smiles, "and they were all there." Picasso and Bakst and Matisse were doing sets for Diaghilev, Erik Satie and Stravinsky were writing the music, Cocteau the book. Picasso loved being a member of the Russian Ballet; he married one of the dancers, Olga Koklova. The 1917 ballet *Parade* was the company's most obvious modernist manifesto. Picasso created a cubist decor and cubist constructions as costumes for two of the dancers, contemporary motifs and events—Charlie Chaplin, the sinking of the *Titanic*—were suggested in the mime, while Erik Satie's tinkly score featured simulated sounds of a typewriter and a foghorn. For *Oedipus Rex,* Cocteau translated for Stravinsky, Picasso did the costumes, Diaghilev directed and Jeanne Lanvin's daughter picked up the tab.

The 1925 Exposition des Arts Décoratifs was the one event that Yves considers the crucible of it all and perhaps the high point of this century's tumultuous art. "It's not until '25 that the look we think of as typical twenties was achieved," he says, "and the exhibition gave its name to the style." He can describe the exhibition as if he had been there. Abstract design had replaced the exuberance of Art Nouveau, and there was not a curve in sight; the buildings were rectangular and the interiors austere. The art deco style, which was called modernist and functional, was defined as including Erté on the one hand and Le Corbusier's "architectural nudism" on the other. It was inspired by cubism, Bauhaus and Aztec art, and the designs were often intended for mass production, as the aim was to combine art and industry. Enormous fountains of glass played among life-sized cubist dolls, and music washed down from four huge towers. Instead of the dummies usually used for fashion exhibitions, André Vigneau had made formalized wax or composition figures, Modiglianis with sculptured hair. The lines of Emile-Jacques Ruhlmann's furniture, of Sue and Mare's interiors, or René Lalique's all-glass dining room or the quiet elegance of André Groult's designs were carried out in rare woods, covered with costly shagreen or executed in crystals. Other objects were in plastics and "ferroconcrete." The lamps, which had lost their metal curves and flounced shades, were by Giacometti. Curtains hung straight and were of hand-woven fabrics and brocades designed by Dufy and Charles Martin. Sonia Delaunay worked with Jacques Heim to apply cubism to clothes. Poiret walked through it all, saying it could have been so much better. At the Théâtre des Champs-Elysées, Josephine Baker and the Revue Nègre were the smash hit. Serge Lifar danced *Zephyr et Flore* in sets by Braque; Stravinsky put on his one-act ballet, *Le Chant du rossignol,* in sets by Matisse; economist Maynard Keynes staggered the intellectual world by marrying Diaghilev's star ballerina Lydia Lopokova. Ina Claire was the first actress to dress natural in her movies, in clothes signed *Chanel;* Vionnet was opening her new premises on avenue Matignon, and on Montparnasse the surrealists held their first exhibition and noisily celebrated their latest convert, Cocteau.

In many ways, Cocteau is Yves's ideal of an artist, not so much for the elegant thumb print he left on poetry, theater, illustration, novels and filmmaking, but because he was the jack-of-all-trades and the tightrope walker who could frolic from one art form to another while being the favorite of gossip writers and magazine editors. Cocteau could introduce others to the avant-garde because he was always three or four steps ahead (he didn't long remain a card-carrying surrealist). He believed in renewal, in surprise, in danger, liberty and the value of beauty for its own sake. Appropriately, a Modigliani drawing, willed to Yves by Cocteau, dominates one wall of the library, opposite works by Bérard, Max Ernst and Jean-Louis Forain, who was Proust's friend.

Rue de Babylone is one of those long, faceless streets that

guard their secrets behind nineteenth-century *portes co-chères* and across inner courtyards. It is an arrow-straight street that runs from the edge of Saint-Germain-des-Prés past the aging Bon Marché department store, the Sisters of Saint Vincent de Paul convent and the Babylone police barracks to the depth of the seventh arrondissement rectitude and opulence. The garden apartment at number 55 is a few stately chestnut trees from La Pagode, the venerable *arts et essai* movie house with its Mandarin forecourt and tradition of avant-garde playbills that stretches back to the unruly surrealists.

The two-story garden apartment is past a nondescript building and a cemented courtyard and comes as a stunning surprise. It is a country place, complete with inner garden and beautiful lawn stretching to the back wall of a convent in rue Oudinot. "It represents the countryside and vacation-time there is never time for," says Yves.

American fan magazines like to say that Jean-Michel Frank designed the place for a great American lady who never got to live there, her fortune having declined dramatically on Wall Street in 1929. In reality, Frank created the duplex apartment for Marie Cuttoli, a *pied noir* of persuasive charm and great wealth who needed an appropriate setting for her extraordinary collection of art. The wife of a senator from Algeria, Madame Cuttoli had discovered North African handicraft in eastern Algeria, set up an embroidery workshop and, guided by the young painter Jean Lurçat, created a sensation at the 1925 Exposition des Arts Décoratifs with very modern, abstract tapestries. With Lurçat as her adviser, she persuaded Braque, Léger, Miró and Picasso to let her make tapestries for some of their canvases. Her friend Helena Rubinstein thought she was Picasso's mistress because she helped him in countless ways (and almost got him to do a portrait of the makeup millionairess), but Madame Cuttoli said she simply liked having artists indebted to her.

For Yves and Pierre, it was love at first sight when they bought the apartment in 1971, three years before Madame Cuttoli died at the age of ninety-four. The renovation of the six-hundred-square-meter (5,600 square feet) apartment was done with reverence. There are still Jean-Michel Frank touches—copper-edged window frames and doorknobs and radiator covers in molded metal with linear grilles—yet the apartment is not a museum but a lived-in oasis.

From the threshold, life is filtered, softened. Impassive butler, lacquered walls and the mixture of whimsical pieces, personal bibelots, art deco furniture and antiques give the visitor the impression of both order and voluptuousness, of a passion for fine workmanship, detail and the relationship of things. The dining room is cool, severe and functional in whites with China-blue accents of seventeenth-century vases. When Yves gives dinner parties, he likes to eat at a round table where he can see everyone he is talking to and have a feeling of closeness. A Lalique glass balustrade leads to Yves's favorite room, freesia white and colored by books, plants, sculptures and drawings. "This shows the other side of my nature and is the room I prefer in the house," he says, "the room where I am the most comfortable and spend most of my time."

He says he needs the apartment as a refuge, as a place to be alone. "I need freedom; I can no longer allow myself to be constantly assaulted. Too many people solicit me."

François-Xavier Lalanne, his sculptor friend, has added to the decor in stages, first providing a flock of mock sheep that stand around the one modern area—the all-white living room. White slipcovers, sheer white curtains, books, records, an earth-brown 1930s carpet and a view of Lalanne's dove chairs on the terrace and the lawn stretching to the convent wall give an overall impression of planned peace. The chromium-framed wood panelings add a hint of a great transatlantic luxury liner. One corner is strewn with lamé pillows and presided over by a K'ang Hsi goddess. There are four new, large orientalist canvases and a new art deco armchair in taupe leather with Nile-green legs carved like ibises. "You know in France we don't have the same passion as in America for harmonizing," he told *Architectural Digest* when the glossy Los Angeles magazine made the rue de Babylone residence part of its Celebrity Homes series. "Here is the best and the worst. Life itself."

Life is an affectionate private world. A Senufo totem

perches in front of a five-panel pastel by Burne-Jones next to a Corbusier console, Ballet Russe frivolities, crystal obelisk and books fighting for space. The combination of sensuous art nouveau floral motifs and the geometry of the cubist patterns contrasts with the warm opulence of soft paisleys and animal skins covering the furniture. The love of art is everywhere: in the great wooden sculpture of a bird by Brancusi, Ruhlmann's piano and table, a cobra lamp by Edgar Brandt illuminating a Lalanne mirror, an Assyrian statue and 1930s metal vases on either side of the chimney by Jean Dunand. A prancing, nude Josephine Baker shares walls with paintings in dark, rich colors—exotic scenes set in Arabia, decadent scenes of ancient Rome. There is also an original photo of a Harlem ghetto wedding by Martine Barrat, with whom he has stayed friends since she did the documentary on him. One wall is dominated by a huge Ivory Coast sculpture of a bird ("It was the first thing I bought when I had money. It's a hundred and fifty years old and on very humid days smells very bad").

"I like the twenties and the thirties because they represent the last days of the great artisans," he says, mentioning that Dunand designed the winged horses on Pont Alexandre III before becoming the chief stylist of art deco and designing, among other things, Vionnet's salon.

Visitors have described the atmosphere as one of exquisite fin de siècle refinement and decadent luxury but without the heavy, cushioned upholstery or lugubrious drapery of real Victorian interiors, and Yves will readily admit that Proust, Huysmans, Redon and other turn-of-the-century artists would feel comfortable here. Proust has remained not so much the favorite as the necessary writer. Yves can quote from many parts of *Remembrance of Things Past*, which is perhaps the longest narrative in existence, and feels that the sixteen-volume work is a unique expanding autobiography, a masterpiece of sensibility and an epic of a single person's mind. "I am a passionate, fanatical admirer of Proust," he says. "Most of all I would like to have lived in the world of Proust."

Before Proust immured himself in neurasthenic seclusion and spent the last fifteen years of his life writing in a room lined with soundproof cork, he was a social climber captivated by the aristocracy. If there is one great difference between Proust's Paris and today's, it is that there is no longer a Count Robert de Montesquiou-Fezenac, the model for both Proust's sinister Charlus and J. K. Huysman's delirious pervert Des Esseintes in *À Rebours;* no Countess de Chevigné or Princess Mathilde, Napoleon III's sister, at whose feet Proust literally knelt. Today even rich women work, if for no other reason than to gratify their egos, and, says Yves, women who set style really no longer exist. But it is not Proust's fascination with high society and dissolving nobility that makes Yves say he would like to have lived in Proust's world. It is Proust's intuition that all illusion must be extinguished before a work of art can be created. *Remembrance of Things Past* is not a confession; it is by modifying his inner feelings and thoughts that Proust made them into art. The most vivid insights of *Remembrance of Things Past* are not wisdom but chance sensations—the famous "madeleine" cake dipped in a cup of tea, the look of three old trees, the tinkling of a spoon against a plate—and the search for reality that dominates the end and remains with the reader long after the last volume has been put down. "In the last volume, *The Past Recaptured,* Proust finds only a shadow of what he once knew." Yves feels Proust regarded time as a destructive, not as a creative, force.

The leatherbound Pléiade edition is in the library—minus the volume Yves is currently reading in his cluttered bedroom. Here, above the headboard of the austere double bed is his personal collection of souvenirs—Japanese prints, thumb-tacked postcards of six-armed shivas and a necklace of rectangular, almost Aztec proportions. On the nightstand, next to a sculpture of a rearing cobra and a metal lamp that might have been at the 1925 exhibition, stand crayons in a blue mug on trop of a sketch pad, ready perhaps for jotting down nocturnal inspirations. Also on the night table is the manuscript of the book he says he may not finish unless, like Proust, he is forced by illness to spend most of his time in one room.

The Ruhlmann baby grand in the music room is badly in need of tuning—when Anthony Burgess visited and played part of Wagner's *Liebestod* on it, he said it sounded as if Isolde were made of tin foil. But Yves loves music, from pop to *Tosca,* Wagner to Nino Rota. He religiously selects all the music for the collection shows and would like to call himself a habitué of the Salzburg festival, but time, again, prevents him from making more than sporadic visits to the festival at Mozart's birthplace.

Food doesn't interest him—friends say he could subsist on boiled rice—but like most people from the Mediterranean basin, he goes home for lunch. Usually he eats alone, in a tranquil moment away from the bustle of avenue Marceau. His only bad habit, he says, is having breakfast in bed. "I never take naps in the afternoon or work in bed. But I love going to sleep at night. It's comforting. Sleep is also a way of recharging your batteries and I really need eight hours." To be sure he gets the eight hours, he takes a sleeping aid prescribed by his doctor. Before a collection, he doubles the dose.

The villa in Marrakesh is the retreat where he tries to spend as much time as possible. Called Es Saada la Zaria (Arabic for "the house of happiness in serenity"), the two-story house is hidden behind a high wall, and Yves and Pierre have decorated it in a "curious" (Yves's word) half-Moorish, half–art deco style and furnished it in dazzling white and beige. Instead of a pool, it has a water basin where reeds of papyrus sway in the evening breeze. He is attracted to Islamic culture, he says, to exotic faces and sunlit civilizations, and when he talks about North Africa, he likes to remind you that he was born at the ocean's edge.

"Marrakesh is a magic city," he says. "It's a city of the desert. The Moroccans are kind and amiable people." In 1970, he did the costumes for Euripides' *The Bacchae* for the students at the University of Tangier. It was in Marrakesh that, six years later, he began sketching the fantasy look. "For the first time, I did my drawings in color," he remembers. "The light there is exceptional. It was the first time I expressed myself as a painter."

He paid for that burst of creativity, returning to Paris to enter the American Hospital in Neuilly, and there are times when he loathes art and the hold it has on him. With Nietzsche and Malraux, he believes art is Promethean, that creativity is a struggle, that the artist isn't so much the sum total of his past, as Freudians like to believe, as the end result of combat and challenge. Children are often artistic, but they are not artists. Why? Because their gift controls them, not they their gift, whereas the great painters of history were locked in mortal combat with their own talent and reached perfection by challenging the works of those who preceded them. The difference between El Greco's early drawings and the splendors of his maturity is not perfection, it is that in the interim, he measured himself against the Venetian masters.

Yves likes to paint when there are no collections to do. "It's a nice solitary occupation," he says modestly. His work is representational, figures not so much in landscapes as in settings. Here it is costumed men and women executed in primary colors and angular lines that remind one of those marvelous 1920s *Vogue* covers by George Lepape and Edouard Benito. There it is a woman in full-length profile in sienna against a white background. There it is more theatrical—four elongated men in browns, whites and blacks, with masks and tricornered hats and, between them, a small, turbaned character.

Color means everything, but Saint Laurent distinguishes between the colors he uses in fashion, in interior decorating and in his private paintings. The Chinese reds and khaki greens of the Opium palette are, like the fuchsia, sapphire and disco-dazzling sequins that followed them in his collections, as perishable as the whites, reds and emerald greens they replaced. Interior decorating reminds him of Monet's water lilies painted at different hours of the day. Certain rooms are lovely at dawn or at dusk, in candlelight, overcrowded or virtually without furniture, and he prefers pale shades that match skin color with touches of eye-popping brilliance. There are timeless colors for dressing—beige and navy blue—and in interior decorating, the golden rule of taste is to know when to stop.

Fashion is, of course, a minor art, he says. Fashion combines the manual skills and perceptions of the artisan with a flair for fetishist objects, and it tends to confuse the beautiful with the useful. "Also, fashion is so perishable," he sighs, adding that so, perhaps, is the performance of a violinist or an actor or a dancer; never quite the same two nights in a row. He may be venerated at avenue Marceau, but in private, he has no delusions about the comparative lowliness of fashion designing in the ranks of the arts. The word *genius*, so often attached to him, is an embarrassment.

"To make fashion on schedule doesn't amuse me," he admits. "All those dresses that die in one year and all those I have to make. It's both graveyard and womb, charnel house and matrix. I feel torn between life and death, between past and future. Each time I must challenge everything, but I can never allow myself to be wrong. You can't allow yourself the luxury of being right every three or four years. You must be 'plugged in' constantly. You are asked to 'feel' what is happening, what *will* happen and to translate that. I've made enough of a noose here to hang myself. I'd love to do fashion when I feel like it, but I'm tied hand and foot to my commercial empire."

So he dreams. While ten thousand persons labor in his name, and the number of articles produced and consumed each year approaches the half-billion mark, he dreams about the theater, about spellbinding catharsis and avant-garde stagecraft, and about travels, about India and the Caribbean he has never seen. And he dreams about an era when people would have time for intricate social dealings and complex human relationships, an era in which the Duchess of Guermantes and the Baron de Charlus could discuss mundane trifles while watching a passing Tadzio under his straw hat and covertly and languidly exploring the inner maze of each other's sensibilities.

Or he has himself driven to avenue Marceau, sitting up front next to the chauffeur, and, together with his collaborators and models, locks himself into his studio and, with armfuls of scintillating fabrics, drapes and shapes an already certain personal future. Others call it work. For him, it is mortal combat with what was and what may be.

17

MAKING
US
TICK

*A*lthough Saint Laurent frequently loses money on designer pieces that sell for as much as $10,000, it is in the very special universe of haute couture that he expresses himself with the least restraint. Today he is rich and famous and living on top of the world of fashion, as not too many years ago Chanel and Dior were looked to for divine guidance.

Like Chanel, Yves feels that charm is a gift, a form of grace that is almost hereditary, and he wonders if Dior wasn't right when he said women don't know how to dress until they are thirty. Fashion is never reasonable. Both Plato and Thomas More thought citizens of the ideal state should all dress alike, in a togalike garment of plain, undecorated and durable cloth, and both admitted that if left to themselves, humans would invent clothes to disguise their egos and to underline the distinctions of sex, breeding and wealth. The annals of fashion are not a chronicle of common sense, but the history of power-consciousness and, yes, of beauty. Clothes are a disguise intended to give others an image of ourselves, to show ourselves in precisely the way we want to be seen. And our choice of clothes is profoundly revealing; the way most of us dress allows others to understand many facets of our character, psyche, beliefs and attitudes toward life.

But this choice is never completely individual. Society also plays a role. Cultures and times have always imposed certain codes of dress that reflected the degree of development, relations with neighboring people, social structure and politics of the given region and period. We have come a long way already, despite the contradictions of our times. Clothes are no longer a blatant sign of social inequality; the uniform has lost some of its fetishist character; sexual taboos no longer weigh too heavily on our dress habits—which doesn't mean that we have reached the millennium when the ideal mix of physical comfort, social usefulness and personal fantasy is no longer a problem. Clothes still have two basic and apparently contradictory functions—permanence and evolution. In buying clothes, a modern person tries to express both, to be "in" with current styles but also to show a little distance from the latest modes and fashion magazine photographs. Accessories-for-effect—funny, oddball hats, gloves, shoes, and junk jewelry intended to play to the big crowds at the shows—get picked up by the consumer, but weeded out for real dressing.

It is within a given code of conventions that individuals are daring and innovative enough to come up with something new. The best of the new ideas have a tendency to be adopted by others and to end up becoming the next set of conventions. In 1979, YSL's shirts of a few seasons back and his jackets "that work with everything" became the items women bought; his very narrow pants and shoulder pads the things women backed away from. Fashion is created by a gentle and persistent tickling of society's ribs and by offering choices. What all women want is options that are flattering and wearable. What is best is what *works* best.

It is society that decides what a beautiful woman looks like. The Renaissance admired a woman for the whiteness of her skin, and elegant women took great care not to expose their faces and hands to the sun, whereas modern westerners, especially in northern climes, go to extraordinary lengths to acquire an off-season tan. The nineteenth century admired a certain feminine fullness—still appreciated in Arab countries—whereas slimness, if not outright emaciation, is the modern western ideal. North American males prefer generous bosoms; Frenchmen generally have a preference for small breasts. There is always a great diversity in human anatomy, and beauty, it seems, is always rare. The ideal of feminine beauty is rarely the most common type of womanhood in a given place or time but some abstraction of nature, sometimes the traits of a celebrity of the time. The women who look like the ideal profit from this resemblance, and those who don't must try to add or subtract kilos, platform shoes or sandals, and, if nothing helps, simply deny the existence of current fashions.

Saint Laurent is convinced that the designer who is modern and meaningful to a majority of his contemporaries is the designer who can reconcile permanence and evolution, that is, the designer who, within the parameters of what is considered socially acceptable and even chic, can invent novelties that end up becoming the next parameters. He can never stand still. If, for one reason or another, the majority of women, or at least an important number of them, get tired of a trend that doesn't evolve fast enough, they will invent their own novelties, turn to "the street." As he has said, a designer can never be too far-out. Fashion is both excess and second nature, and the designer must stay ahead of the accidents of evolution.

Yves's private, inner self is not optimistic. He has a keen sense of living in a dying age. We are witnessing radical changes, he believes, in the decadence of social strata. The end of an era is not Wagnerian but Proustian, a sensation of shifting sands and geological transformations. In the face of it, he has chosen to look backward, toward the 1920s, and 1930s, which, he says, continue to vibrate in all the arts. He is very conscious of change, and in emphasizing what is becoming rare, in making us aware of luxury that is disappearing, he hopes not so much to make us stand still as to make us accept whatever happens. His success, he feels, depends on his ability to tune in to the life of the moment, even if he doesn't really live it. There is no age for the appreciation of beauty.

He knows he must remain infinitely open and that he must constantly create and constantly assimilate what he creates. The jacket may be his permanent success story, but it, too, must evolve and become different, its shape move from waist to the top of the hip, its texture change from tweed to silk and suede. And he is honest and logical enough to see that the flip side of adjusting to the times is the refusal to accept *any* value, any principle that pretends to be lasting; that it is impossible to find the parameter that will contain all possibilities.

If he more or less agrees with Dior's remark that women don't know how to dress until they are thirty, and if he finds a nineteen-year-old's face uninteresting because it is unmarked by life, it is because women—and men—not only have to know themselves pretty well in order to express themselves but in order to have anything to express at all. Young people's modes of dress are rarely inspiring despite the contemporary hype, he feels. It takes time to acquire taste, and even when it is acquired, it never replaces brilliant intuition.

Men are the most important group to liberate, he feels. Men have come a long way, but society is not yet ready for the transformations YSL and other designers would like to see happen. He disliked the unisex fashion of the early 1970s—the word, too; he would have preferred to call clothes that can be worn by either sex *bisexual*—but regrets the experiment was not given a better chance. A robe for a man is no more silly than a pair of pants for a woman. Turkish women wore pants for centuries, and Arab and African men wear robes. Yet if such fashions are not yet here, it is because men are frightfully conventional. It is now over a hundred years ago that the necktied two-piece suit became the correct masculine attire. Even if men have now largely escaped the total gray-flanneled uniform, they still are far from even catching up with women's freedom of dress. He likes to remind those who think the "peacock" revolution is a sign of contemporary decadence that history is full of precedents of manly coquetry. Perhaps once men have liberated themselves, society will discover an equilibrium between a new virility and a new femininity we can only dream about. He wouldn't be surprised, however, if this new virility and femininity turn out to be pretty similar.

Clothes have always had an erotic function, and Yves is very much aware of the old couturier adage that if you cover one erogenous zone, you must uncover another. Long robes demand plunging necklines; diminished décolletés mean legs must become visible. Because the part of the body that is temptingly covered has almost always excited the most interest, clothes that are supposed to be a triumph of modesty are often the most seductive. The modern acceptance of sexuality as something positive and healthy has had evident consequences in the way we dress, as exemplified in a Parisian lingerie slogan he likes to quote: Adorn your nudity. The next step is obvious. Equality of the sexes means that men must learn to please, to be seductive and attractive, which means that their fashion must change. We will soon see both a narrowing of the gap between mens- and women's wear and an idea of beauty that plays with clothing and nudity, a phenomenon already apparent in leisure clothes. With the exception of the need to dress protectively for cold climates, clothes will be the adornment, not the veil, of the body.

Feminist emancipation has meant that intelligent women refuse to be pawns of the rag trade. "We have more on our minds today than what goes on our backs," goes the saying, and fashion has come to mean personal style and something that touches a woman's life. Strident militancy died in 1977, the year warnings against designer manipulation were good magazine copy everywhere except *Vogue* and *Harper's Bazaar*. "Women pay dearly, up to $1,000 per Saint Laurent peasant outfit, for the privilege of looking like a New York streetcorner hot dog vendor," headlined *Working Woman*, while *The New York Times Magazine* tried to prove with pictures of Jackie O, Gloria Steinem and Barbara Walters "then" and "now" that feminism had cured women of their penchant for giving in to fashion dictators. In Paris, *GAP* editorialized that young people's *"Non à la mode"* was not so much an open rebellion as a defensive, and no doubt temporary, refusal to be conned. "This isn't a political reaction against the consumer society, but an ecological reaction against contrivance," the trade paper said, inviting the industry to pause and think before it reacted. Noting that it was perhaps a sign of the times that popular boutiques were selling more Cuisinarts than French-cut jeans, New York's *Village Voice* wondered whether ecology was the real reason designers were getting into sheets and towels. The erosion of faith in new and dynamic fashion seemed to reach the very people whose livelihood depended on producing and promoting novelty, as writers and buyers increasingly seemed to see through the clothes on the runways to a network of messages as complex, as contradictory, as perplexing and dispiriting as modern life itself. Increasingly, they declared themselves immune to showbiz stimulation and expressed the feeling that novelty might have little to do with the real style they professed to admire.

On the consumer level, the erosion is not so much of faith as of pocketbook. Even women in upper-income brackets shake their heads when they leaf through fashion magazines and see rtw where jeans start at $90, white cotton piqué shirts sell for $180, silk kimonos for $690 and a silk charmeuse bias-cut pants-plus-top outfit comes to $1,100. The ravages of inflation and the "me decade" hedonism may explain some of the the-more-it-costs-the-more-it-sells psychology, but a suspicion persists that much of YSL's turnover comes, like the success of *Star Wars*, from the repeat business of fashion "junkies" rather than the spreading of new consumers.

Neither Yves nor the House of YSL seems to be aware of this. His standard answer is that he *knows* his clothes are too expensive. When Gabrielle Busschaert is asked, for example, she says her boss is too removed from the dollars-and-cents responsibilities to be aware of any price details and that, anyway, the house has no "profiles" of rtw clients. Bergé is certainly aware of money, but in the French business tradition, he is more than reticent when it comes to cost breakdowns, and even competitors have a hard time imagining them poring over computer readouts to establish consumer profiles in distant Rive Gauche lines.

Yves expresses the overview. He doesn't think himself so far removed from "everyday women" that he has no concern for their comfort. He embraces the increased freedom, responsibility and mobility of the modern woman. It is his favorite subject, but he thinks women have sacrificed a lot in the recent struggle for liberation. Feminism imposed its own party line that was a contradiction in terms, insofar as it is the opposite of freedom of choice. He believes that women's power over men lies in a deep, veiled and enigmatic mystery, and that by denying those things that attract men, women may also destroy the essential distance between the sexes. The difference between men and women accounts for the attraction of the sexes, and the difference implies tension and even rejection. Beautiful clothes and makeup are part of a woman's allure, and Yves is not at all astonished to see the idea of treating women like men becoming passé again. If anything, he senses a relief in many women from the pressures of being challenged by feminist rhetoric.

"Women who want to be men, to look like men, are not truly free," he said in 1978. "On the contrary, they are suffering from an inferiority complex about them. Women who feel in control of their situation don't wish to be men; they are sufficiently free to enjoy being women—a condition they don't experience as inferior but as different." In recent years, he has put his money where his mouth is and introduced unexpected and provocative pointers—cinched waists and spiked heels, the glitter and allure of a woman as sex object past—saying that women are now confident enough to wear frankly sexy fashions.

There are indications that even fashion leaders are not taking these pointers too seriously. While Geraldine Stutz could say that "clothes do matter, but the vital interest that women have always had in clothes has enlarged," Grace Mirabella could write that the 1978–79 Paris couture collection should perhaps be viewed in "a totally abstract manner, that none of it was intended to be taken literally and indeed possibly very little of it *will* be taken seriously."

But all fashion is a denial of what is, and, as Balmain says, "to work too cravenly for the street is esthetically unhealthy." All designers' authority rests on public acceptance, and Yves says he doesn't know one woman who doesn't want to look good. He will admit the new provocative chic is perhaps also the result of designers being bored, but then again, we are living in a boring time. Also, the new chic reflects women's emancipation and sense of knowing who they are and what they can do. "They know they can be very bright and successful—and sexy—at the same time."

We are at the dawn of an era where women—and men—will want to be more appealing. We dress to please, for work, for the weather and to express our personality. Dressing is increasingly a matter of the individual's frame of mind, and moods and feelings will no doubt be even more important in the future. "How do you dress," *Vogue* asked in 1979, "to stop a crowd, feed a fantasy or to look serious?"

And, Yves likes to remind antifashion arguers, there are many women, and even more men, who feel bewildered by a surfeit of choice, people who, in effect, like to be *told* what is right for them. He sees many of them and likes the story an American retailer told him about the daughter who wants to wear the same as Sue and Debbie and Ann and Jane and tells her mother, "You don't understand, if you don't look like everybody else nobody will pay attention to you." Contemporary fashion offers a variety of choices never known before.

Yves thinks most women over thirty-five probably look younger than women their age ever looked before, and he believes women can learn from men when it comes to mixing ephemeral styles with a basic wardrobe. The revolt against consumerism and conspicuous waste was particularly virulent in post-1968 France, and he was not among the cynics who said of counterculture kids that it was easier to change clothes than society. If anything characterizes recent years, he feels, it is that too much has been improvised and not enough has been thought through, which doesn't mean that the burst of creative ideas hasn't been an asset. But the artist in him rebels against a successful style that doesn't last and the craftsman in him against throwing away what has been perfected. His greatest satisfaction is to see an impeccably cut jacket live on a thousand shoulders in the street. He has lamented the four-times-a-year grind. He knows all about the desperation of deadlines, of never having enough time.

The very special universe of haute couture is not just a laboratory for ready-to-wear merchandising; it is *other*. Dreams do not contradict reality; they are refractions of reality, subjective playbacks and sometimes future perceptions. For Saint Laurent, haute couture is the increasingly fragile world where the undertow of the times can be captured for one brilliant season, since haute couture depends a tiny bit less for its effect on immediate public consent than ready-to-wear.

And he knows all about the need to win immediate consent and all about the cutting edge of time. The seventies are the "me decade." Personal growth, therapy, physical health, the home, ecology, creative relationships and the arts are the positives. The flip side is the breakdown of consensus, withdrawal, selfishness and a shallow pessimism. These are not exciting times, and since dress design draws its inspiration from world news, the arts and changes in people's activities and attitudes, contemporary fashions shouldn't be exciting either.

The irony is that while the profound desire for individual freedom has always been the prime mover of evolution in fashion, this same desire also works against it. In a mass-produced, consumer society, freedom to dress is the answer to the imperious need in each of us to be more than a uniformed number in a utopian paradise. Societies which, like China under Mao Tse-tung, felt compelled to make everybody wear the same clothes, are reacting to a caste-ridden past, and their reaction means they are already halfway through the cure. Yves is convinced that as soon as such people feel certain that past inequities have been overcome, they will return to the diversity that allows each to express, within the limits of available options, his or her own personality. The language of fashion is universal and convergent, and while fashion may lose its four-times-a-year lockstep, it is, in its widest sense, the visible common denominator of the period that an increasingly global society is living through. Discoveries are still ahead because, in its search for beauty, fashion is its own end.

18

MASTERY

There has always been a fairly derogatory attitude among intellectuals toward fashion and a corresponding defensive manner among those dealing in fashion. Louis Auchincloss once observed that academic writers seem to find the courage to write about society, in the sense of fashionable society, only from a great distance.

Saint Laurent is not the one to help when it comes to describing the inner soul of his talent. Like Chanel, he has always been on guard against indiscretion—against intrusion, also; and spending nearly twenty-five years in the limelight has taught him circumspection and reinforced his natural reserve. He has never been on a talk show and has never made any of those don't-quote-me confessions. The people surrounding him—and that really means Pierre Bergé—have made access to him limited, cleverly imposing a distance and a last veil that cannot be penetrated, as if the ultimate secret might be that there is less to YSL than we want to think, as if they don't dare trust us with the naked Yves.

It is no wonder that Yves is insecure. His work is intuitive, and he is under the constant pressure of being number one. He must constantly hope that what he makes will be appreciated by the media, the buyers and the consumers, all of whose motives for liking or rejecting his work are rarely identical. There is probably no other area in the commercial arts in which the game is played for higher stakes or where an established artist must risk his career four times a year. The House of Saint Laurent is, of course, powerful enough to survive a couple of bombs, and Yves can no doubt coast for a year or two on the punch of accumulated success. But fashion is pitiless. YSL, Lagerfeld, Kenzo, Bohan, Montana and Givenchy command today's Paris headlines; Cardin and Courrèges no longer do so. An added trump in Yves's royal flush is his logical mind. There are reasons for what he does, which may explain why so many of his ideas stay around as long as they do.

To imagine him exhausted is not difficult. Each collection includes a hundred-plus novelties, and year-round he must create ideas for the advertising people and fashion directors whose hunger for novelty is insatiable. To be the trend setter means walking on the knife's edge. If he comes up with designs that conflict too much with his previous "statements," there is consternation and confusion among the buyers. If he doesn't change from last season's style, buyers complain they are not given a decisive lead. As a modernist, he believes beauty doesn't have to make sense and that every new style is essentially a reaction. Fashion is the universal teacher of modernity. Its current lesson is a certain ease in dressing that has to do with the way clothes look and the way they feel. Very little can stand between the line and the body, between a mood and its expression: "Whatever I have done has always been based on the concept of clothes that work and move with the natural way of a woman's body, not against it. My sense of structure is not to build a false concept of a woman's body, but to make the clothes, even pared-down clothes, move with shoulders and hips."

As designers' childhoods go, Yves's early years were not

exceptional. The infant Chanel was inclined to cut up her aunt's curtains for her dolls, the boy Dior used to dress cardboards and Givenchy offered practical advice on fashion to his mother when he was seven; Lagerfeld did so when he was four. Some designers love women, some hate women, and as children, say the Freudians, were involved in too-intimate relationships with their often too beautiful, too youthful mothers. But mom or supermom is a too-easy fetish for those who need to explain away talent. John Fairchild, when confronted with the theory that designers are a bunch of homosexuals out to destroy womanhood, said, "That old argument that designers are just queers who want to make women look ugly, is silly. They want to make clothes that sell. That's all. To make money."

At least two non-Freudian explanations are advanced in Paris to account for the predominance of male designers. The shift from the 1920s and 1930s dominance of female designers to that of postwar male couturiers is attributed to history and technology. The prewar fashion was more *flou*, more detailed and therefore more propitious for feminine creativity. It was woman-created—Vionnet, Lanvin, Chanel, Schiaparelli, Ricci—and needed a feminine presence to continue. World War II brought about the austerity of the suit, which brought tailors to feminine dressmaking. Despite the tendency of women's clothes to more fluid, softer lines, the tailors were men, and, perhaps unconsciously, they created a fashion relying on masculine talent. Cutters, says Chambre Syndicale trade school director Olga Saurat, work "*à plat*" (flat out, on a table), not, like Vionnet, Lanvin—and YSL—on dummies and live models. An even more prosaic explanation for the preeminence of male designers is that they don't have to wear the clothes they create and therefore can ignore practical considerations and come up with striking designs. Women designers, say Saurat and Sonia Rykiel, remain less inspired, less tyrannical also, and more modest and realistic.

In the grander overview, Saint Laurent's impact is associated with the feminization of men's clothes—jackets, suits, pants—and his auspicious beginning coincided with the triumph of the Dior look, which was structured (and tailored, and was to be seen in retrospect as a great leap backward, since it allowed women to look as they had before the war and not like ersatz soldiers and factory hands). The sexual ambivalence that has characterized women's clothes for twenty years is new only in its dimension, however. Elizabethan women experimented with doublets and jerkins, and Marie Antoinette flaunted the rigid dress codes of Versailles by having a portrait made of herself in a guard's uniform, but the wearing of men's clothes was confined to well-known exceptions such as George Sand until Chanel's heavy borrowing from menswear made the erotic combination of mannish clothes and feminine charm a chic new possibility, although only in sportswear. In 1937, Marlene Dietrich could still scandalize Hollywood's nouveaux riches by appearing at dinner parties in her satin tuxedo, and it was not until 1967 that *Elle* could report that female employes of Parisian insurance companies and banks were allowed to come to work in pants.

Saint Laurent's thumb-tack reputation is that he is the designer whose sharply tailored blazers and straight-legged trousers put millions of women into pants, and his success is associated with an elegance of fabric, workmanship and fit—qualities that were at their height on avenue Montaigne during his short apprenticeship with Dior. He acknowledges this and thinks that women can adapt men's entire wardrobe, uniforms included, as long as they don't look like transvestites, as long as they don't look aggressively masculine. The George Sand look, he says, is no longer necessary, because the difference between the sexes is what is attractive, and the woman who is truly free has no inferiority complex about men and therefore no wish to appear to be a man.

From his earliest childhood, Yves has been instinctively sure of his talent. When he was four, he sent his aunt back to change before she could go out with his parents, and as a blushing eighteen-year-old, he commanded the immediate attention of Michel de Brunhoff and Dior. Rarely has a designer so early and so decisively dominated fashion. When asked why all the couturiers end up with the same trends each year, he has said that, with the exception of Kenzo, they quite simply copy him. "Each season they copy my things from the previous season," he said in 1976. "I was tired of being copied. That's why my last collection was an explosion of fantasy. While I did that, the others did me—blazers and simple things." From the beginning, his mind has been clear, his gaze steady, and his work shows none of the terrors and few of the hesitations that characterize his profession, even though he likes to say his designs are born in a "crucible of pain." If he has to sum himself up, he likes to say that his career has oscillated between the classic look of what men wear and fantasy.

He realizes that those formative years at Dior are, for better and for worse, still with him. He is not so sure that if he had been a little younger, he wouldn't have opted totally for ready-to-wear, but overall, he is who he wanted to be. "If I chose this trade, it was because I wanted to be the greatest. I wanted to mark my era because I think fashion is very important. It reflects the state of mind, the evolution and the future of civilization. Every seven, ten years there's a great change in how we live that is first expressed in the way we dress."

If he has shaped the era in which we live, the march of time has also molded him. "You cannot improvise a career," he reflected in 1978. "The world was quite different when I chose my profession. At one point, I was very tempted to design for mass manufacture, to quit couture, but it was too late. I had too much responsibility toward the people who helped me establish the house."

There are times when this responsibility feels like a stone around his neck, and there are moments, especially of late, when he feels elated by the burden, when he is convinced that it is only now that he finally and totally controls his craft. The inspirations have been many—films, a girl passing in the street, art, books and the very collapse of traditional values themselves—but the latest, and most gratifying, has been the métier itself. Since the fantasy look, a sense of virtuosity, of the-sky-is-the-limit ability, has permeated his work. The mad Mongols, female samurais and Chinese empresses continued in 1977 as fashions turned softer and fluid, and tailored jackets in plain velvet replaced the blousons, and pants began to give way to a variety of skirts. The winter of 1976–77 was quite mild in Europe, and the muffled look—a matter of survival in much of North America—was more fad than necessity, but shawls and hoods, all part of the ethnic look, were everywhere, enhanced by lavish braid trimmings and bright embroidered bands. Yves thought nothing of mixing a huge orange damask jacket with satin harem pants tucked into cavalier boots fastened with cords that ended in circus pompoms, or adding a full feather headdress that almost tickled the ballroom chandelier. The ready-to-wear message was bubbly, bloused and billowy as he piled ponchos and scarves over bloused and belted voluminous dresses. The summer couture was pure theater and he was the first to admit it, quoting Cocteau's famous sally that madness is wisdom, if you can afford it.

As Bergé had said in his March 1977 denial of the death rumors, Yves still needed therapy, and the summer rtw and couture collections were created under the added distraction of Loulou's marriage, celebrated in a marathon of month-long minicelebrations. The couture collection was pulled together in one week, with round-the-clock efforts and multivitamins, which Loulou was reported as saying were "for nervous people and hard-to-manage children."

The reviewers loved the long-ago-and-far-away romance. Eugenia Sheppard wrote in her syndicated column in 43 newspapers that since YSL's name carried more fame and prestige than any in the fashion world, "he can afford the sumptuous satins, velvets and the beautiful, eccentric headdresses, gilt-edged boots and especially-designed jewelry that builds up the fantasy mood of his show." *Time* called him "the Sun King of fashion" and revealed that the soft opiates of Oriental opulence were the harbinger of "a perfume he will introduce next year, named, appropriately, Opium."

By fall, Yves left other designers to outdo themselves in the flamboyance he now abandoned. Gone were his taffeta fantasies hung with gold and silver, his wild paisley and feathers and his rich peasant look. While Montana's storm-trooper collection caused a brawl, Kenzo's eye-patched pirates in jodhpur pants and his miniballoon dresses had his girls looking like leggy lollipops, Lagerfeld went for softness on the borderline of negligee and Bohan elaborated on his *jeune fille* frocks with straw boaters, white stockings and party shoes, Yves pulled off the coup of abandoning folklore altogether. Instead, he offered a muted collection of soft blouses, skirts and dresses in basic browns and khakis. There were still what he called opium jackets, but his evening wear was soft and classically elegant, with ample offerings of flowing muslin gowns baring legs and shoulders. The simplicity of his designs and fabrics, *Newsweek* reported, had the effect of making some of his colleagues' clothes look vulgar and silly.

His inspiration, Yves said, was New York, not so much as an American city, but as a global idea everybody can love. Calling it "a pulse point," he said he had seen women in the streets of New York wearing T-shirts, some form of jeans and beautiful hair that made them look wonderfully modern. He carried the Big Apple theme into the 1978 summer rtw and couture, when he and Bohan were suddenly the twin stars of Paris, both coming out with highly styled simplicity. For both, feminine forms were back in clothes that were clean-lined, pared-to-the-body, uncluttered, soft, and supple. For the couture collection, Yves chose music by George Gershwin and, for the finale, *When the Saints Come Marchin' In*. The showstopper was a black satin tuxedo suit opened to expose a decorative strapless bra. By April, *Women's Wear Daily* called all this the Broadway classic, Exaggerated Chic and, finally, High Chic, and said Paris was dreaming up moods of Noel Coward glamour, a return to Hollywood drop-dead entrance clothes, sleek dinner dressing in a new mix-up approach to the suit.

Yves was in top form. He liked his high glamour for its combination of simplicity and theatricality. "Today haute couture must reflect what is seen in the streets, just like ready-to-wear. It is totally passé for a couturier to make something too grand and dull. Cheerfulness, humor and provocation are today. Humor is a vital element. My message is humor combined with total refinement."

Even though he was working with his usual high-adrenaline anxiety and lack of sleep, friends found Yves looking crisp, relaxed and positive. In 1976, he had looked puffed and bloated; now he didn't hesitate to show his toned-up physique on night escapades with Loulou and Betty, where the alcoholic intake was moderate. When he was out, he was often prancing around, Fred Astaire–style, and humming *When the Saints*. To *W*'s André Leon Talley, he complained he had never discovered life in his youth. "Life is to be lived when one is young. And truly, I've never lived." Others found him playfully teasing and impish. He had something of a mischievous elf's inner grin, *Femmes* magazine's Rolf Bigler decided, when he said that sincerity and honesty were important for a designer.

Success—the annual turnover was approaching $400 million—also relaxed Bergé. Besides becoming owner of the Théâtre de l'Athénée (Cardin also acquired a theater) and taking helicopter-flying lessons so he could take intimates in his own chopper for luncheons in Deauville, he began dabbling again in his old trade of launching people. As an amateur impresario, he involved himself in the disco scene and promoted several nightclub singers. As demonstrated in reverse by the slow fade of Bernard Buffet since Bergé had dropped the painter, Pierre's riveting powers of persuasion were undiminished. Buffet was now an unknown, even in the anthology section of the new Beaubourg Art Center bookstore in Les Halles.

Showbiz took over the runways in 1978, but Yves was making order out of chaos (and Kenzo joyous fantasy out of fairy-tale kingdoms). Exaggerated Chic meant glamorous dressing for day and evening. The summer rtw featured electric-bright charmeuse dresses, broadened shoulders, shortened skirts and a straight silhouette. The *International Herald Tribune*'s Hebe Dorsay called Yves's daytime clothes "a clever rehash of all his past hits," and Marie-Josée Le Picard of French TV's second network called them "a clever rehash of Schiaparelli 1938–39," but everybody else loved the dash and the out-and-out sensuousness. It was all right to be a sex object again—in America, Bella Abzug bleached her hair and lost forty-five pounds, while Betty Friedan said feminists were playing around with eye shadow again. Designers showed short dresses for after dark, blends of architectural shapes and very soft fabrics mixed with redefined and extended shoulders, narrowed waists and the nonstop line of legs seen through slits and slashes. Adornments were all-out glitter, big chunks of junk jewelry worn on everything. The naughtiest skirt was a deceptively demure and dignified wraparound that kept opening up as the model walked, exposing a tiny triangle of satin pants.

Yves carried provocative allure over into his haute couture, working tirelessly through the summer.

His new *flou* swept the field.

"It's the most beautiful collection I've ever done because there's something new for me in relation to my work," he beamed at the July 26 unveiling. "It's a mixture of architectural, structured shapes and the very soft and feminine. I had waited all my life for something I didn't know how to create." He credited Balenciaga and Vionnet with inventing the true *flou*, which, by his definition, should make soft, sensuous, floaty dresses look as if they would drift off the body at any moment. For two hours, the largest crowd ever watched the collection, packed five rows deep in the Intercontinental's ballroom. The excitement kept mounting, and from the moment the first model strode out in a blue plaid coat, the applause grew in intensity. The drama, delight and dressed-up mood of the evening look beguiled the audience. Here, it was a bias-cut, one-shouldered evening dress in rose satin, slit to the thigh and caught with black velvet bows. There, it was a bolero dinner suit in black velvet, worn with a sheer evening blouse embroidered in gray lace. The acclaim reached fortissimo when Mounia Orhozemane walked down the runway in what was essentially a simple two-piece black dress. She wore diamond bracelets over black gloves and a handbag in the shape of a heart on a long chain slung over her shoulder, all topped with a jeweled pillbox with feathers pointing toward the ceiling. The crowd called her back for an encore, and she obliged, something that hardly ever happens in a fashion show.

Nothing in the collection appeared without something on the head, and after the YSL mixes of black with all sorts of other colors, hats were the big story. The climax was passibly theatrical, with clothes that were tributes to Zizi Jeanmaire, Carmen and other greasepaint heroines and to Loulou and Betty in the audience. "If you haven't seen Saint Laurent, you haven't seen Paris," announced Geraldine Stutz of Bendel's, while *The New York Times*'s Bernardine Morris wrote that the trouble with being Saint Laurent "is that everybody loves a winner, so a number of his ideas, such as the bow tie, turned up in other collections earlier this week (word gets around). Sometimes they served as parodies, debasing his ideas." Eugenia Sheppard wrote that it was the most wearable collection he had ever made.

The pace was grueling. The trip to New York to launch Opium aboard the *Peking* was all work, and Yves hardly saw any friends there. "There is no time for friends or my family," he said in September. "I love my family, but I don't even have time to see my mother. Ten years ago, I had a huge open house for all my friends. Now, I think about them more often than seeing them. Now that I've reached maturity, it's my work that possesses me. And I am possessed by my work. This is at once sublime and awful."

Exaggerated Chic continued into 1979 as provocative styles crept into new areas of pop culture. Again, Yves was leading. American designers put away the Annie Hall big tops and full skirts and unveiled a spring look that paid homage to a female form that hadn't been fashionable for years. They adopted the hot colors and made everything narrowed and sexier, and although the 1940s and 1950s *rétro* look was a dirty word along Seventh Avenue, the soft padded shoulders, tapered short jackets and basic black cocktail dresses were something of a recycled Joan Crawford look.

Yves passed up opportunities to design the wardrobe for Audrey Hepburn, Michelle Phillips and the rest of the cast of *Bloodlines* (he was now so famous that the screenwriters instead wrote in a scene where Phillips buys her clothes in a Rive Gauche boutique) and the new uniforms for Air France's three thousand cabin attendants. Instead, he plunged into his summer line. While other Parisians came out with Marilyn Monroe and Mae West revivals, he continued man-tailored sportswear for daytime and, in ready-to-wear, reinterpreted the sailor look of the first collection he did under his own name in 1962, and again in 1972. Middy overblouses, tunics, flyaway tops and knee-length skirts were counterbalanced by a naughty look of see-through chiffon off-the-shoulder blouses and transparent evening dresses. There were red, white and blue separates for daytime wear, with first-mate stripes, anchor appliqués, bows tied under collars, bermudas and pants with mother-of-pearl buttons up the sides. As the year progressed, the switch from the loose and layered look continued toward a more clinging and more constricting look that emphasized breasts, waists, hips and legs and was a distant and very modern echo of the fifties, hugging the body with belts, darts and seams.

Yves likes to pluck a flower from the past, as with the nautical look. He likes it because it gives him a sense of transcendence, continuity and evolution. His retrospective mood set him smartly apart in the winter 1979–80 ready-to-wear, which buyers generally called the least appealing Paris season in memory and the media called a circus extravaganza that had little to do with clothes.

While Givenchy was on a Highland fling, Mugler and Montana were off in neon-colored sci-fi fantasies, Miyake showed black taffeta flying-nun hats, Lagerfeld showed halfmoon hats and bustles, Rykiel offered superwoman —the word knitted on a white, above-the-knee chemise dress—and Kenzo's heroines went from a Minnie Mouse costume he had worn himself on his fortieth birthday, to the ultimate *rétro:* a cavewoman with fake animal skins belted or slung all over her black leotarded body, the YSL collection was subdued and filled, *The New York Times'*s Bernardine Morris commented, "with clothes for people to wear who are not obsessed with clothes." The two-hundred-piece collection included quilted Chinese jackets and taffeta evening gowns, new twists to blazers, pants, skirts and pullovers and, for the media hoopla, a thigh-baring sidewrapped skirt. "Fashion is now a circus; the atmosphere is absolutely abominable," he told the media, adding that what journalists wanted from a collection was not what women looking for clothes wanted. "People always come to Rive Gauche to find something that perpetuates, that adapts to things they already have. Nothing could be more of a compliment than a woman who arrives with a blazer from me that's ten years old, a blouse that's three years old and a well-cut pair of pants that are a year old. Clothes that don't date are modern." In couture, he also offered clothes to the 1980 woman that were simple, flattering and enduring. He has enjoyed his recent work, especially the feat of mastering *flou,* and has come to terms with his responsibilities toward his corporate self. "The work hangs on my shoulders," he said. "After all, I couldn't do it without the house. The workrooms are vital and it's my responsibility to create."

He is happy to hear such an astute observer as Yvonne Deslandres of the Centre de Documentation du Costume describe his impact as also being that of designing clothes that are free of class and age and almost of social functions. Fashion is a business of change, but Yves is gratified when others can see the red threads running through his career. On the eve of his fortieth birthday, he summed himself up as having molded our era little by little, just as his style developed and gradually imposed itself.

"If you look at all my collections, even the first ones at Christian Dior, you can find themes which I continued, developed and enriched and which formed the modern woman. There were scarves for women instead of hats. Afterwards, I put women in slacks. Courrèges was perhaps the first couturier to do this but he didn't know how. His slacks were rigid and unfeminine. So then I did it. After May '68, my entire collection was pants. You shouldn't forget that when I brought out that collection, we got turned away from restaurants and nightclubs in New York because the women were in pants. This big change was all because of me."

He will admit to one failure only—the year of Courrèges. "I don't recognize the second one: the forties line in 1971. Wide shoulders, high heels, black stockings; it was all too daring, but later my line imposed itself." He doesn't believe in the perfect embodiment of anything, because fashion is composed of parts, and its triumph is merely a better rearrangement of attributes. Ultimately, the foundation of any art rests on its buried life. Although he is sure he has exorcised most of his private demons, he is not so sure he can unravel the reasons behind his ideas and his craft. In his own mind, his latest triumphs are almost inner-directed, giving him the satisfaction of not only being right and of understanding his time, but of finding himself and of knowing how to accept himself.

19

MUSIC
OF THE
FUTURE

The reason the huge portrait behind Bergé's desk on avenue Marceau features an Yves Saint Laurent without glasses is that when they and Betty Catroux went to New York to present the 1972 couture collection in the Hotel Pierre ballroom, Yves had shaved off his beard, cut his shoulder-length hair and tried on contact lenses. Everybody said he looked younger than ever. When Andy Warhol put on *his* glasses and made sketches for the portrait, he thought Yves's eyes looked bluer without spectacles. But the contact lenses irritated Yves and, he said, it was more important for him to see without tears than to exhibit the blue of his irises, especially since he was falling in love with a Burne-Jones at the Metropolitan Museum.

The power of the artists, say art historians, is becoming increasingly enigmatic. To see rather than to be seen, to understand rather than to be understood, are the growing concerns of the maturing Saint Laurent. Art is narcissistic insofar as it amounts to a gift for seeing oneself, and Yves's most recent work has been an attempt at exploring his own talent, to reinventory his own career. For 1980, he planned to sum himself up by building a couture collection based on the best of all his past collections while at the same time give timelessness another try. The idea, he said following a month-long vacation in Marrakesh, is to find the important personal themes and the best and most significant shapes, and to restate them in contemporary clothes. If he could accomplish this, he felt he might be able to accomplish the feat of creating a form of dress that is both truly modern and ageless.

All art is a new way of saying old things, and the art of dressing is enriched by reinterpretation. "My past is my *rétro* style," Yves said as he selected fabrics for going back to his roots. Clothes, for any designer, are a kind of transcendence by which we—and he—ultimately change. The long history of costume has had its periods of effervescence, followed by periods of calm, which have turned out to be periods of extraordinary ferment. Yves's intuition is that we are living in a twilight of a new era in which this ebb and flow of inspiration and its expression is perhaps being superseded by a questioning of society itself. The grand enterprise of our time is not to redefine the way we look, but who we are. Yet if fashion—and the story of Yves—has taught us anything, redefining the way we look should tell us who we are.

Saint Laurent has tried to reflect the complexity of our time and of the fractured society we live in. His recent collections have been accompanied by mixtures of all kinds of music—the throb of disco interrupting cabaret twang interrupting opera. This breaking up of expected rhythms, he feels, is characteristic of today. Since the mid-1970s, he has keenly felt that he is the last couturier, that the designers of the generation following him think of clothes and fashion differently, that clothes have different values and meanings to them. "I don't know what, but I feel great changes are coming," he has said. "My antennas tell me there will be a kind of nonculture, but the way we're expressing ourselves is being reinvented." In the meantime, he expresses himself in ready-to-wear with disciplined altruism and in haute couture with the abandon of the painter or the writer he never quite became.

He believes that the main function of the creator when he isn't creating is to embellish his mind, as one would adorn one's house, and to accumulate artistic wealth, whether borrowed from museums or from nature's beauty. When asked to define himself, Saint Laurent has said, "I'm the sage of fashion," meaning that he considers himself not so much a designer full of wisdom who is venerated for his judgment, but a prudent and perhaps somewhat solemn individual. His work is his central obsession, and he has said that he never loved anyone the way he loves what he is doing. But he will not admit to being a prisoner of his empire. Rather, he says, it is a question of responsibility toward the people whose livelihood depends on his talent and whose skills are very much part of the success. He has chosen to be responsible. But his responsibility often goes beyond the primary trade of designing. He knows how to surround an object with a theme, an ambience, a concept. And he knows how to play out his private fantasies in current fashions, how to transform passion into novelty.

It *has* occurred to him to give it all up. "Yes, I have wanted to drop everything," he told *Saga* in 1978. "Since ready-to-wear allows me to keep this huge thing going, I must continue. You must always exceed yourself in this business, which is inhuman, exhausting. I'm the last of the big couturiers. Haute couture ends with me.

"I want to be the mirror of my time, to give back to women their reflected self. Today, women don't have to change their wardrobe every six months. Today, women no longer become obsolete, out of date. In fact, when I see some women mix old things of mine with what I've just created, I find that just marvelous. Women are more and more liberated; no one should try to make them prisoners again." His aim, he has said on another occasion, is to free, to glorify and to enhance a new feminine consciousness of the possibilities of self-expression.

There are moments when he thinks fashion, as opposed to style, is on the wane, despite the new tolerance for self-gratification. "Appearance will be much less important in the future," he predicts. "What counts most is what a human being is, what you are within yourself." He wonders whether Lagerfeld can be right in thinking that a weird, strange fashion may be coming, like a cloudburst, because Yves feels society is too fractured to be swept up by any one storm. The creative givens are narrower than they were twenty years ago, for example, because so many people want to say something with clothes—designers, coordinators, advertisers, stores, as well as the wearers themselves. The "echo" has been tremendously amplified.

On the eve of the eighties, Yves wishes for an exciting decade. The revolution of manners and mentality was exalting and inspiring in the sixties, he felt, and there was nothing like that in the late seventies. Orientalism was one way of staying modern, at least in Europe. Another was the "adulterous mix of everything," the universal availability of all cultures—ponchos over Eskimo boots, sombreros with jeans, rhinestone cowboys. But there are moments when he wonders if tomorrow's fashion couldn't be the Maoist blue—if not exactly the single, totalitarian uniform for one and all, at least a severely restricted wardrobe. As a designer of ready-to-wear, this wouldn't bother him. On the contrary, he likes the rigor and perfection that ready-to-wear should imply while resenting the commercial imperatives that say rtw must constantly change. "Designing clothes demands a lot of patience," he says, "and a designer cannot really go for perfection and for novelty at the same time." His goal in rtw is no longer to create shock waves but clothes women can count on, even though a $90 price tag on a pair of jeans still keeps them outside the reach of most consumers. In haute couture, he expresses himself with little regard for the monied few who can think of dressing in made-to-measure. Since his creation is underwritten by the ready-to-wear and the franchises and not the elite who can afford couture, he regards this as his right. "I am really involved in expressing something that perhaps someday I could express in other ways—in painting or in writing. I suppose it sounds egotistical, but I express myself personally in terms of the female body."

After Poiret had lost everything, he wrote in his memoirs that what fashion needed was a new tyrant who could both give it a thrashing and free it from its self-doubt. "Whoever renders this service will be loved and become rich." Glory and wealth have come to Saint Laurent, who, alone, has known how to carry on the difficult heritage of Poiret, Chanel and Dior. If he hasn't so much chastised the industry as profited from its perpetual insecurity, he has remained one of its outstanding figures. With him, designers seem to have begun to go beyond mere clothes toward the intangible attitudes and subliminal instincts that shape our moods and needs. Influences reach items and behavior patterns that were relatively immune to the rhythms of fashion in Poiret's, or even Dior's, time. We demand "design" from salad forks and conceptual integrity from city skylines. We want imaginative utilization of the possibilities that new forms offer, and we are beginning to apply a kind of idealized gold standard to the relationship between quantity and quality, and to want to tax visual pollution. Utilitarian objects are seen as the expression of a culture's attitude toward itself.

For Yves, awareness of his own potential came in adolescence, in response to theatrical enchantment and in reaction to the taunts of classmates. "One day I will be stronger than you," he told himself in the hallways of the Oran *lycée*. The "one day" became cumulative and sustained a centripetal quest that, in his maturity, he would call at once sublime and awful. One day . . . Through the difficult late teens, it helped him move in from the colonial hinterland with instinctive energy and dogged drive.

From the beginning, his talent has been powerful enough to both reflect and impose upon the complexity of the times. That January afternoon in 1958, the people crowding into Dior's salons to see the heir apparent thought they were going to a wake—a *"défilé d'outre-tombe,"* some of them whispered maliciously. He was still in mourning for the master, but sported a furtive sprig of lilies-of-the-valley in his lapel.

One day . . . Hubris was followed by ignominy, catharsis and a second, more modest debut in his own name. He made his breakthrough as the sixties turned splashy and revolutionary, and everything his precocious and protected childhood had taught him crumpled while most of what he had learned from the master of highest fashion was dismissed. He was twenty-six and young enough not only to adapt but to be inspired by upheavals. He was also clever enough—or Bergé and the crew that success assembled for him were smart enough—to realize that if style alone couldn't impose him on his own generation, increasing affluence brought youth closer to his spell.

He stumbled only once, erring on the conservative side the year Courrèges set the decade's tone. A year later, he led the way into high-fashion ready-to-wear. Technological advances made many new fashions possible, and the widespread use of synthetics did more than stylish innovations to diminish the gap between the rich and the not-so-rich, and even to break down the notion of seasons. The fallout from fame put couture names on an increasing variety of consumer goods, but the Paris couturiers came in for an explosive notoriety that they couldn't all live up to. By the end of the decade, Yves was the only Parisian of any real international significance.

During the listless, perplexing mid-1970s, he lived through the crisis of turning forty and feeling his ascendancy not so much challenged as appearing uninteresting in his own eyes. The crisis necessitated psychiatric attention, but it also provoked a liberating, egotistical and extravagant burst that left the pros of the gilded chairs awestruck when they were not reduced to tears. The fantasy look didn't alter the way women would dress for a decade, as the immediate predictions had it, but it led Yves to a new concentration, to a new mastery of his métier, that opened new directions. It led him to an unerring reliance on instinct, to the conviction that proof of influence is not in being convincing but in being contagious, and to being possessed by work in a way that was at once awful in its all-devouring exclusivity and misanthropic craving for privacy and sublime in the wonderment of the vistas it offered. Novelty is both imitation and opposition, and he showed that together with wit and humor, a certain existential anguish is part of the elusive process. Yves knew where he stood in relation to his talent and to tradition, and he knew that although he was adaptable, maturity inevitably meant a narrowing of activities and interests. At the dawn of the eighties, he was a unique world influence, powerfully articulating the fragile and transitory impulses of our time.

Saint Laurent was also a living contradiction of popular notions of who and what a designer is. With him, it has become modern not so much to measure oneself against current obsessions as against past excellence, and to realize that the future is more complex than its logic. His loyalties are inconsistent, first shifting from the elitism of haute couture to the popular front of ready-to-wear, then back again from the constrictions of mass manufacture to the tonic of art for art's sake. In the traditional notion of artistic progression from inexperience through excellence to decay, he is proof that creativity upsets more than it perfects, that the history of fashion is not the history of its perfection. Progress doesn't come in straight lines. That the satin tuxedo came after the trapeze line, the Mondrian look before high chic, has nothing to do with the presence of these ideas. His nostalgia for a Proustian past filled with civility, languor and a very different sense of time and relationships deflates the idea that "now" people must live in an intoxicated spontaneity and trade on amplified vapidity. His belief that we live in a twilight era has given his backward glances extraordinary beauty, as well as an insouciance that may be prescient. We must imagine him bent over his desk at avenue Marceau late at night, locked in combat not only with the greats among his predecessors but also with the imaginary rivals of the future.

His awakening came with the discovery of adult make-believe, with the enchanted locus of a thousand prestidigitations. Louis Jouvet in wig and funny clothes gamboled in a fairyland setting, pretending to be Arnolphe, who pretends that his love for Agnès made him bring her up to total innocence. But Jouvet and Dominique Blanchar were more than fleshed-out cardboard in a farce written "to show ourselves as others see us." The theater was the ceremonial place of magic, where imagination took preplanned flight, where incarnation was supremely true and where society judged its collective wisdom and whimsy. In the beginning, fashion was a detour for him, an oblique expedient and indirect means to his true calling. One day . . . But fashion, too, proved to fulfill sensibilities, to be capable of incarnating imagination, to create its crowds while at the same time intoxicating them. Dior was a teacher of exquisite taste, but overwhelmed and driven in late success, and his sudden death rolled the dice. Yves reached the theater anyway, on off nights and between collections, while his name came to mean sensual allure, deliberate assertion and the soul of luxury that provokes seductive responses.

Since then, fashion hasn't lived in a vacuum but has come to consider the whole world its stage. It has become the essential microcosm of the visual arts, and Yves's authority and influence have been part of the change. His contributions have been powerful enough to modulate the appearance of modern woman and, like the tailor in *The Emperor's New Clothes,* have transformed some of that by which we invisibly change ourselves. With Yves, fashion has acquired what Henry James called "the music of the future."

Not that there is any one age for living beauty, says Yves. "I'd like to think that fashion of the future will inspire a need for beauty and that it will supply that beauty. After all, the world of fashion is a total illusion."

ACKNOWLEDGMENT

I could not thank all the people who took time to help me prepare this unauthorized biography—and not all would want their names to appear. Let me thank at least:

In Paris: Pierre Balmain, Anne-Marie Beretta, Francine Crescent, Augustin Debadie, France de Dieuleveult, Colette Gros, Laurie Heim and her boss Kenzo Takada for running their film, Svante Loefgren, Maud Molyneux, Olga Saurat, Madame Bougouin at *France Soir* and, for an overview and sense of history, Yvonne Deslandres.

In London and New York: Jacintha Alexander, Maxine de la Falaise, Anita Gallo, Duane Michals, Steve Rubell, Geraldine Stutz, Cynthia Vartan and Diana Vreeland.

In San Francisco and Los Angeles: Sonja Caproni, Artis Lane, belatedly Sandy Orgolini and John Schnetzler. I am also grateful to Margot Greenberg for having read the final manuscript.

—Los Angeles
February 1979

BIBLIOGRAPHY

W hile no book exists on Yves Saint Laurent or, indeed, on any of the living Parisian designers, in French or English, fashion is an oft-treated subject, if more often in pictures than in text.

The following books contain valuable information on contemporary or past aspects of Paris high fashion and sometimes illuminate the work and ideas of Yves Saint Laurent.

Alsop, Susan Mary. *To Marietta From Paris 1945–1960*. Garden City: Doubleday, 1975.

Barthes, Roland. *Système de la mode*. Paris: Seuil, 1967.

Bergé, Pierre. *Horreur de la guerre de Bernard Buffet*. Paris: Parenthèses, 1953.

———. *Bernard Buffet*. Geneva: Cailler, 1958.

Cabanne, Pierre. *Pablo Picasso*. New York: William Morrow, 1977.

Chonez, Claudine. *Giono par lui-même*. Paris: Seuil, 1956.

Deslandres, Yvonne. *Le Costume image de l'homme*. Paris: Albin Michel, 1976.

Dorner, Jane. *Fashion*. London: Octopus Books, 1974.

François, Lucien. *Comment un nom devient une griffe*. Paris: Gallimard, 1961.

Garland, Madge. *The Changing Form of Fashion*. New York: Praeger, 1970.

Haedrich, Marcel. *Coco Chanel*. Boston: Little, Brown, 1972.

Hamburger, Estelle. *Fashion Business*. San Francisco: Canfield Press, 1976.

Howell, Georgina. *In Vogue*. New York: Schocken, 1976.

Kelly, Katie. *The Wonderful World of "Women's Wear Daily."* New York: Saturday Review Press, 1972.

Konig, René. *A la mode: On the Social Psychology of Fashion*. Translated by F. Bradley. New York: Seabury Press, 1973.

Lee, Sarah Tomerlin, ed. *American Fashion*. New York: Quadrangle, 1975.

Poiret, Paul. *En habillant l'époque*. Paris: Grasset, 1930; re-edited, 1974.

Roselle, Bruno du. *La Crise de la mode*. Paris: Fayard, 1973.

————. *Un Siècle de couture parisienne*. Paris: Editions Léonard, 1976.

Saint Laurent, Yves. *La Vilaine Lulu*. Paris: Tchou, 1967.

Waltz, Barbara, and Morris, Bernardine. *The Fashion Makers*. New York: Random House, 1978.

INDEX